Hugh Williamson

"This excellent book tells the remarkable story of one of America's great but lesser known sons, a polymath and scholar, who was at various times a physician, politician, educationist, mathematician, merchant, divine and spy. Pupil of John Hunter the founder of scientific surgery, friend of Benjamin Franklin, witness to the Boston Tea Party, surgeon-general in the Revolutionary War, congressman in the House of Representatives, scientist and philanthropist. What a life! For those who have an interest in the founding of America or in the history of military medicine, or just like a well-written and entertaining biography, this book is for you."

—Sir Barry Jackson, MS, FRCS, FACS (Hon),
past president, The Royal College of Surgeons of England

"George Sheldon's biography of Hugh Williamson is a joy to read. Dr. Sheldon provides his readers with an enlightening and delightful account of a physician who was one of the framers of the US Constitution. Along the way, Sheldon makes substantive contributions to colonial American history and the history of medicine during the eighteenth century."

—Howard Markel, MD, PhD,
George E. Wantz Distinguished Professor of History of Medicine and Director, Center for the History of Medicine, The University of Michigan, and author of *When Germs Travel* and *Quarantine!*

"Professor Sheldon has done a great service in bringing to life this surgeon pioneer in his meticulously researched book. A great contribution to medical history."

—Wendy Moore, freelance journalist and author of
Wedlock: How Georgian Britain's Worst Husband Met His Match and *The Knife Man: Blood, Body-snatching and the Birth of Modern Surgery*

Hugh Williamson

Physician, Patriot, and Founding Father

George F. Sheldon, MD

an imprint of Prometheus Books
59 John Glenn Drive, Amherst, New York 14228-2119

Published 2010 by Humanity Books, an imprint of Prometheus Books

Inquiries should be addressed to
Humanity Books
59 John Glenn Drive
Amherst, New York 14228–2119
VOICE: 716–691–0133, ext. 210
FAX: 716–691–0137
WWW.PROMETHEUSBOOKS.COM

14 13 12 11 10 5 4 3 2 1

Library of Congress Cataloging-in-Publication Data

Sheldon, George F., 1934–
Hugh Williamson : physician, patriot, and founding father / by George F. Sheldon.
p. cm.
Includes bibliographical references and index.
ISBN 978–1–59102–770–6 (pbk. : alk. paper)
1. Williamson, Hugh, 1735–1819. 2. United States. Declaration of Independence—Signers—Biography. 3. United States. Continental Congress—Biography. 4. North Carolina—History—Colonial period, ca. 1600–1775. 5. North Carolina—History—Revolution, 1775–1783. 6. United States—History—Revolution, 1775–1783. 7. United States—Politics and government—1775–1783. I. Title.

E302.6.W6S447 2009
973.3'13092—dc22
[B]

2009032813

Printed in the United States on acid-free paper

Dedication

Family is undoubtedly the biggest influence on historical projects. My wife, Ruth, is a history major; my older brother, Richard, is a retired professor of Russian language and literature at Dartmouth; and my younger brother, William, has a PhD in German history and retired as director of the German America House in Nuremburg, Germany.

Many of the Founders had daughters whom they valued, Thomas Jefferson's Maria and Martha and John Adams's Nabby, for instance. Nancy Isenberg's fine new book about Aaron Burr, *The Fallen Founder,* shows him to be clearly advanced among the Founders in his appreciation of the intellectual potential of women. His daughter, Theodosia Burr Alston, was taught language, mathematics, and philosophy and was considered by him and others as an intellectual equal or superior.

I continue to learn from my daughters as they mature in their chosen professions, Anne as a secondary school teacher, Betsy a health and human services administrator, and Julia as a doctor of veterinary medicine.

Students at the University of North Carolina and other fine state universities are beneficiaries of Hugh Williamson and the Founding Fathers. In addition to numerous other contributions to the founding of the United States in the Age of Enlightenment, Williamson participated in the evolution of pre–Revolutionary War academies into or the founding of nondenominational, publicly supported universities: the University of Delaware, the University of Tennessee, and the University of North Carolina.

Contents

Contents

Contents

Foreword

It isn't every year that an individual who has distinguished himself as a highly competent surgeon and teacher of medicine will turn and in the fullness of his career write an important biography of a significant figure of the Revolutionary period in American history. George Sheldon has done so. On these pages he brings an authentic Revolutionary hero, Hugh Williamson, into your acquaintance.

Dr. Sheldon rose to unusual levels of achievement in academic medicine. Because of self-imposed standards of quality of teaching and excellence of performance as a surgeon, those same qualitative personal demands have produced a most readable and exciting story of a unique, relatively unknown, yet quite important figure of early American history.

Hugh Williamson was different; he had a fine education

and he used that great asset fully in the service of the spirit of revolution in his time. Signer of the Constitution, Williamson came by his role as patriot out of service as a university professor; a scholar of medicine and science; colleague of Jefferson, Washington, Madison, and Franklin; and a molder of government in North Carolina in the late eighteenth century.

George Sheldon's scholarly work clearly establishes the vital relationship Hugh Williamson had to the emergence of the fledgling democracy in the New World. In North Carolina he stands with William R. Davie and others who gave this state its very proud role of builder of a new nation of free people.

Here then is the story of a true Revolutionary spirit, an authentic patriot. You will enjoy getting to know him.

William Friday,
President Emeritus Honorary
The University of North Carolina

Preface

Hugh Williamson (1735–1819) was a product of the eighteenth-century Enlightenment. He was a Founding Father, one of the thirty-nine signers of the Constitution of the United States, a citizen-soldier, and legislator. During the Revolutionary War, he was a spy, a courier for Benjamin Franklin, and surgeon general of the North Carolina Revolutionary War militia. After the war, he became a politician and served in the North Carolina legislature, the Continental Congress (1782–1785), the Constitutional Convention, and the first United States House of Representatives (1790–1793).

Unlike many Revolutionary War leaders, Williamson had a formal education. He held bachelor of arts and master of arts (mathematics) degrees from what is now the University of Pennsylvania, an MD degree from the University of Utrecht, and an honorary LLD degree from the University of Leiden for his work in astronomy. He was a learned scientist who was active in the American Philosophical Society. He supported academies and the nascent universities of the Atlantic Coast, such as the University of North Carolina, the University of Delaware, the University of Pennsylvania, Princeton University, the University of Tennessee, and Davidson College. He was a faculty member at what are now the University of Pennsylvania, the University of Delaware, and Princeton University. He was a colleague of George Washington, Thomas Jefferson, James Madison, and Benjamin Franklin and was influential in developing land policies that shaped the national domain.

I discovered Hugh Williamson in the course of research for a named lectureship, the Fitts Oration of the American Association for the Surgery of Trauma. The topic for that lecture was *John Hunter and the American School of Surgery*,[1] a topic based on the post-London careers of the American students of John Hunter. Hunter was the leading surgeon-biologist of the Enlightenment. Study at his anatomical school (actually a museum and zoo) on Leicester Square and Great Windmill Street in London was the goal of all students of medicine who could attain it.

European medical schools, dominated by the University of Edinburgh, were the only route to professional education for physicians from many countries in the eighteenth and nineteenth centuries, including America. American students during that period would finish their baccalaureate degrees at existing schools in colonial America. Many would then pursue the only medical education available in the colonies, which consisted of "reading with the doctor" and then "riding with the doctor." They would then take a Continental tour, which in the latter years of the eighteenth century evolved into an axis where they would obtain a medical degree at a Continental university before or after time spent studying in the anatomical schools in London. Especially fortunate students would live in Hunter's compound as a place of surgical practice; Edward Jenner, discoverer of the vaccine for smallpox, was the first of these "resident pupils." Hunter's anatomical museum and zoo functioned in effect as an early form of a medical school (many of its original 15,000 or so specimens from this period are still to be seen in the Hunterian Museum at the Royal College of Surgeons in London at Lincoln Fields Inn). Hunter kept a register of the students who worked with him, which included the majority of the faculties of the first five medical schools in the United States; among them were the first professor of surgery in America, John Jones, at King's College (now Columbia University); the father of American surgery, Philip Syng Physick; and Benjamin Rush, the University of Pennsylvania physician patriot who signed the Declaration of Independence. The register also included Hugh Williamson.

As my quest for information on the careers of Hunter's American students came to a close, I had not found any details on Hugh Williamson's post-Hunterian career. The search for him in Philadelphia, where much of his early education and career occurred, did not reveal his activities during the Revolutionary War period. I was surprised, though, to find that he had returned from France about six months after the Declaration of Independence and was nearly captured by the British while carrying dispatches to the Continental Congress from Benjamin Franklin. Williamson surprisingly was not given a commission in the medical department of the Continental Army during the war, and the reason seems to be that before he delivered the dispatches to the Congress, it had received a report from Silas Deane, its first official emissary to France, stating that he thought Williamson was a British spy or sympathizer. Deane's suspicions were most likely based on Williamson's several meetings with Lord North in the run-up to the war, after the Declaration of Independence had been adopted. Meanwhile, Williamson was becoming engaged in shipping with his brother, a South Carolina ship captain, and, as the Chesapeake Bay was blockaded by Lord Howe, which thus cut off commerce between North and South, he did not return to Philadelphia but instead moved to North Carolina.

In my own backyard of North Carolina, I discovered more about Williamson. His brief but important nine-year career in North Carolina in addition to his serving as surgeon general of the North Carolina Revolutionary War militia, included serving as a delegate to the first North Carolina legislature, delegate from North Carolina to the Continental Congress, and delegate to the Annapolis Convention on trade issues and then the Constitutional Convention. Following his important role in ratification of the Constitution by North Carolina, the twelfth state to do so, he became a member of the first two federal Houses of Representatives.

Williamson was an early secretary of the board of trustees of the University of North Carolina, the first state university in the United States to graduate students in the eighteenth century. The founding of this university fulfilled George Washington's dream of having a publicly supported, nondenominational institution of higher education in America. Williamson wrote the first chronicle of North Carolina, in two volumes as *The History of North Carolina*;[2] it was not well received because it did not discuss much history. He may have intended more, as notes of his appear in William R. Davie's journals that suggest material about events not discussed in his chronicle, but if he did intend to do so, he never got around to it. Moreover, he, as others, saw North Carolina as a backward state in contrast to its two neighbors, Virginia and South Carolina. It was often referred to as "Poor Carolina." Williamson noted that the early political life of North Carolina was "a history of disasters, misrule, and oppression," and that North Carolina lagged behind its neighboring colonies economically, socially, and politically. Local civil strife included the 1771 Battle of Alamance and the Regulator conflict. Williamson said, "If I had been disposed to record disputes that originated in pride, resentment, the spirit of party, avarice, or dishonest temper, I might have swelled this work to a considerable bulk. Such details of follies and vices cannot be interesting."[3] That opinion, written in 1812, was from a man who witnessed the Boston Tea Party, spied for the Revolutionary cause, was wartime surgeon general, and was active in politics both in the legislature and the Constitutional Convention! He certainly witnessed conflict and avarice in all of his public life.

Williamson was active in the formation of complex land policies of the postwar period, which involved a fair amount of speculation. During this activity, he became a close friend and business associate of the Blount family. After the war, Williamson recommended to President George Washington that William Blount, his friend and fellow delegate to the Constitutional Convention, become governor of the Tennessee territory, and he was appointed to that position. Unfortunately, Blount later became involved with an Aaron Burr–type of conspiracy to establish a country out of the remaining Spanish territories in what is now part of the United States and the incompletely defined Louisiana Purchase. While a United States senator, Blount became the first official impeached under the new Constitution.

One of my sources was the excellent master's thesis of Helen Jenkins in 1950, awarded here at the University of North Carolina. The historical societies of Pennsylvania and Boston were very helpful. Some useful material exists in the North Carolina State Archives in Raleigh. The National Archives in Washington, D.C., is a rich source of Williamson's correspondence with Jefferson, Madison, and Washington.

Concerning the Constitutional Convention of 1787, Madison's notes of its debates are the acknowledged, accurate, and detailed account, from the minutes he took. Madison had studied past governments in studying the classics and was a true student of the eighteenth-century Enlightenment. He went to Philadelphia prepared to write a constitution that corrected faults of prior governments emerging from military conflict. Of interest is his having his notes posthumously published in spite of great urging to do so earlier. They were published with his other papers in 1840, four years after his death. The reason he offered for delaying publication was to save them for the value they would bring as revenue to his will. One wonders if he had other reasons. A motive may have been to allow the Supreme Court to ponder the meaning of the constitution as it built American law on that document, testing it, melding it with English common law, and so on. Had the notes of the convention been available, it is possible that delegates might have been called to be involved in opinions, especially in areas where they had disagreed. The first "student" to evaluate the printed constitution in depth was Abraham Lincoln. Lincoln pored over the constitution for the better part of a year, in preparation for the Cooper Union speech that secured the Republican nomination and ultimately the presidency for him. In it he cited the opinions of the Founders, all then long dead, and their opinions on slavery.[4]

Much of the "hands on" work was done by work-study students. Graduate students in history at the University of Pennsylvania scoured and copied many of the archives in Philadelphia, from the College of Physicians of Philadelphia, the American Philosophical Society, the Library Company and others. Here at the University of North Carolina, Chapel Hill, Leah Whittington, Jennifer Meyer, Jennifer Kagarise, and Courtney Schumacher all worked on reading the downloaded letters from the Internet on various founders. Dr. William "Bill" Powell, the historian of North Carolina, was always interested in the Williamson biography and read early drafts.

Special thanks are due Mary Jane Kagarise, RN, MSPH, who drafted most of the work on Williamson's North Carolina experience. She read drafts and was offered a coauthorship. In the latter phases of preparation of this book, I enlisted the superb assistance of Chris Crochetière, editor of BW&A Books, Inc. of Durham, North Carolina. I have previously published with their assistance and value their input. Robert Milks assisted us, a copy editor of great skill.

I am grateful for the editorial patience and assistance of Prometheus Books, and especially its editor in chief, Steven L. Mitchell.

Williamson has deserved a biography for many years. I hope this one does him justice.

Prologue

"He Was No Ordinary Man"

As a physician and scientist, Hugh Williamson was one of the best to be found in the United States. As an army surgeon, he succeeded in practice and recommended inoculation against smallpox for civilians and military troops before they entered active service. Immunizations are now routinely given in all modern armies. As a scientist, Williamson was admired in both America and Europe. As a commercial man, he was active in the building up of the carrying trade and was one of the first to have a correct idea of the practicability of the Erie Canal. He endeavored to establish a plan of social insurance for sailors. As a legislator, he was active in the interest of his state and nation. As a philanthropist, he gave generously to worthy causes. As an educator, he took much time in establishing and maintaining schools. As a statesman, he endeavored to guide the nation into safe channels. He warned against the possible division of the states and did his best to defeat legislation that tended to this end. As a servant of the people, he gained their confidence and thanks. In view of Dr. Williamson's constructive ideas and unselfish service, we may well say that he was "no ordinary man."[1]

Chronology

1718	Blackbeard is said to have captured the ship in which Hugh Williamson's mother, Mary Davison, crosses the ocean from Londonderry to Pennsylvania at the age of three, with her father, George Davison
1730	Arrival in America of Hugh Williamson's father, John W. Williamson, from Dublin, Ireland
1731	Marriage of Hugh Williamson's parents
Dec. 5, 1735	Birth of Hugh Williamson (HW) in Chester County, Pennsylvania

Chronology

1753	College of Philadelphia chartered; HW enters first class
1756–57	HW employed by the College of Philadelphia as a teacher of Latin and English
May 17, 1757	HW receives a BA degree at the College of Philadelphia's first commencement
1757	Death of John Williamson
1757	HW returns home to Shippensburg, Pennsylvania, to settle his father's estate
1758	HW pursues theological studies in Connecticut with Dr. Samuel Finley
1759	HW licensed to preach; resigns because of ill health
1760	HW receives an MA degree from the College of Philadelphia
1760–63	HW serves as a professor and chair of mathematics, College of Philadelphia

Chronology

Oct. 8, 1763	HW gives notice of intended resignation from professorship to study medicine
1764	HW enters University of Edinburgh for one year, to study medicine full time; continues studies at London with John Hunter, eventually obtaining MD degree from University of Utrecht
Jan. 19, 1768	HW elected to membership in American Philosophical Society
June 3, 1769	HW studies transit of Venus for American Philosophical Society
Nov. 9, 1769	HW studies transit of Mercury for Society and evolves own theory about comets
1769	Newark Academy incorporated by Penn charter; HW one of the original trustees and incorporators and first secretary of the board
Dec. 1771	HW publishes "On the Variations of the Compass" in *Pennsylvania Gazette and Journal*

Chronology

1771	HW's "An Essay on Comets" published in the first volume of *Transactions of the American Philosophical Society*
Dec. 1773	HW concludes a trip to the West Indies to raise money for the Newark Academy in Delaware; attends planning meetings for, and observes, the Boston Tea Party; on another fund-raising mission for the Newark Academy, he sails to England in one of John Hancock's fast ships, carrying word of the Boston Tea Party event to London
Feb. 19, 1774	HW interviewed by the British Privy Council about Boston Tea Party and colonial matters
1775	HW studies electricity with Benjamin Franklin and John Hunter; publishes "Experiments with Observations on the Electric Eel" in *Philosophical Transactions of the Royal Society of London*; anonymously publishes *The Plea of the Colonies*, which solicits the support of the English Whigs for the American cause

Chronology

1776	American Colonies proclaim independence; HW sails for America from France after spending some months in Europe
Apr. 12, 1776	Halifax Resolves, supporting independence from England, unanimously adopted in North Carolina
May 27, 1776	North Carolina voices support for independence from England at Continental Congress
June 7, 1776	Motion made in Continental Congress for an independent United States
July 2, 1776	Independence resolution adopted by Congress
July 4, 1776	Approval of the final draft of the Declaration of Independence by Continental Congress
Oct. 1776	HW sails from Nantes, Frances, to America; escapes British blockade; delivers dispatches from Franklin; denied commission in Continental Army

Chronology

Mar. 1777	HW evades British blockade of sea trade by relocating to Edenton, North Carolina; prospers in mercantile business trading with French West Indies; returns to practice of medicine
July 28, 1778	HW affirms loyalty to North Carolina and the colonies by signing the Book of Allegiance in Edenton
Oct. 1779	HW appointed surgeon general of the North Carolina troops by Major General Richard Caswell; serves until 1781
Fall 1780	HW serves under command of General Isaac Gregory at Battle of Camden in South Carolina; frequently crosses British lines to tend to wounded; prevents sickness among troops through attention to food, clothing, hygiene, and shelter; enhances reputation as a patriot
July 1781	HW resigns from North Carolina militia and returns to Edenton
Apr. 17, 1782	HW elected to North Carolina House of Commons from Edenton, begins his political career

May 3, 1782	HW elected by General Assembly as delegate to the Continental Congress at Philadelphia
July 19, 1782	HW assumes seat at Continental Congress; serves until 1785; resumes active participation in American Philosophical Society
1783	HW argues for a southern location for the federal seat of government, preferring Falls of the Potomac, near where Washington, D.C., now located; takes position against slavery
Apr. 30, 1783	William Blount resigns from Continental Congress to return to North Carolina General Assembly to represent Craven County; replaced by Richard Dobbs Spaight, also from Craven County
May 14, 1783	General Assembly of North Carolina thanks Hugh Williamson and William Blount for their address to the minister of France on the birth of the dauphin of France
Sept. 3, 1783	Definitive Treaty of Peace and Commerce with Great Britain concluded, officially ending the Revolutionary War

Chronology

1784	HW votes in favor of Thomas Jefferson's Land Ordinance Act of 1784, the only Southern congressmen to do so because of restrictions on the slavery expansion provision
May 24, 1784	General Assembly of North Carolina expresses state's appreciation of faithful services to Hugh Williamson and Benjamin Hawkins
Sept. 30, 1784	HW writes letter on Cession Act to Governor Alexander Martin of North Carolina
1785	The Ordinance of 1785 includes HW's grid design for western settlement; creation of Davidson Academy (named for his uncle) by the legislature of North Carolina; HW serves as one of its incorporators and trustees
June 15, 1785	HW re-elected from Chowan County to the North Carolina General Assembly for a second term
June 10, 1786	HW elected to be a commissioner to the Annapolis Convention

Chronology

Apr. 3, 1787	HW appointed by North Carolina governor to Constitutional Convention at Philadelphia to be held on May 4, 1787
May 25, 1787	Constitutional Convention gets under way; HW most active representative from North Carolina; attends faithfully; demonstrates keen debating skills; serves on numerous important committees
1787	Shays's Rebellion in Massachusetts demonstrates "disunity" among the United States
Aug. 1787	HW publishes *The American Museum* under pseudonym, Sylvius
Sept. 17, 1787	HW signs the United States Constitution as a North Carolina delegate and one of thirty-nine of fifty-five signing
1788	HW returns to the Continental Congress and serves until the Constitutional Congress commences in 1789
July 21, 1788	Hillsborough Convention in North Carolina fails to ratify Constitution

Chronology

July 25, 1788	Virginia ratifies Constitution assuring the needed majority required for Philadelphia Constitution to become the new governing document of the United States
Aug. 4, 1788	North Carolina declines unconditional ratification of the Constitution
Sept. 17, 1788	HW publishes article in *New York Advertiser* and *State Gazette of North Carolina*, predicting North Carolina will eventually join Union
Jan. 1789	HW marries Maria Apthorp, daughter of prominent member of the king's council of New York, who bears him two sons
1789	HW relinquishes seat in North Carolina General Assembly
Apr. 30, 1789	George Washington takes oath of office as first president of the United States; new federal revenue system takes effect, making North Carolina imports subject to duties and forfeitures

Chronology

Mar. 4, 1789	First Congress under new Constitution submits twelve amendments to the states; ten adopted by requisite number of states
Sept. 25, 1789	Submission and ratification of the ten amendments, the Bill of Rights, by Congress
Nov. 1789	HW is member of the Fayetteville Convention (state ratification convention for Constitution); votes for ratification
Nov. 21, 1789	North Carolina, reassured by the Bill of Rights, ratifies Constitution and joins the Union
Dec. 22, 1789	North Carolina approves all twelve originally proposed amendments to the Constitution
1789–93	HW active with Blounts in mercantile ventures
1789	Ratification of charter of University of North Carolina by General Assembly
Mar. 19, 1790	HW takes seat in federal Congress in time for second session of Congress; serves until March 3, 1793

1790	James Iredell, friend of Williamson, appointed a Supreme Court justice by George Washington; HW compiles map of trans-Appalachian region
Oct. 20, 1790	Maria Apthorp Williamson dies
July 20, 1791	HW an original trustee of University of North Carolina; attends his first meeting
1793	HW moves to New York when term in Congress expires and engages in literary and philanthropic pursuits; founds the Literary and Philosophical Society of New York and is prominent member of the New York Historical Society
1795	Some of HW's maps published in Matthew Carey's *General Atlas*
Feb. 6, 1795	Adoption of bylaws of University of North Carolina; HW starts service as secretary of the Board of Trustees of University of North Carolina, a position he holds until Dec. 4, 1798

Chronology

1796	Land Act of 1796 adopted; originates in a bill introduced four years earlier by HW
1799	Williamson County, Tennessee, named in honor of HW, citing his work as surgeon general of North Carolina troops in the American Revolution, North Carolina legislator, and member of the Continental and United States Congresses; HW publishes *Observation on the Proposed State Road from Hudson's River to Lake Erie*
1807	HW publishes "Of the Fascination of Serpents" in American Repository; HW's older son dies; HW publishes "Observations on the Climate" in *Transactions of the American Philosophical Society*
1812	HW publishes *History of North Carolina* in two volumes
1815	HW's younger son dies
May 22, 1819	HW dies at age 83; interment in the Apthorp tomb in Trinity Churchyard, New York City, near the resting place of Alexander Hamilton

Chronology

1823	Erie Canal project completed, as envisioned by HW
1839	Williamson County, Illinois, formed from Franklin County, Tennessee; named for Williamson County, Tennessee, by immigrants from that area

Chapter 1

Early Years

One of the most detestable skunks in human society.
—Benjamin Franklin, writing of Hugh Williamson in 1764

Hugh Williamson was of Scots-Irish descent. His parents, who married in 1731, were known for their religious faith, integrity, industriousness, and frugality. At the age of three, Dr. Williamson's mother, Mary Davison, came to America with her father, George Davison, from Londonderry, Ireland, and settled in Philadelphia. Family legend has it that the ship that brought them was captured by Blackbeard the pirate.[1] Hugh Williamson's father, John W. Williamson (1709–1757), was a clothier from Dublin, Ireland, who came to America around 1730 and settled in Chester County, Pennsylvania.

Hugh Williamson

Hugh Williamson was born December 5, 1735, in West Nottingham Township on Oterara Creek, Chester County, Pennsylvania. He was the eldest of six sons and four daughters and grew up in a household of thrift and morality. Williamson's earliest education occurred in a country school near his home. At an early age, he intended to become a minister and would visit and pray with neighbors who were sick.[2] His father was decisive in encouraging him to study and become a scholar of the arts. The plan, as with other colonial families that could afford it, was for him to study in England. In order to learn languages and prepare for college, Williamson attended New London Roads Academy, which evolved into one of the most celebrated schools in Pennsylvania and became a lifelong attachment for Williamson. On November 24, 1743, the Philadelphia newspaper the *Pennsylvania Gazette*, announced the academy's opening: "We are informed that there is a Free-School opened at the House of Mr. Alison in Chester County, for the Promotion of Learning, where all Persons may be instructed in the Languages and some other parts of Polite Literature, without any Expences for their Education."[3]

Under the direction of the school's founder, the Reverend Francis Alison, a witty but stern instructor, Williamson learned the classical languages of Latin, Greek, and Hebrew. Alison was born in County Donegal, Ireland, in 1705. As with many of the founding educators in colonial America, he was a graduate of the University of Edinburgh. He later became the first president of what would become the University of Delaware, where he taught English grammar, basing his instruction on the grammatical structure of Latin.

At the New London Roads Academy Williamson also studied logic, moral philosophy (including ethics and political economy), mathematics, mythology, rhetoric, geography, and history. Learning techniques favored at the academy were debate, didactic lecture, and recitation. Most of the books used by Williamson and his fellow students were from Alison's personal library. Books were a scarce commodity and not readily available in New London. Williamson would sometimes walk the forty-five miles to Philadelphia to borrow a book about science or mathematics.[4]

Hugh Williamson continued his education at the same academy when it moved to its new location in Lewisville, about five miles away, where it came under the direction of the Reverend Alexander McDowell, a pupil of Alison's. Classes were largely conducted in McDowell's home, a mile southwest of Lewisville at the northern edge of Cecil County, Maryland. McDowell, like Alison, had considerable difficulty acquiring books. He searched relentlessly, especially for Hebrew books, finally borrowing some from a friend in Ireland. Williamson remained at the academy until his skills were proficient for college, distinguishing himself by his diligence, orderliness, and upstanding moral and religious behavior.[5]

Throughout his adulthood Williamson remained devoted

to securing funding and support for the New London Roads Academy. In 1760 the academy relocated to Newark, Delaware. In 1764 it was incorporated by a Penn charter and became the Academy of Newark. Its reputation for fine learning propelled it to develop into Newark College in 1834, Delaware College in 1843, and the University of Delaware in 1921. Upon its charter in 1769, Hugh Williamson became one of the original thirteen trustees of the Academy of Newark and was elected by the trustees to serve as the board's first secretary.

After graduating from the academy, Williamson returned home, taught himself Euclid's *Elements* and studied mathematics further. His lifelong commitment to order, precision, and mathematical reasoning probably developed during this time. His father arranged for him to complete his education in Europe, but when the College of Philadelphia was chartered in 1753, under the leadership of Dr. Benjamin Franklin, Williamson entered its first class.[6] The College of Philadelphia would later become the University of Pennsylvania, in 1790.

Williamson was employed beginning in 1756 (while still a student) as a teacher in both the Latin and English schools connected with the college. Just before his graduation his family moved to Shippensburg, in Cumberland County, Pennsylvania. The same year as his baccalaureate graduation, Williamson's father died, leaving his eldest son as the sole executor of his estate. So in 1757, Williamson moved to Shippensburg, where he stayed with his mother for about two years to settle the estate and personally collect its widely scattered debts. His father's will left specific monies or properties to his wife, Mary; his sons Hugh, John, David, and Samuel; and his daughters Rachel, Margaret, and Mary. His younger children were to be under guardianship. Of interest was the bequest of a Negro maid slave to Rachel and a Negro slave, Cesar, to his wife, Mary, or "if he survives Mary then . . . to David, Samuel and John."[7] Hugh Williamson himself never owned slaves and was against the practice. In later years, when the Constitutional Convention was struggling with the slavery issue, Williamson was instrumental in the Three-Fifths Compromise, the methodology adopted for the counting of slaves for census taking.

Hugh Williamson was quite distressed by his father's death, and became ill and fatigued while serving as executor of the estate. "His constitution received a shock which induced an alarming hypochondria that was only relieved by traveling, and a release from the anxiety and care which his attention to business had imposed."[8]

When not occupied with administering the affairs of the estate, Williamson studied divinity under the direction of Dr. Samuel Finley, who preached at East Nottingham Township in Chester County. Williamson was drawn to the ministry from a sense of duty, believing that his piety and education uniquely qualified him for it.[9] In 1759 he progressed to formal theological studies in Connecticut, and was licensed to preach.

Upon his return home from Connecticut, Williamson was

admitted to the Presbytery of Philadelphia and preached for two years. He was never ordained or placed in charge of a congregation. He continued activities with the Presbyterian Church and served on a committee under the articles of the Presbyterian denomination to enable that the church act as a body in regard to the conflict among the Presbyterian Old and New "Lights." Among the group in addition to Williamson were William Allison and William Rush. Ill health and his growing disgust over the doctrinal controversies in the Presbyterian Church between the more evangelical followers of George Whitefield ("New Lights") and the orthodox party ("Old Lights") were factors in his decision to change his vocation from theology to medicine. Medicine had been one of Williamson's favorite subjects during divinity training. During the colonial period medicine was often practiced by religious leaders, as for example Cotton Mather. Hugh Williamson's nephew later remarked: "My mother can give but little information respecting the doctor's study of medicine; she however believes that this science must have been a favorite study with him long before he had determined to attend to it regularly, as she found him, when studying divinity, giving directions respecting inoculation for the small-pox."[10]

Returning to the College of Philadelphia, Williamson received the degree of master of arts in 1760. He was immediately appointed to a professorship and served as chair of mathematics from 1761 to 1763. Having begun his study of medicine while teaching mathematics, he gave notice of his intended resignation from the professorship on October 8, 1763.[11]

In 1764 Hugh Williamson entered the University of Edinburgh to pursue the full-time study of medicine, where he studied for a year before transferring to the University of Utrecht, which had been the leading medical education site in the early eighteenth century. He studied with the famous Herman Boerhaave and completed his medical education there, receiving the degree of doctor of medicine. He then toured northern Scotland and went to London, where he remained for twelve months pursuing further medical studies as a "resident pupil" of the dominant scientist of the eighteenth century, John Hunter. Following a tour on the Continent, Dr. Williamson returned to America with vastly improved health and practiced medicine successfully in Philadelphia for a number of years.

Dr. Williamson entered politics in the mid-1760s as a partisan of the proprietary government in Pennsylvania and initially a political opponent of Benjamin Franklin. Williamson's authorship of the scurrilous pamphlet *What Is Sauce for a Goose Is Also Sauce for a Gander, An Epitaph on a Certain Great Man* (1764) along with other essays had positioned him in opposition to Franklin. He charged Franklin with supporting the Stamp Act, and in turn was called by Franklin "one of the most detestable skunks in human society."[12]

> In time the controversy, which had originated in questions of frontier defense, merged in the more general issue of the virtues or weaknesses of the Proprietary government. Franklin asserted, in Cool Thoughts on the Present Situation of our Public Affairs, that 'the political body of a proprietary government contains those convulsive principles that will at length destroy it.' He was ably answered by Hugh Williamson, professor of mathematics at the College and an ardent Presbyterian, who in his three 'Plain Dealer' papers claimed he could see no advantage in a change from 'Proprietary Slavery to Royal Liberty.' What we need, he declared, is to advance from 'Quaker Slavery to British Liberty.' Williamson further accused Franklin in his article, 'What is Sauce for the Goose is also Sauce for the Gander,' of having deserted the interests of the frontiersmen for reasons of his own political advancement. So deeply did the schism cut into popular feeling and prejudices that reason soon gave way to bitterness, satire to personal abuse, and good taste to outright scurrility.[13]

Of interest during this period of time in Philadelphia, a debate over Parliament's prerogative ultimately involved colonial independence. The debate's origins lay in religious division over the issues of the Great Awakening, which—in Philadelphia—occurred with the coming of George Whitefield in 1739, a division that produced a flood of sermons and pamphlets attacking or defending the new faith. This debate individualized and democratized religion in nondenominational dimensions. What began as a religious issue broadened into acrimonious debate that assumed an increasingly secular tone. Two wars, the French and Indian War (1754–1763), followed by Pontiac's Rebellion, sometimes called Pontiac's Rebellion or War (1763–1766), further mixed religion in the issue with the matters of defense, Indian policy, and relations between the assembly in Pennsylvania and the proprietors. Moreover, also in 1763, the Paxton Boys (a group of men from Paxton, Pennsylvania) raided a settlement of peaceful Conestoga Indians, massacring many and adding to the further destabilization of the frontier. In response, Governor John Penn issued warrants for the Paxton Boys' arrest. British imperial policies gradually swept all provincial controversies into a continental tide of revolution.[14]

The intensity of the social cleavage of the 1760s that occurred in both the "Great Awakening" and the Quaker Assembly was especially poignant during Pontiac's Rebellion. In 1763 a mob of frontiersmen massacred Christian Indians at Conestoga Manor and then marched on to Philadelphia. Even the Quakers took up arms in self-defense against them. A committee of clergymen and assembly members, headed by Franklin, met them at Germantown and invited them to disperse. The proponents of all factions, Quaker, Presbyterian, Anglican, and Proprietary, rushed into print to provide a point of view on the so-called Paxton Boys, the name of the rebellious group. Franklin spoke for the Pennsylvania Assembly and posed the query "are we government described in a narrative of the late massacres in Lancaster County?" He characterized the rioters as unpopular and obvious. David James Dove, defending the Paxton Boys in the pamphlet *Quaker Unmasked*, inquired "whether the affection which some principles of that sect have shown to Indians can be owing to the charms of their squaws, or advantages of trades." The Quakers did their utmost to demolish Dove in print, and a deluge of writings occurred. "The religious clash merged with the general political unrest. It all would lead to the general unrest, increasing democratization which became directed at British colonial policy."[15]

During those years, the narrow ecclesiastic arguments of the 1740s advanced into the dignified presentation of principles by John Dickinson, John Galloway, and James Wilson. The public matured in its understanding, and the press was active on the issue. A lot of controversy came out of a variety of "new side" Presbyterians boldly preaching in a stronghold of "old side" conservatism ("side" being equivalent to "light"). The Reverend William Smith, with whom Williamson would work on scientific studies, was pragmatic and political and had all the zeal and love of battle of a good combatant. He enlisted in the proprietary ranks.

Chapter 2

Scientist

> Knowledge only is of value which exalts virtue, multiplies the comforts, Soothes the sorrow, and improves the general felicity of human intercourse.
>
> —Hugh Williamson, recounted by David Hosack

Williamson made significant scientific contributions while in Philadelphia, England, and, in his later years, New York. His development as a scientist and educator was evidence of a strong intellectual curiosity that eventually drew him to the philosophical and then practical concepts that led to revolution. Another natural evolution from his scientific interest was a commitment to education. He eventually held faculty positions at what became the University of Pennsylvania, the University of Delaware, Princeton University, and Columbia University. He was a trustee of the University of

Pennsylvania, the University of Delaware, University of Nashville, many academies, and the University of North Carolina.

Williamson began nine years of medical practice in Philadelphia in the midst of political, religious, scientific, and social turmoil that existed in the run-up to the American Revolution. When again his delicate health began to interfere, this time with his medical practice, he devoted increasing attention to scientific, literary, and philosophical pursuits. He found practicing medicine "emotionally exhausting."[1] His acute awareness of the suffering of his patients made him prone to the insomnia and frequent fevers he would commonly suffer when caring for the seriously ill.[2]

Williamson had been well prepared by his education for these intellectual pursuits. Williamson was in the first graduating class of seven from the College of Philadelphia, all of whom became distinguished scholars. Williamson was mentored and influenced by Theophilus Grew, a professor of mathematics, who made the calculations for the almanacs published at Philadelphia, New York, Annapolis, and Williamsburg. Grew also wrote a text on the *Use of the Globe* for students in the academies and colleges. He contributed mathematical puzzles to the newspapers and was active in making surveys and setting boundaries. When he died, he was succeeded by Hugh Williamson as teacher of mathematics at the college. The Reverend John Ewing became provost and Williamson would follow him to Delaware and England as a fund-raiser.[3]

On January 19, 1768, Williamson was elected to membership in the American Philosophical Society, founded by Benjamin Franklin. He attended his first meeting January 26, 1768, at the famous Indian Queen Tavern, along with sixteen other initiates who, like Williamson, had all been named trustees of the College of Philadelphia. Williamson enjoyed the meetings; he attended regularly and was an active participant. Franklin and other founders of the Society doubted the worthiness of these newly elected members, which caused some consternation. The Indian Queen Tavern, where the Society generally met, would also lodge Williamson nineteen years later during the Constitutional Convention in 1787.

In 1769 the American Philosophical Society appointed Williamson to serve on a commission with David Rittenhouse, Dr. John Ewing, and William Smith, among others, to study the transit of the planet Venus across the sun on June 3. His report, preserved in volume 1 of the *Transactions of the American Philosophical Society*, was pronounced by the astronomer royal of Great Britain to be "excellent and complete."[4] Williamson served on a similar commission to study the transit of the planet Mercury on November 9 that same year. His work for these commissions was important in settling the longitude of Philadelphia, among other places.

The equipment used by these amateur scientists was quite surprising, considering Franklin's doubt that a single tele-

> scope adequate for making the observations could be found in the entire province. Four telescopes were assembled at Philadelphia. Ewing planned to use the new one which the [Pennsylvania] assembly had provided for the occasion. Joseph Shippen had obtained permission from the proprietors to use a small reflecting telescope belonging to them. Thomas Prior had a telescope of his own and a large refracting telescope was borrowed from Miss Polly Norris for the use of Dr. Hugh Williamson.[5]

Carl and Jessica Bridenbaugh, in *Rebels and Gentlemen,* addressed Williamson's accomplishments in astronomy. Observation sites for a scientific observation of the planets were three: the city, the residence of Rittenhouse at Norriton, and the lighthouse at Cape Henlopen. Hugh Williamson, Colonel Joseph Shippen, and others assisted Dr. Ewing, an accomplished mathematician, astronomer, and friend of Hugh Williamson. Owen Biddle was an instrument maker, and made an instrument for the sightings. An altitude instrument, a transit telescope, and a chronometer were also there. The Philosophical Society encouraged making of other observations also. The successful calculations of these Philadelphia scientists were the first demonstration of American cooperative scholarship by scientific men. The study was "The Transit of Venus Across the Sun."[6]

Williamson did not confine his scientific interests to participation in studies; he helped lead attempts to educate the broader public, as the Bridenbaughs noted. The Reverend John Ewing and Dr. Hugh Williamson asked the College of Philadelphia for the use of rooms for adult education. This was denied, and a course of natural and experimental philosophy at the Masonic Hall in Lodge Alley was done. It was a semiweekly meeting and very popular. Philadelphians became inveterate lecture goers, as Bostonians of a later date did.[7]

As he studied the planets of Venus and Mercury, Williamson evolved his own theory about comets. He came to characterize comets as cool, solid, and opaque bodies that are probably inhabited, rather than destructive masses of fire. Williamson also proposed the existence of multiple solar systems. Despite widespread objections to these views, Williamson persisted and was not proven wrong. His original ideas on comets were also published as *An Essay on Comets and an Account of their Luminous Appearance: together with some conjectures concerning the Origin of Heat* in the first volume of *Transactions of the American Philosophical Society* in 1771. Williamson would later consider his theories on comets to be among his most significant scientific conjectures. His astronomical theories were the basis of his being awarded an honorary LLD from the University of Leiden and being elected to the Society of Science in Holland.[8]

Williamson had a wide variety of scientific interests in addition to astronomy. He navigated the Susquehanna River for about 120 miles in order to inform the Society about how river navigation could be improved. He obtained information from the Society of Sciences at Haarlem on the way the Dutch constructed canals, which supported performing surveys for canals between the Cooper and Santee rivers in South Carolina, through the Great Dismal Swamp to connect North Carolina and Virginia, and from Lake Champlain to the St. Lawrence River. He was among the first to describe the practicality of building a canal from Lake Erie to the Hudson River.[9]

The interest in canals during the formation era of the United States was intense. One outcome of negotiation as the new nation formed was the location of the federal capital. Washington City, was central to the river barge system as a communication link among the thirteen new states along the Chesapeake Bay and inland waterways. States became interested in extending the navigation of rivers,[10] which led to plans for the surveys for the proposed canals between the Cooper and Santee rivers and between North Carolina and Virginia. In the Great Dismal Swamp area of North Carolina, difficulties were encountered.[11] Williamson's information on techniques and equipment the Dutch had used in canal building, along with similar information Thomas Jefferson obtained from France, proved useful in dealing with the difficulties.[12] Williamson described a "castern machine for cleaning canals, and rivers which [he noted] may be usefully employed on some of the slips in Philadelphia."[13] In a letter of June 29, 1795, Williamson conveys extensive survey information from scientific instruments as to the suitability of draining and producing canals from the Great Dismal Swamp.[14] In fact, the remnants of a canal system exist to this day at Foggy Bottom in Washington, D.C. Ultimately, however, his idea of a water system as an essential component of uniting the colonies was replaced by the technology of railroads after 1820.

George Washington, Thomas Jefferson, Hugh Williamson, and others formed the Dismal Swamp Company to capitalize on the transportation network for the thirteen original colonies by waterways. Later, following Williamson's move to New York City in 1793, he became an advisor and advocate to Governor DeWitt Clinton of New York on the planning and financing of the Erie Canal.[15] This was the first federal project dealing with transportation.[16]

Williamson's large network of scientific contacts made it possible for him to acquire unusual items and artifacts. Williamson presented the curator of the American Philosophical Society with a shark's jaw, a skin of a shagrum fish, a porcupine fish, and a specimen of asphalt, obtained from a friend in western Florida.[17]

During the early nineteenth century, in a long letter to Jefferson, Williamson proposed using canal technology to alter the geopolitical situation with France, Spain, and Great Britain after the Louisiana Purchase. Supposing (incorrectly) that West Florida had been ceded to Louisiana, he suggested that a navigable canal be cut through the Bear River producing a conduit between the Tennessee River to Bear River in Mobile with the hope that the Spanish would give up Florida, and that eventually Spain, perhaps through war, could be compelled to give up New Orleans.[18]

On August 17, 1770, Williamson presented to the American Philosophical Society a paper titled "Attempting to account for the change in climate in the cultivated parts of North America." He linked populating and clearing the land to climate changes, since trees impede wind, making for warmth. He explained that land warms and cools more quickly than water. Williamson was primarily concerned about climatic change from a medical point of view. He related remissions of pleuritic and inflammatory fevers to the more temperate winters that resulted from populating the land. His studies on climate also helped lead to his election to the Holland Society of Science and the Society of Arts and Sciences of Utrecht.[19]

Williamson by nature was progressive. He was interested in all devices and ideas that would improve the quality of life and make America better. He published his findings from serving on an American Philosophical Society committee to examine specimens of flint glass manufactured by W. H. Stagle in Manheim of Lancaster County, Pennsylvania.[20] He presented another paper to the American Philosophical Society in December of 1771, "On the Variations of the Compass," which was published in the *Pennsylvania Gazette and Journal.* He and others had noted the variation of the compass from true north, which seemed to change depending on where one was on the Earth. Hugh Williamson submitted a plan to the American Philosophical Society for collecting data on this variation from information that was known in the colonies. Although the results were not conclusive, William Alexander, a scientist, thought sufficient data existed to formulate the general rule that the eastern side of the line had no variation, and variation would increase predictably as one moved to the North East.[21]

After August 20, 1773, Williamson could not attend the American Philosophical Society meetings again until 1782 due to his travels. He sailed for England in 1773 and remained there until 1775, continuing to devote his time to scientific inquiry. While in England he became interested in experimenting with electricity.[22] Hugh Williamson, Benjamin Franklin, and John Hunter worked together on many electrical experiments, Franklin having been a patient of John Hunter and Williamson a resident pupil. Eventually Franklin and Williamson forged a close friendship in England. Their relationship evolved to collaborative research on electricity and electric eels.

> In electricity, the sensation of the early 1770's was the electric eel, a fish which could transmit electric shock to anything it touched. Philosophers on both sides of the Atlantic were amazed and delighted; naturalists as well as academic

> men and physicians began to study this curiosity. William Walsh, one of the leading students of electricity in England, ran a series of experiments on the torpedo, as it was named, in order to determine whether the shock it delivered was electrical in nature. The surgeon, John Hunter, happily dissected one, absorbed in its anatomy. . . . Hugh Williamson carried out another series of experiments on electrical eels from Guiana which he felt to be different from the torpedo used by Walsh.[23]

The electric eel, a fresh-water variety, had been brought to London from Surinam. It could kill prey at a distance and exert painful electrical shocks at will when touched.[24] Williamson performed more than twenty experiments on eels. In the tradition of pure science, he was meticulous in attending to procedure and recording his observations. His "Experiments with Observations on the Gymnotus Electricus, or Electric Eel" was first published in the 1775 edition of the *Philosophical Transactions of the Royal Society of London*, and it was read before the Society.[25] He participated in these experiments with an outstanding group of collaborators, including Jan Ingenhouze in addition to Hunter and Franklin. In 1774, while officially raising funds in England for the Academy of Newark, Dr. Williamson again worked with Benjamin Franklin, who was serving as a colonial agent for the colonies and an agent for Pennsylvania. Williamson served as a courier for Franklin for, like Franklin, he came to support independence for the colonies.

Williamson's scientific career continued throughout his life, except when he was active in the Revolutionary War and in his legislative career. He resumed active participation in the American Philosophical Society in 1782 when he returned to Philadelphia as a delegate from North Carolina to the Continental Congress. He continued to be an active member through 1804 when his final paper, "Of the Fascination of Serpents," was adopted by the Society. It was published in the Society journal *Medical Repository* in 1807.[26] In it Williamson explained that a snake overcomes his prey sheerly by fear, which Williamson called "dementation." When an animal is terrified, it cannot turn its eyes away from the object of its fear, a conjecture he proved through personal experimentation and observation.

Williamson's interest in promoting science and philosophy extended into his career as a legislator; he proposed a bill to secure literary property, which was one of the earliest copyright bills. It gave the author of books, maps, and so on the sole liberty of publishing or printing the work for fourteen years. The title was to be recorded with the secretary of state and a copy provided for use by the state.[27]

Williamson moved to New York in 1793 upon retirement from Congress. After moving to the North, he focused his attention on forming the Literary and Philosophical Society of New York. His work for it covered such topics as the 1792 fevers that prevailed along the Roanoke River in North Carolina; the incorrect manner in which iron rods were being installed against lightning; the means to preserve the commerce of New York; the benefits of civil history; and navigation and navigable canals, published as *Observation on the Proposed State Road from Hudson's River to Lake Erie* (1800).[28] He continued to work during this period with Washington and Jefferson to promote the draining of the Great Dismal Swamp. Scientific, medical, and philosophical papers Williamson wrote were published in the journals of numerous scientific societies.

Williamson had conversations and correspondence with Thomas Jefferson about their mutual interest in natural history. Jefferson had a special interest in mammoth bones and probably dinosaur bones.[29] He even theorized that some of the large animals might still live in the trans-Mississippi West and instructed Lewis and Clark to ascertain that possibility when they went on the Corps of Discovery in 1802.

While in England, Williamson's relationship with Franklin moved him beyond his interest in science to another field; it exposed him to the increasingly fragile relationship between England and America. He became an active pamphleteer and advocate for the American cause and an active participant in the complex activities leading to the American Revolution.

Chapter 3

Revolutionary War Spy

"We have had great pleasure in his company for a few weeks. He favored the meeting with his presence," said Samuel Adams in describing Hugh Williamson's attendance at the planning meetings for the Boston Tea Party.

—*The Writings of Samuel Adams*

"I doubt not the veracity of Dr. Williamson's account of the agency in procuring those letters," said John Adams alluding to the disputed role of Williamson in the Hutchinson-Oliver affair.

—John Adams, quoted in *The Evening Post*

The Newark Academy dispatched Williamson on a fund-raising mission to England in the fall of 1773. It occurred as tensions between England and colonial America were increasing. While preparing to leave from the port of Boston, Williamson's ship was delayed in the harbor, perhaps by accident but more likely by plan, as he then attended the planning meetings for the Boston Tea Party. Immediately after the Boston Tea Party he sailed on one of John Hancock's fastest ships and was the first person to deliver the story of the event to England. It was reported in newspapers and in Parliament via the Privy Council. The background of these events and Williamson's role in them are part of the run up to the American Revolution.

Background to Revolution

The Townshend Acts of 1767 were the last of a number of attempts by the British Parliament to raise revenue through taxation of the American colonies. The irony of this set of taxes, none of which were really very severe, was that it was based on the logic that British monies had been spent on the French and Indian War (the Seven Years' War) fighting the French in colonial America, an expensive war that resulted in depletion of the British treasury. The British, not illogically, thought that some of the cost of paying that war debt should come from the colonies where the war was fought, and where the British Army protected the colonists. France, America's ally in the Revolutionary War, also became financially challenged with its support of the American Revolution adding to that deficit. This was a significant factor that led to the French Revolution.

Politics in Great Britain was quite complicated at the time. Prime Minister William Pitt, who was sympathetic to the Americans, was forced to resign in 1762. The members of Parliament who had backed Pitt's ministry during the Seven Years' War joined the ranks of the parliamentary members who supported King George III's firm position of insisting on the colonies' compliance with British regulation and taxes. The hardened British position toward the American colonies on a variety of issues occurred at a time when the thirteen colonies were increasingly questioning the value of being colonies.

In testimony before Parliament in 1766, Benjamin Franklin, colonial agent for Pennsylvania, Massachusetts, and Georgia, advocated repeal of the Stamp Act, which was part of the Townshend Acts. He suggested that the colonists had denied only Parliament's right to levy internal taxes on the colonies and implied that they were not opposed to external taxation. The position stated in the Declaratory Act passed by Parliament was that it had the right to legislate for the colonies in all matters, including external taxation, but the colonies reserved the right to levy internal taxes. Lord Townshend, chancellor of the Exchequer, denounced that division of authority while at the same time seeing an opportunity to impose a revenue-producing tea tax on the colonies, tea being among the commodities taxed in the Townshend Acts.

The British treasury was heavily dependent on the tea monopoly for tax revenue. An important feature was the East India Company's monopoly over the British colonial markets. In 1767 Parliament had before it a series of proposals dealing with the East India Company. Among them was the Indemnity Bill, which provided that for tea shipped to America, the company be granted a full rebate of all customs duties.

The Townshend Revenue Act of 1767 had several principles that stirred up opposition in America. The stated purpose, to raise revenue from the colonies, brought the strongest negative response. Second, the act provided that tax proceeds would support a colonial civil servant list that required the colonies to pay for British-appointed government bureaucracy and leadership, such as governors. Finally, collecting duties in America underscored the fact that the colonists were paying for their government directly but were subject to "taxation without representation."[1]

Resistance to this legislation occurred as soon as the details of the acts were known, and it took a variety of forms, such as the tea parties. The Boston Tea Party is the most famous of the tea parties, but in fact they occurred in other colonies, including North Carolina, where ladies in Wilmington and Edenton refused to drink tea. Resistance also took the form of buying tea from smugglers who got their tea from Holland. Patriots conveniently justified purchase of smuggled, nontaxed tea from Dutch merchants or smugglers as striking a blow against British tyranny. The conflict over taxation, eloquently expressed by the Sons of Liberty and propagandists, such as Samuel Adams, Isaac Sears, Charles Thomson, and James Otis, provided the most inflammatory issue the American colonies had with England.

The thirteen colonies varied in their degree of disaffection with England; Massachusetts was the colony in greatest conflict. The method of communication among the colonies had no truly formal administrative structure, taking place mainly through the Continental Congress and the postal service. There was no national government, but there was an important and highly functional mail service, led and organized by Deputy Postmaster Benjamin Franklin, whose appointment as colonial postmaster was from the Crown. The Committee of Correspondence, the Sons of Liberty, and an expanded group of anti-British sympathizers shared through extensive correspondence the events and problems of one state with the others. Moreover, when Franklin became colonial agent for Pennsylvania, and later for Massachusetts and Georgia, he used familiarity with postal resources to maximize correspondence among a variety of secret committees formed by the Continental Congress.

Franklin's political orientation went through a spectrum of evolution, initially favoring rapprochement with Great Britain but evolving to support colonial independence. After being removed as deputy postmaster by the British government in the wake of the Hutchinson-Oliver Affair and reprimanded by Lord

Wedderburn in the Cockpit, as we'll see, he was appointed by the Continental Congress as an unofficial emissary to France.

As the Townshend Acts snuffed out hope that there would be an indemnity act, they offered a boon to the general importation of tea. With the retention of the Townshend Acts after 1770, the East India Company's tea trade continued to be saddled with an almost impossible burden. In 1773, the company brought 600,000 pounds of tea to the ports of Boston, New York, Philadelphia, and Charleston. The Townshend duty of three pence per pound was intended to allow tea to be sold at a price low enough to compete with smuggled tea from Holland. The colonists were determined that the tea should not be landed. At Charleston it was seized and stored by customs officials; in Philadelphia and New York, the ships were turned back.[2]

As resident agent for Massachusetts, Pennsylvania, and Georgia, Benjamin Franklin had just achieved some amelioration of the crisis of 1773. Specifically, he had presented a petition in August of 1773 calling upon the Crown to remove Governor Thomas Hutchinson and Lieutenant Governor Andrew Oliver of Massachusetts from office. The petition went to Lord Dartmouth, the colonial secretary, and the issue seemed to be evolving to conciliation. However, less than a week before the Boston Tea Party, Thomas Cushing, speaker of the Massachusetts Assembly, wrote to Franklin about the rage of Boston over the Tea Act and called it a serious crisis.

Mass meetings had been held by the Boston Patriots for most of 1773. The British colonial Governor, Thomas Hutchinson, who was born in the colonies but was out of favor with the Massachusetts citizenry, was concerned about extralegal meetings. He reported that a lawyer and high-placed Son of Liberty, probably John Adams, was advocating a conciliatory approach. Hutchinson assured his superiors in London that no meddling with the shipments of tea would occur. However, over five hundred people attended protest meetings in November, which resulted in attacks such as "tea parties." Colonists also continued to buy smuggled tea from the Netherlands, which they justified as acts of patriotism.

The Hutchinson-Oliver Affair was an inflammatory event on both sides of the Atlantic. Thomas Hutchinson and his lieutenant governor and brother-in-law, Andrew Oliver, had confidential letters intercepted by someone who delivered them to Benjamin Franklin. He, in turn, sent them to Thomas Cushing, the House speaker of the Massachusetts Assembly, where they elicited a strong response. There were nineteen letters by seven different authors. Lieutenant Governor Oliver wrote six of the letters, and six were from Governor Hutchinson. The person who obtained the letters is unknown, but Williamson is one possibility.[3]

The incident centered around the content of the letters and, equally important, whether they were obtained improperly as private correspondence or whether they could be considered public documents. The letters, written between 1767 and 1769, described the tumultuous conditions from the arrival of British troops in Boston allegedly sent for mob control. Other issues discussed included proposed reforms to make the provincial government less dependent on the British Crown. The letters implied a conspiracy of the Americans pursuing a course contrary to the interest of Britain. That suspicion was reinforced by the belief that Hutchinson and the others also stood to profit financially from their efforts to further the British trade required by the Townsend Acts. When House Speaker Thomas Cushing, an enemy of Governor Hutchinson, received the letters, he broadcast them to the Massachusetts Assembly, which was outraged. The Massachusetts Assembly instructed Franklin to ask the Crown for Hutchinson's replacement.[4] Meanwhile, in Massachusetts, Hutchinson was set upon by mobs, his home burned, and he eventually moved to England.

The dispute over who stole the letters resulted in a nonfatal duel fought December 11, 1773, between the brother of Mr. Thomas Whatley, a British bureaucrat, a putative recipient of the letters, and Mr. John Temple, a secretary to Franklin. The duel was inconclusive and a second was in the offing. Meanwhile, on December 25, 1773, Franklin, from his Craven Street address in London, assumed total responsibility for the publication of the letters, citing the unfortunate result of the duel and noting that he would not divulge who had given him the letters. His letter asserted the public nature of the letters while his

British detractors claimed he had violated the private mail of gentlemen. The letters created as much of a furor in England as they did in Massachusetts.

The public revelation of the Hutchinson-Oliver Papers was regarded by the British as reflecting dishonor on Franklin. He was subsequently summoned on January 29, 1774, to the famous philippic event in the Cockpit, immortalized in a painting, and attended by many notables, including Joseph Priestly (discussed below).

Both Franklin's and Hutchinson's hopes for reconciliation were dashed by the Boston Tea Party. Hutchinson's home, as noted, was destroyed by a mob and he was forced to move to England. The Coercive Acts that followed basically placed Boston under a state of martial law. General Thomas Gage, the British commander in North America, was appointed governor-general by the king to replace Thomas Hutchinson. Lord North, George III's prime minister for almost a decade, led this repressive approach to America.

Hugh Williamson and Covert Activities

Hugh Williamson entered the complex politics of the period at this time. In December of 1773, he concluded a fund-raising trip for the Newark Academy to the West Indies and prepared to embark for England on a similar mission. His involvement with the evolving radical separatist movement at that time was probably well established. In Boston, he participated in the meetings planning the Boston Tea Party, whose leaders were Samuel Adams, James Otis, Joseph Warren, and others. Williamson wrote of the planning meeting (as noted in *The Papers of Benjamin Franklin*):

> Of interest, observers noted the calm deliberation of the body of the individuals participating in these meetings. Hugh Williamson, who happened to be on his way to England from Philadelphia, reported that few men made inflammatory speeches, and that the leaders were determined to prevent any measures that would endanger the tea. He would have thought himself to be in the British Senate . . . were I not convinced . . . that they were not yet corrupted by venality, or debauched by luxury, Williamson added.[5]

Samuel Adams, commenting on Williamson's attendance at the tea party planning meeting held in the Old South Meeting House, said: "We have had great pleasure in his company for a few weeks past; and he favored the meeting with his presence."[6]

On December 16, the Boston Tea Party occurred; Samuel Cooper described two to three hundred persons in dress and appearance like Indians dumping 340 cases into the Boston Harbor. Williamson, on his way back to London after witnessing the tea party, was entrusted with several letters to Dr. Franklin.[7] Williamson sailed from Boston on the *Hayley* on

December 22, 1773, and arrived at Dover one month later. The *Hayley*, owned by the rich patriot John Hancock, was among the fastest of his fleet, thus assuring that Williamson would arrive in England with the revolutionaries' version of the Boston Tea Party before the colonial government's version of the event reached London. Williamson delivered his account to Franklin, who, as the representative of Massachusetts, was called to report to the Privy Council. The official version of the Boston Tea Party was eventually provided by the unpopular British colonial governor, Thomas Hutchinson. It reached London a week after Williamson's arrival. The official report from the colonial governor was substantially different from the version presented by Williamson.

Franklin was in a tenuous position at this time. He had lived in England for most of sixteen years. He had been summoned to explain to the British government American resistance to the tax policies, and to this uncomfortable task were added instructions by the Massachusetts legislature to present a petition that Hutchinson be removed as governor. The meeting Franklin was summoned to occurred on January 11, 1774. To this petition dispute about Governor Hutchinson, an inflammatory issue was now added, the insulting news of the Boston Tea Party! The meeting was basically a trap, as Franklin was subjected to public interrogation in the Cockpit, by Solicitor General Lord Wedderburn, a seasoned and acerbic prosecutor. The Cockpit was a public interrogation center. It was a large hall with a gallery. The British Privy Council sat as jury while Lord Wedderburn pilloried Franklin. In the audience were Joseph Priestley, Edmund Burke, and a large crowd that jeered. Franklin, portrayed as a betrayer of confidence, was soon removed as deputy postmaster and returned to Philadelphia.

Williamson, Franklin, and the Hutchinson-Oliver Affair

When the king denied the petition for removal of Governor Hutchinson, Franklin was summoned to appear in the Cockpit, a public interrogation site designed to humiliate and destroy the reputation of the person examined. The examination was conducted by Lord Alexander Wedderburn, a solicitor general of famed rhetorical skills who considered the conflicts with the colonies from the Boston Tea Party and other events to be treason. The person in the Cockpit, Benjamin Franklin, was to be the source of most of this treason. The accusations were punctuated with hoots and insults from a gallery. Franklin refused to respond to the accusation; he remained standing and silent through the reprimand. As a result of these events, Franklin was removed as deputy postmaster and eventually replaced by Arthur Lee as colonial agent. Franklin returned to Philadelphia as a hero and soon was requested by the Continental Congress to represent it in France.

David Hosack's obituary of Williamson, published in 1821, was reported in newspapers as solving one of the minor mysteries of the Revolutionary period, the name of the person who gave Franklin the inflammatory Hutchinson-Oliver letters. John Adams noted, "I was one of the first persons to whom Cushing communicated the great bundle of letters of Hutchinson and Oliver, which has been transmitted to him, as Speaker of the House of Representatives [Massachusetts] by Dr. Franklin, their agent in London. I doubt not the veracity of Dr. Williamson's account of the agency in procuring those letters."[8] Hosack, surgeon to Alexander Hamilton after the Burr-Hamilton duel, student of John Hunter, and leading surgical educator at Columbia University, was Williamson's friend. The obituary included the statement that Williamson, late in life, confided to a friend that he had obtained letters that he believed to be the Hutchinson-Oliver letters:

> He [Dr. Williamson] had learned that Governor Hutchinson's letters were deposited in an office different from that in which they ought regularly to have been placed; and having understood that there was little exactness in the transaction of the business of that office [it is believed it was the office of a particular department of the Treasury], he immediately repaired to it, and addressed himself to the chief clerk, not finding the principal within. Assuming the demeanor of official importance, he peremptorily stated that he had come for the last letters that had been received from Governor

> Hutchinson, and Mr. Oliver, noticing the office in which they ought regularly to have been placed. Without a question being asked, the letters were delivered. The clerk, doubtless, supposed him to be an authorized person from some other public office. Dr. Williamson immediately carried them to Dr. Frank [*sic*], and the next day left London for Holland,—"I received this important fact [writes Hosack], from a gentleman of high respectability, now living, with whom, as the companion and friend of his early days, Dr. Williamson had entrusted the secret."[9]

Other scholars, however, dispute Williamson's role in obtaining the letters.[10] Williamson did not leave Boston until December 1773, which is significant because Samuel Adams had written Arthur Lee from Boston on June 14, 1773, acknowledging receipt of the Hutchinson-Oliver letters, which had already been submitted to the Massachusetts legislature and were at that time in the hands of the Committee of Correspondence.[11] Archived letters of Franklin also cast doubt as to Williamson's direct involvement. A January 5, 1772, letter written by Thomas Cushing quoted a letter from Franklin: "I did myself the honor of writing you on the 2nd of December past, enclosing some original letters from persons at Boston which I hope got safe to your hands."[12]

It seems unlikely that Williamson procured those letters. The most likely explanation is that Williamson, coming from the Boston Tea Party and meetings with the Sons of Liberty, took letters of a secret nature to deliver to Benjamin Franklin. He briefed Franklin on the Boston Tea Party, and he may have probed the security of the British postal service to obtain letters that he delivered to Franklin. He may have obtained confidential letters of the British colonial office, but not the Hutchinson-Oliver letters.

The fallout from the Hutchinson-Oliver letters resulted in Franklin's loss of his position as deputy postmaster, put him in danger of being tried for treason as a British subject, and forced his recall back to the colonies. The Hutchinson-Oliver event, however, raised Franklin's popularity in the colonies and removed him from being a conciliator between the colonies and England. Previously, he was regarded as "too English by the Americans, and too American by the English."[13]

Williamson's Report to the British Privy Council

With Franklin in difficulty with the British government, Williamson delivered the correspondence to him from the Continental Congress including the details of the Boston Tea Party. He then testified or reported to the British House of Commons Privy Council as the first witness of the Boston Tea Party to arrive in London. When Williamson was interviewed by the Privy Council, he provided a candid and sobering view of the relationship between England and the colonies. Williamson's defensive responses were undoubtedly out of concern that he might be charged with treason or implicate others and, after all, he was still a British subject. The report was more pessimistic than those London had been receiving from Governor Thomas Hutchinson and other British colonial officials.

Williamson was interviewed by Lord Dartmouth of the Privy Council on February 19, 1774, about the tea incident and other colonial matters. "Dr. Williamson declared that, if the coercive measures of Parliament were persisted in, nothing short of civil war would be the result. It appears that the incorrect information on the part of the British ministry, as to the public sentiment in America, was almost incredible. Lord North himself has said that Dr. Williamson was the first person who intimated in his presence the probability of civil revolt."[14]

The Privy Council attempted to require Williamson to submit a sworn written transcript of his testimony. When Williamson objected to signing one, he was informed by the lord president that they would receive his narrative unsigned, but they asked him to answer some additional questions. The clerk transcribed his answer to one of the questions inaccurately. Williamson objected and the clerk was reprimanded. When the examination was finished, the attorney general handed him a pen to sign an attestation. Williamson indignantly let them know that he was not in the habit of lying and laid down the pen. As he had undoubtedly been asked names of people in the colonies, he was unwilling to sign a document that might endanger another's life. Williamson noted: "But if the measures were about to be pursued by Parliament against America, which out of doors were said to be intended, the time was not far distant, when his native country would be deluged with blood. This hand, said he, shall be guiltless of that blood."[15] After receiving assurances that the sworn statement could not be used in any type of prosecution, he signed the document.

Official testimony about the tea party was received some days later from three other tea party witnesses who were representatives of Thomas Hutchinson. The official government version was that the Selectmen in Boston (much like city council members) placed a guard over the tea ships to prevent the tea from being smuggled onshore or destroyed. In fact, the Selectmen wanted to turn the tea ships back and not let them unload. However, the official version of the tea party was accepted by the Privy Council and communicated to Parliament. Williamson's version of the Boston Tea Party and the description of the conflicted environment in Boston were suppressed. The result was more restrictive measures for Boston, called the Intolerable Acts, which basically established martial law. This was the point at which General Thomas Gage, the ranking head of the British Army in the colonies, was appointed governor general, replacing Thomas Hutchinson.

In the period following his testimony to the Privy Council (1774), Williamson continued fund-raising efforts for the Newark Academy. He also was an active pamphleteer advocating for the American cause within the context of the British Empire. Dr. Williamson solicited the support of the English Whigs for the American cause by anonymously publishing in 1775 *The Plea of the Colonies on Charges Brought against them by Lord Mansfield and Others*. This was a pamphlet in the form of a letter published in London that attempted to answer the charges that had been made against the colonies accusing them of disloyalty and distrust. Williamson declared that if Parliament continued its unreceptive position, war would result. His *Plea of the Colonies* answered two speeches made by Lord Mansfield, who urged that the Americans be subdued because "The Americans do not wish for peace, they have been long aiming at absolute independence and will be satisfied with nothing less." Williamson also warned in his *Plea of the Colonies* that Great Britain would lose a war with the colonies because "people contending for liberty have never been subdued . . . the Americans say the Lord hath helped them . . . that Providence is on their side."[16]

The stated purpose for Hugh Williamson and the Reverend John Ewing of the Newark Academy's being in England was to raise money for it. Fund-raising for colonial colleges and academies was complicated, requiring endorsement by the college and often by its religious affiliate.[17] Despite obstacles, Williamson and Ewing were successful in obtaining funds for the academy, even from George III! The fund-raising efforts allegedly raised at least £1400 for the academy, a small amount compared to that raised for Princeton, King's College, and the College of Philadelphia. Williamson claimed that their mission was handicapped by the enmity of the Princeton president, Dr. John Witherspoon, who was also engaged in fund-raising and was felt by Williamson to be in competition with Newark Academy.[18]

> One evening at the home of Mr. Dilly, a London bookseller, with Samuel Johnson in attendance, "he [Dr. Ewing] began to defend the cause of the colonies. Johnson looked at him with sternness, and said, '*what do you know, Sir, on that subject?*' Johnson's prejudices against the Americans were strong; he considered them, as he always called them, rebels and scoundrels. . . . Johnson had rudely said, 'Sir, what do you know in America. You never read. You have no books there.' 'Pardon me, sir,' replied Dr. Ewing, 'we have read the *Rambler*' [a Johnson publication]. Civility returned, with Ewing and Johnson conversing until midnight."[19]

Johnson, in fact, made a contribution to the academy.

With the onset of war in 1775, their fund-raising efforts were at an end. Williamson's associate, Professor Ewing, returned to America in 1775. Williamson would not return until 1777. In a letter to his wife, Ewing noted that Williamson had found a romantic interest and traveled north to Scotland to meet with a wealthy widow:

> Dr. Williamson has cast his eyes upon a pretty widow in town with fine eyes and about as tall as yourself she is well bred, sensible and sprightly, with two sons and an old mother about 70 years of age. After saying so much need I say that she has about six thousand Pounds Sterling and is 29 years of age. Each of her children has as good a fortune left by their Father in the Hands of Executors who have ye sole Direction of their Education and consequently will not permit them to be under her management, if she should marry. It is no small sacrifice for her to give up her native Country and her mother and children and go with him to America. However, I believe she will do so. The matter is almost concluded. Upon saying this to the Doctor, he replied that it was more than *almost concluded* and my next will give you account of its accomplishment.[20]

Dr. Williamson's potential marriage to the British widow, however, did not come to fruition.

Americans in London were often thought to be disaffected colonials. In reality many were Anglo-Americans who sought recognition of their colonial status. In February 1775 Lord North made his final effort to avert war with Britain's American colonists. His Conciliatory Proposal and the response from the colonies, called the Olive Branch Letters, were the final communications before the Declaration of Independence officially severed ties between England and the colonies.

Lord North's proposal is usually considered clumsy or even

duplicitous. Nonetheless, in June 1774, for the first time since conflicts had arisen, the Continental Congress felt the environment favored negotiations with Great Britain. The proposal was taken seriously by Americans living in England at the time. The terms of the Conciliatory Proposal, as written, were considered inadequate by the colonists since those terms really did not address their objection to the taxation proposal. They were optimistic, however, as they believed it could be a step toward the British government acceding to their demands. The temporizing feature that the Continental Congress could serve in an extraconstitutional role, however, was tantamount to amending the British government. Dr. John Fothergill, a friend of Franklin's and John Hunter's, and a mentor to a generation of medical students who founded medical schools in America, was enthusiastic about rapprochement, as was Edmund Burke.

A variety of secret negotiations occurred, with Franklin being central to most. The Boston Tea Party, however, had escalated events and had begun to close the door on peace efforts of the Anglo-Americans in England, who included Franklin, Josiah Quincy, Jr., and Thomas Bromfield. Arthur and William Lee were on the more radical fringe. Franklin's protégé, Dr. Edward Bancroft, became a British spy and lived on an English pension in England after the war.

Williamson is considered of the moderate view and had been associated with a number of Philadelphia patriots, such as Joseph Reed, Charles Thomson, and John Dickinson. Williamson stated his belief that Americans were not complaining of governance by England, but of not being accorded the same rights that the British in England enjoyed. Williamson also was in communication with Lord Dartmouth and in January 1775 was encouraged by information that Dartmouth was considering sending a commission to America.[21]

In London, however, Williamson became associated with the extremists, such as the Lees and John Wilkes. Williamson was regarded as a person of valuable opinion by the British prime minister, Lord North, and with the Declaration of Independence almost assuredly meaning war, Lord North summoned Williamson in October 1776 to ask his opinion of the operation of the laws of Parliament in regard to colonial policy. (Where the meeting took place is uncertain, possibly in France.)

In January 1774, in a letter to Benjamin Rush, Williamson noted:

> I ventured to express my apprehension of what could be certainly accepted by Administration if the next congress should think themselves safe in offering it. The Motion made toth [*sic*] Day by Lord North, which seems to have been very unexpected either by outs or ins, very nearly confirms my opinion. Give me leave to add, I am absolutely certain that the Ministry will receive much less than Ld. North has just held out, provided the Colonies shd. make an Offer. But the Scots party in the Cabinet are so violent that nothing more could be held out at present.[22]

Revolutionary War Spy

In the fall of 1775, Williamson and two other Americans living in London at the time, Ralph Izard, senator from South Carolina, and Henry Cruger, a merchant from New York, were brought into last-ditch talks with Lord Dartmouth and Lord North. Williamson and Izard were corresponding with the Continental Congress as late as November 1775 that Lord North was about to give in. Others never thought that was likely.[23] The Olive Branch petition, if conditions had been granted, would have meant that the sovereignty of the British government would be diminished.

In Paris, Lord Stormont, British ambassador to France, closely watched the American courtship of France. Although he was repeatedly lied to by the French, he was not duped. In August 1776 Williamson met with Lord Stormont. Williamson informed him that he could be of help in modulating the conflict if he could get home. At the meeting "in which Williamson stated that the Americans were incorrect about the expected help they could expect from European powers, Williamson offered that he could be of assistance if he could get assistance in returning to America"[24] (he did return home not too long afterward, as we'll see). Silas Deane, newly arrived as the first official envoy from the Continental Congress, had a major instruction to *purposely* inflate the level of support the Americans enjoyed from Spain, Prussia, and other European powers, so he could not have been pleased when Williamson offered Lord Stormont a contradictory analysis.

Chapter 4

Continental Congress and Secret Committees

As the seemingly inevitable escalation to war evolved, the thirteen colonies, represented by the Continental Congress, created secret committees for special intelligence functions. These included the Committee of Secret Correspondence and the Committee on Spies established on September 18, 1775. These committees were charged with procuring arms from abroad. Its members included Benjamin Franklin, Silas Deane, John Langdon, and Robert Morris. On November 29, 1775, the delegates created the Committee of Correspondence, later known as the Committee of Secret Correspondence, for "the sole purpose of corresponding with our friends in Great Britain, Ireland, and other parts of the world." The Committee of Secret Correspondence included Benjamin Harrison, Benjamin Franklin, Thomas Johnson, John Dickinson, John Jay, and Robert Morris.[1]

When the Committee on Spies was created June 5, 1776, it was intended "to consider what is proper to be done with persons giving intelligence to the enemy or supplying them with provisions." Its members were John Adams, Thomas Jefferson, Edward Rutledge, Robert Livingston, and James Wilson.[2]

The spy network focused on activities abroad and operated in conjunction with congressional committees, as well as with General Washington and his staff. When the American constitutional order was established in 1787, this authority would be delegated to the executive branch and the president, but during and before the Revolutionary War, it was a function of the Continental Congress. As the war approached, the Congress, positioning for covert action, relied heavily on communication through Franklin's network, the postal service.[3]

In September 1775 a motion was made in the Continental Congress that envoys should be sent to France to solicit support for the American conflict with England, a move supported by John Adams. The motion was initially defeated as many Americans still hoped for reconciliation with England. As events escalated toward war, Franklin, now in France as a representative without official portfolio from the rebellious British colonies, established an important intelligence network as a founder of the Committee on Secret Correspondence. He was known to that committee by the code number 72 and to British Intelligence as "Moses." His ambassadorial residency at Passy, in southern France, near the Swiss border, was America's first intelligence "station."[4] Operating under the Committee of Secret Correspondence, Franklin actually had a flotilla of small Irish and French privateers that preyed on British shipping.

Franklin became the center of clandestine meetings with the French, who were sympathetic to the Americans but did not want to engage in open hostilities, as they were at peace with Britain under the treaty that concluded the Seven Years' War (French and Indian War in North America).

In March 1776 the Continental Congress sent Silas Deane to Paris to request military supplies such as clothing, uniforms, arms, money, and other assistance. Deane sailed from America by way of Bermuda and Spain in order to avoid the English cruisers patrolling the Atlantic Ocean. Deane was specifically instructed to *inflate the degree of support* that European powers held for American independence.[5]

Soon after arriving in France, Deane wrote John Jay, president of the Continental Congress, a long letter, partially reproduced below, that describes his activities to recruit resources for the newly declared, independent United States. He also describes his concern about Williamson's loyalty, which later (see below), was conveyed in his first dispatch, cosigned by Franklin, to the Continental Congress. His suspicions directly determined Williamson's role in the Revolutionary War and his ultimate political base in North Carolina.

Hugh Williamson

From Silas Deane to John Jay President of the Continental Congress.

Dear Jay, Paris, December 3d, 1776

If my letters arrive safe they will give you some idea of my situation, without Intelligence, without Orders, without Remittances, yet boldly plunging in to contracts, engagements, and negotiations hoping something will arrive from America. By General Coudry I send 30,000 Fusils, 200 pieces of Brass Cannon, 30 mortars, 4000 tents and Clothing for 30,000 Men, with 200 tons of gunpowder, Lead, Balls, etc., etc., by which you may judge I have some friends here. . . .

I presented the Declaration of Independency to this Court after it had indeed become an Old Storey in every part of Europe. . . .

Tell Mrs. Trist that her husband, and Capt. Fowle were well, the 16th instant I had a letter from the latter. Pray be who You trust in Europe. One Williamson, a Native of Pennsylvania, is here as a spy, yet, I believe he corresponds with very good People on your side of the Water. The Villain returns to London once in a bout six weeks to discharge his budget.

Doct. Bancroft has been of very great service to me. No man has better Intelligence in my Opinion, but it cost something. . . .

Have sent this in secret hand, and am with the utmost impatience to hear from you. Dear Sir Your's,

S. Deane[6]

Deane's suspicions concerning Williamson are detailed in Julian Boyd's articles on Silas Deane, "Death by a Kindly Teacher of Treason."[7] The irony of the distrust of Williamson and endorsement of Bancroft is apparent. Williamson was a patriot. Bancroft was Deane's pupil shortly after Deane graduated from Yale in 1758. At Franklin's suggestion, Deane met Bancroft in Paris in the summer of 1776 and secured his collaboration as an informant. He was unaware that Bancroft was in the pay of the British government and reported to George III within forty-eight hours of significant meetings.

Deane recruited Europeans, such as the Marquis de Lafayette and Baron von Steuben, for service in the American cause in the Revolutionary War, often to high rank with minimal qualifications. Meanwhile, the British made efforts to recruit spies within the American commission in Paris. A complex double agent, who was primarily a British spy, was Dr. Edward Bancroft. Bancroft became friends with Benjamin Franklin in England, and Franklin recruited him as a spy. On Deane's arrival in France, Franklin instructed him to contact Dr. Bancroft as a source of information about British policy and activities. Deane arranged the meeting, which led to a complex relationship in this context. Deane was directed by Bancroft in a number of commercial activities, which were at best war profiteering and at worst treasonous.

The contact recommended by Franklin suggests "writing a letter to him under cover to Mr. Griffiths of Purnum Green near

London and desiring him to come over to you in France or Holland on the score of old acquaintances. From him you may obtain a good deal of information of what is now going forward in England and settle a mode of continuing correspondence. It may be well to remit a small bill to defer his expenses in coming to see you, and avoid all political matters in your letter to him."[8]

Meanwhile, Bancroft was recruited as a double agent for the British by William Eden, chief of the British Secret Service, who arranged a meeting with Paul Wentworth, an old friend of Bancroft's and also an acquaintance of Deane's.[9] When Benjamin Franklin arrived in Paris to take over negotiations with the French, Lord Suffolk, British envoy, told Bancroft to move to Paris and inject himself into Franklin's circle, and for that he was given a lifetime pension of £200, later raised to £500. The spy doctor, Edward Bancroft, was not exposed until seven years after his death, when access to diplomatic activities of the British was provided. Paul Wintler, a British secret agent, was sent to Paris to be Bancroft's handler.

The method of communication was complex. Letters were put in bottles, a string placed around the neck of the bottle, and the bottle anchored to a hollowed-out tree. There even was a special type of secret writing used by Silas Deane and Dr. James Jay, British sympathizer and brother of John Jay. They used cobalt chloride glycerin and water stain as secret ink. Washington actually used this same method in the Culpeper Ring, his group of spies in New York. It is said that the French-American Treaty was in King George's hand forty-eight hours after its signing, courtesy of Bancroft and compliments of Deane and Franklin, who sent Bancroft on secret missions to London not being aware of his betrayal. Franklin was remarkably blasé about the potential of spies and commented in response to a friend's warning about British spies:

> I have long observed one rule which prevents any inconvenience from some practices. It is simply this, to be concerned in no affairs that I should blush to have made public and do nothing but what spies may see and welcome. When a man's actions are just and honorable, the more they are known, the more his reputation is increased and established. If I was sure, therefore, that my valet de place was a spy, as probably he is, I think I should not discharge him for that if in other aspects I liked him.[10]

Even though Franklin trusted Bancroft, he probably used Bancroft to pass false information to the British.

Arthur Lee was appointed deputy postmaster by the British government and was located in London, replacing the discharged Franklin in that position and also as colonial agent. Deane and Lee, the two agents sent by the Committee of Secret Correspondence, began a campaign of inflating American strength to a French secret agent in London.

Silas Deane became the main American contact with Pierre

de Beaumarchais (author of the play *The Marriage of Figaro*) and the French foreign minister, Comte de Vergennes. On December 3, 1776, Deane wrote to John Jay about the operation. As well as being president of the Continental Congress, Jay was later a diplomat to France and Spain and was a participant in many secretive foreign operations of the war, including a front to transmit supplies from France to the colonies. This involved meetings with the French government, which stipulated that meetings and assistance be secret, so as not to breach the official peace with England.

John Jay was elected president of the Congress in December of 1778 and had been active on the Committee to Detect Spies. As president of the Congress, he reviewed counterintelligence and classified information. He discovered that information about Deane's unofficial access to the French government through Beaumarchais had been leaked. He also discovered treasonous activities of two members of George Washington's personal guard. In the same period, the propriety of Deane's expenditures was questioned by Arthur Lee. He accused Deane of war profiteering, based on some of his activities with Dr. Bancroft. He also accused Deane of spending French donations on items he used as personal gifts. Accusation of foul play was traded back and forth between rival groups supporting Arthur Lee or Silas Deane. On his return to America Deane was eventually considered culpable, was disgraced, and died in England. Years later, in 1842, his family received a pension and an apology from Congress. Bancroft lived in England after the Revolution on his pension from the British government.[11]

The newspaper *De Leide* in Holland was penetrated by a secret American operative and was useful in getting favored credit for the United States in Dutch financial markets. Hugh Williamson had spent substantial time in Holland in this period, and may have been involved.

Williamson's Role in the Twilight War

When hostilities between Great Britain and its American colonies resulted in the Declaration of Independence on July 4, 1776, Williamson was still in Europe. He had first become involved in covert activities in the prelude to the war, beginning with his participation in the planning of the Boston Tea Party and carrying dispatches to Franklin from the Continental Congress afterward. He had become a pamphleteer for the American cause during his fund-raising activities for the Newark Academy. However, he was clearly under scrutiny regarding covert activity. Silas Deane was duped by Bancroft into thinking that Williamson was a British agent.[12] Deane had received a letter from Bancroft of September 13, 1776, stating flatly that Williamson was "secretly a spy in the service of government." Deane wrote of Williamson: "Under the pretence of being an American, this man is doing prodigious mischief. . . .

Let his name be known in America and everyone be put on their guard how they deal with him."[13]

During Williamson's eulogy, Dr. Hosack noted that after Williamson delivered the Hutchinson-Oliver Papers, he left the next day for Holland. It is known, however, that Williamson's connection with the Hutchinson-Oliver Papers had occurred earlier, so it is possible that the event in obtaining confidential mail by probing British security occurred in the spring or summer of 1776 instead of 1775. Williamson remained in England for months afterward as pamphleteer and provided information to the British about the conflict.

Dr. William Willcox, editor of the Franklin papers, interpreted Williamson to be either well grounded as a double agent or to be duplicitous.[14] Other interpretations, however, are more likely. Peace efforts did continue into 1776. Although Lexington, Concord, and Bunker Hill had occurred, the Second Continental Congress, on July 10, 1776, sent a letter to Lord Dartmouth, carried by Richard Penn, which proposed reconciliation of America and England, the Olive Branch Letter. The letter did not get to Lord Dartmouth until September 1. Lord Dartmouth answered that the king would not accept that petition; that response did not get back to Philadelphia until November 9, 1776.

Williamson would have known of the effort at reconciliation, through the Olive Branch Letter, and probably offered to be a diplomatic intermediary. More likely, he was hoping to find passage to America, which was increasingly difficult with the British Navy's owning the seas and impressing seaman. Deane would understandably be annoyed and suspicious of Williamson meeting with Lord Stormont. So in Deane's first official communication as envoy to France from the Continental Congress, he repeated his earlier assertion to Jay on the possibility that Williamson was a British agent.[15]

This letter in response to Deane's of October 1, 1776, was the first word to him in Paris from Philadelphia. The letter covers many topics related to state of the war, foreign relations, and so on, and it notes:

> We shall pay proper attention to what Mr. Deane writes concerning Dr. Williamson and Mr. Hopkins, and we think the ill treatment this country and Mr. Hopkins and Mr. Deane have received from these men strongly, suggests the necessity of invincible reserve with persons coming to France as Americans and Friends to whom most irregrable profess have not removed all doubt about.
>
> Signed Benjamin Harrison, Richard Henry Lee, Will Hooper, and Jno Williamson endorsed by Benjamin Franklin.[16]

One wonders if Franklin and Williamson ever discussed this letter that deprived Williamson of participating in the Revolutionary War as a medical officer in the regular Continental

Army and in the war in any form until he became surgeon general of the North Carolina militia when the British invaded the Carolinas as part of the Southern Strategy. It is unlikely that Franklin would have thought Williamson a British sympathizer. The best explanation is that letters were sent by Deane and others of his staff without his endorsement.

Williamson's whereabouts during the months after the Declaration of Independence are unclear. He was in Holland for part of that period, perhaps working to obtain a favorable financial position for America. It is likely that he was engaged in activities directed by Franklin and may have been involved in influencing the Dutch newspaper *De Leide*, which supported the Americans. He was eventually able to secure passage to America, as advised by Dr. John Fothergill, who also counseled Dr. James Hutchinson, who traveled back with him. Both carried dispatches from Franklin to the Continental Congress.

Fothergill's letter to James Hutchinson of September 9, 1776, describes the dynamics of the period. The letter advises Hutchinson to return to America via France to a destination near Boston, believing the British general Lord Howe would focus military action on New York. Fothergill hoped that his relative, Benjamin Waterhouse, would accompany Hutchinson. (Waterhouse was an original Harvard Faculty member and brought Jenner's vaccination technology to the United States. He remained in Edinburgh in medical school during this period.) Hutchinson went to France and at Nantes met Benjamin Franklin, who entrusted him with the dispatches to the Congress. The passage was slow and the food poor. But he had the companionship of another young mentoree of Dr. Fothergill, and Franklin, and John Hunter, namely, Dr. Hugh Williamson.[17]

Hutchinson and Williamson sailed on the *Sally* from Nantes on October 26, 1776. When the American coast was sighted, an American naval vessel, the *Wasp*, took the two doctors with Franklin's dispatches on board to a feast of claret and rum plum pudding. A small boat landed them near Lewes, Delaware. Their luggage, medical books, and belongings were lost when the *Sally* was captured by the British and taken to New York.[18]

Williamson and Hutchinson proceeded to Philadelphia and delivered their dispatches to the Continental Congress. Hutchinson also carried a letter from Fothergill to Governor John Penn, dated October 9, 1776, urging an appointment for him to the Pennsylvania Hospital. Hutchinson was appointed and then given a staff position in the Flying Corps* of the Middle Department. His first assignment was to inoculate the troops at Valley Forge for smallpox. After the war, he taught chemistry at the medical school of the University of Pennsylvania. Waterhouse, a student of John Hunter, continued his studies at Edinburgh and did not return until 1778. He returned to become one of the founders of the Harvard Medical School and is called the "Amer-

*A medical organizational unit of the Continental Army.

ican Jenner" for his efforts to inoculate for smallpox, including doing so for Jefferson and his family.

Williamson unsuccessfully applied for a position in the military. He had impeccable credentials with his medical education in Edinburgh and Europe, as well as his surgical training with John Hunter. Moreover, he had been a successful medical practitioner in Philadelphia before the war and an active member of the American Philosophical Society. In addition, his education and scientific involvement were similar to others, such as Benjamin Rush, William Shippen, and John Morgan, who were valued medical leaders in the Revolutionary War.

However, the Continental Congress had by this time received its first official report from Silas Deane mentioning Williamson as a possible British sympathizer or spy. The question of Williamson's *reliability* arose, undoubtedly due to the belief of Deane. A few days after seeing the report, John Adams wrote:

> This much I may say, that we have letters from Dr. Franklin and Mr. Deane; both agree that everything is as they could wish but the Doctor has just arrived, and had not been to Paris and therefore could know nothing of the cabinet. The noted Dr. Williamson is arrived, full of encouraging matter; but what confidence is to be put in his intelligence, I know not. Franklin, Deane, and Williamson all agree in opinion that a war will take place.[19]

With the Continental Congress receiving this information, it is not surprising that Williamson was denied a commission.

In February 1778, Williamson wrote a Philadelphia merchant:

> I am not in a haste to return [to Philadelphia]. What have I to do in Pennsylvania? Is it that I may try for some Employm^{t} that I ought to have been solicited to accept? Is it that I may be pestered by answering numberless objections proposed by some insidious Knave who have heard the Dreams of some fool who could not tell whether I (am) of the Country that gave me birth? There is not in America a Man who has served it more faithfully or disinterestedly. I am still ready to serve it if an Occasion should offer. I see none at Present.[20]

Williamson, raised in Pennsylvania, a graduate faculty member at the College of Philadelphia, a member of the American Philosophical Society, and a nine-year medical practitioner in Philadelphia, certainly had reasons for returning to Philadelphia. Having been denied a military commission, he joined his brother, Captain John Williamson of Charlestown, South Carolina, in shipbuilding, commerce, and related business ventures. However, Lord Howe had blockaded the Chesapeake Bay, limiting shipping commerce to Philadelphia from the South. The peevish tone of the letter, however, suggests that the suspicion cast over his patriotism by Silas Deane, reflected in John Adams's letter, was a deeply felt insult. In fact after the Revolutionary War was over, both Deane and Williamson were investigated.

The congressional investigation cleared Williamson of suspicion. Silas Deane, however, was not exonerated, as noted earlier, and he died in England after hostilities ceased.

Failing to secure a military appointment, Williamson pursued other options. He and his brother, Captain John Williamson of Charleston, became active in shipbuilding and commercial trading with the West Indies during the early years of the Revolutionary War when most hostilities occurred in the northeastern colonies. Because the Chesapeake Bay was blockaded by the British, Williamson could not implement his plan to engage in commercial operations from Philadelphia with his brother. Accordingly, he located the center of his activities in Edenton, North Carolina.

When the British Southern Strategy was implemented in 1779–80, both Hugh and John Williamson became combatants, Hugh as surgeon general of the North Carolina militia, John as a captain. (Years later, during Jefferson's administration, Hugh Williamson wrote a letter of introduction to Jefferson, who met with John.) The movement of the war to the South brought new responsibilities. Williamson resumed medical practice in Edenton, where he became a respected practitioner. He was soon summoned to care for victims of a smallpox epidemic by the North Carolina governor in addition to serving as the surgeon general.

Chapter 5

The War for Independence in North Carolina

There was not in America a man who served it more faithfully or disinterestedly.

—Hugh Williamson, chafing in a letter in 1778
over the questioning of his loyalty by
Deane's report to the Continental Congress

Book of Allegiance: [I] pledge to truly support, endeavor to maintain and defend the independent government against George III, king of Great Britain.

—Signed by Hugh Williamson, July 28, 1778

The diverse population and patterns of immigration along the Atlantic coast contributed to different loyalties. In the lowlands known as the Tidewater, the descendants of the earliest settlements had profitable plantations. The government in London and taxation policy most closely affected these citizens. Inland North Carolina was populated by a number of Scots-Irish immigrants who did not share the same political philosophy as the coastal dwellers. The Piedmont dwellers, those who lived between the coastal areas and the mountains, believed that the Tidewater planter aristocracy was ignoring their needs. In fact, the Regulator movement in 1770 and 1771 was actually a conflict with the British colonial government over the same issues that led to the Revolutionary War, such as government taxation without representation.[1] The Tidewater planters were mainly Patriots and the Piedmont farmers were more likely to be Loyalists supporting the British. In the Appalachian Mountains, a third group of settlers consisted of the rugged frontiersmen, so called Over-the-Mountains men. Dealing with Indians on an ongoing basis, these independent people were usually supporters of the Patriot cause.

Several of the British American colonies had an almost entirely English citizenry. North Carolina had more English than any other nationality, but the colony also had more non-English white people than any other southern colony. North Carolina's population was less concentrated in coastal towns, its settlers having pushed westward. In North Carolina, a colony larger than New York, there were Swiss, German, Scots-Irish, French Huguenot, American Indian, and Black inhabitants, as well as English.

The disposition of North Carolina was primed to support independence. For at least forty years before the American Revolution, North Carolinians had fought against authority, including against such restrictive measures such as the Stamp Act, the Navigation Acts, the Sugar Act, the Intolerable Acts, and the Townshend Acts. North Carolinians had fought Indians on unfriendly borders, established trade in poorly suited harbors, and banished the Church of England. There were more small industries and small farms in North Carolina than in South Carolina and Virginia. Small industries were more apt than larger ones to support independence.

The sentiment in North Carolina's fourth Provincial Congress, held in Halifax beginning April 4, 1776, favored independence. A committee was appointed to consider the various grievances against England and to draw appropriate resolutions. This report, known as the Halifax Resolves, was unanimously adopted on April 12, 1776. The Provincial Congress of North Carolina instructed its delegates in Philadelphia: "To concur with the delegates of other Colonies in declaring independency, and forming foreign alliances, reserving to this colony the sole and exclusive right of forming a Constitution and laws for this Colony."[2]

A copy of the Halifax Resolves was sent to Joseph Hewes, a North Carolina representative to the Congress. North Carolina newspapers printed the document's text and praised its contents. On May 27 delegates from North Carolina and Virginia presented to Congress their instructions to seek independence. A motion was made on June 7, 1776, that the colonies should be free and independent. Congress adopted the resolution on July 2 and on July 4, 1776, the final draft of the Declaration of Independence was approved by the Continental Congress.

Although periodic Indian conflicts occurred during the colonial period, most of the southern colonies were not involved in the first four and a half years of Revolutionary War activity. Washington's strategy for the war was to keep a core of regular Continental Army troops and coordinate their activities with local militias. Local militias would be expected to control the Loyalists in their region and be available for military operations of the regular army on a call-up basis, as "minutemen," when hostilities occurred in their area.

The war in the South was fought in large part between Patriots and Loyalists, with fewer British Army and Continental Army troops than in the Northeast. In North Carolina the first battle of the American Revolution in the South was a type of civil war, since it was without the regular army troops of either the British or the Continentals but rather between Loyalists under Donald MacDonald marching from the Cape Fear River toward Wilmington and the Tidewater Patriots under the command of Colonel James Caswell.[3] They fought February 27, 1776, in an engagement known as the Battle of Moore's Creek, which was won by the Patriots. This being a neighbor-versus-neighbor battle, it initiated a pattern of violence that eventually polarized the citizenry against the British Southern Strategy and drove them into the Patriot camp.

The battle had an interesting dimension in that a group led by MacDonald was among the Scots who had emigrated to North Carolina after the Battle of Culloden in 1745. In that battle, the Royal Army crushed the forces of Bonnie Prince Charlie (Charles Stuart), who was attempting to reclaim the British throne for the Stuarts. He escaped to the Isle of Skye and ultimately to Europe disguised as a woman, "Betty Burke," smuggled out by Flora MacDonald, the heroine of the Scottish Resistance, whose statue is at Inverness Castle and who was the wife of Donald MacDonald. The paroled Scots from the rebellion were allowed to emigrate, but swore support for the king. Honoring that in America, they joined Clinton's Loyalist forces near Moore's Creek. The Scots were better equipped with kilts and bagpipes than with weapons and tactics.

The Loyalist force, composed mostly of Scots, had 1,700 casualties, half as prisoners, which included MacDonald. The captured were imprisoned in Halifax, North Carolina, and in Pennsylvania. Over the next two years, Flora was summoned before the Committee of Safety, her two daughters mistreated, and their jewelry stolen. Their estate of 550 acres, Killiegrey, was confiscated. Her husband urged her to sell their remaining assets and return to Scotland. On the way to Scotland her ship was accosted by the French; she urged all on board to fight and received a broken arm in the action. She eventually did return to Skye, the North Carolina experience resulting from loyalty to the crown a bitter memory.[4]

The set battle pieces, as might be expected, were won by the British, but the irregular warfare, conducted by Patriot heroes like Francis Marion, the "Swamp Fox," Thomas Sumter, and Andrew Pickens was classical guerilla warfare in which the Patriots harassed supply lines and then disappeared into the countryside.[5] British war planners advanced the belief that a southern Loyalist uprising would win the war. Moreover, their efforts early in the war to secure a naval blockade of the South were successful. This lesson was not lost on Abraham Lincoln in the American Civil War eighty-five years later.

Hugh Williamson became involved as a combatant when the British war strategy changed to a southern emphasis. The Tory ministers in London believed that a major stroke in the South would result in a rising of southern Loyalists. The plan was to obtain a substantial hold in the South by taking the cities of Charleston and Savannah, and then organizing the Loyalists and moving north to conclude the war. In 1779 the British prime minister, Lord North, was receiving opposition from the colonial secretary, Lord George Germaine, who believed the war was both expensive and a failure. The counterargument, supported by King George III, was that the majority of the southern colonists were still loyal to the king, and only some substantial support from Great Britain was needed, following which a Loyalist uprising would evolve, and the war would then terminate. Britain's security was now at risk, in that a variety of foreign mercenaries had to be hired to maintain the war, increasingly British politicians in London who were sympathetic to the Revolutionary War cause claimed that it was time to discontinue the war, and Britain's traditional enemies, France and Spain, were sympathetic to and assisted the colonies.

The campaign of 1780 and 1781 by British General Henry Clinton was based on that strategy and assumption. As the South had been comparatively spared for the first four years of the war, it was difficult to determine exactly how many of the population were Loyalists. The war, especially in the South, was very much a civil war with back-and-forth movement of loyalties and a number of uncommitted. In fact, the Charlestonians even tried to remain neutral when the British initiated their Southern Strategy.

Williamson was in the Netherlands in 1776 when the colonies proclaimed independence. Bringing his travels to an end, he went to France. He did not sail for America from Nantes until late 1776. His traveling companion, James Hutchinson, and he with their dispatches of a sensitive nature from Franklin to the Continental Congress escaped capture by the British and went on to Philadelphia. After they delivered their messages from Franklin to the Congress and Williamson subsequently failed to receive a commission in the Medical Corps, he located in North Carolina in March 1777, where he pursued commercial shipping free from the British blockade in the mercantile enterprise with his brother. With his brother, he had obtained a sloop in Charleston loaded with products from the West Indies for delivery to Baltimore. En route to Baltimore, Williamson ordered the sloop to dock at Edenton, at that time the largest mercantile center in the Albemarle and a flourishing port frequented by smaller ships. He decided to remain in Edenton, with his cargo because he feared it would be captured by General Lord Howe, who had blockaded the Chesapeake Bay. While he was mainly involved with commerce, he also resumed his practice of medicine.

So Williamson settled in Edenton, near Bath, which was chartered in 1705 as the first incorporated town in North Carolina. Considered one of the best towns in North Carolina, Edenton, also known as the Port of Roanoke, was surpassed as a trading center only by Brunswick, North Carolina. Large ships could not enter Edenton's harbor because of shallow water, dangerous sandbars, and quicksand. However, smaller ships from there were able to establish extensive trade with the West Indies, Southern Europe, Boston, New York, and Virginia.

Edenton was inhabited by a number of prominent supporters of American independence. The Federalist leaders around Edenton were led by an unusually strong clique: Samuel Johnston, a lawyer; his brother-in-law, James Iredell, appointed to the first Supreme Court by President George Washington; Hugh Williamson; Stephen Cabarrus; William Hooper, a signer of the Declaration of Independence; Joseph Hewes, another signer of the Declaration of Independence, who served on the Marine Committee and was a patron of John Paul Jones;

and Colonel Edward Buncombe, mortally wounded at the Battle of Germantown. Another Samuel Johnston, originally from Dundee, Scotland, became North Carolina's first senator, served as governor, and was elected president of the Continental Congress. Thomas Jones was one of the drafters of North Carolina's constitution.[6]

> Edenton had had many loyalist merchants, but in April of 1777, all persons who had traded with the British Isles in the past ten years were required to take a loyalty oath to the state. Failure to do so, required them to dispose of property, except for naval stores, and leave North Carolina. A number of the merchants became privateers and became wealthy in the 1777–78 period. Williamson wrote Mr. Mease, a Philadelphia merchant, that a profitable trade was occurring in "Virginia Aboats" and it was difficult to get a carpenter. Williamson however, had two vessels of forty tons, and was building three of seventy tons. Since Williamson was engaged in shipbuilding he was not in a hurry to return to Philadelphia where he would "be pestered by answering numberless objections proposed by some insidious Knave who heard the dream of some fool who could not tell whether I am of the country that gave me birth." He claimed that he was perfectly willing to serve his country should the occasion offer there "was not in America a man who served it more faithfully or disinterestedly." Williamson was among the many who signed the Book of Allegiance in Edenton,

> North Carolina 28 July 1778 which pledged to truly endeavor to support, maintain, and defend the independent government against George The Third, King of Britain.[7]

The oaths of allegiance demanded by the British and the Americans were taken seriously. If one had signed as a supporter of the king and then was found to be fighting for or assisting the rebels, a capital offense was committed, with execution as a penalty.[8]

Although Williamson was involved in shipping, he also practiced medicine in Edenton. He was invited to New Bern to administer the new treatment of inoculation for smallpox when an epidemic of that disease occurred in 1779, preventing the General Assembly from meeting there.

Chapter 6

The Revolutionary War Moves South

In December 1779, General Henry Clinton moved to seize the southern port of Charleston. The new strategy of concentrating the war in the South was intended to break the stalemate in the North, where Philadelphia, New York, and other cities were occupied but the countryside remained unpacified in the typical pattern of guerrilla warfare.[1]

Clinton had left New York City during the Christmas holiday of 1779 with eight to nine thousand troops, ninety transports, and fourteen war ships. Lord Cornwallis went with him as second in command, while the British occupation of New York City continued with over fifteen thousand men. The army landed on Edisto Inlet thirty miles south of Charleston on February 11, 1780. Clinton also had troops in Georgia, having secured Savannah as one of the first bases for the southern campaign. Charlestonians gave Governor John Rutledge dictatorial power, and he mobilized a defense force under Major General Benjamin Lincoln to oppose the British naval landing, having slaves build new fortifications and adding more colonial Continental troops. Rutledge had ships ordered into the mouth of the Cooper River, and sank some using a log-and-boom chain across the river. Clinton called upon Lincoln to surrender and suspended hostilities briefly. Lincoln rejected the demand for unconditional surrender, and hostilities renewed on May 9. The bombardment continued and eventually almost six thousand Americans marched out to lay down their arms. This surrender remains the third largest capitulation in American history, and with it, Lord Clinton had secured the base he desired to conquer the South.

With the capture of Charleston and Savannah, the strategy of obtaining a good stronghold in the South, which was expected to induce a massive recruitment of Loyalists, seemed to be falling into place. However, subsequent events occurred in the Carolinas that turned the population against the British.

After the fall of Charleston, Lieutenant Colonel Banastre Tarleton's Loyalist dragoons pursued an aggressive and brutal pursuit of Colonel William Washington and Colonel Abraham Beaufort. When Beaufort rejected Tarleton's demand to surrender, as he was withdrawing to Hillsborough, North Carolina, Tarleton's dragoons attacked with sabers and bayonets, and continued to kill officers and wound men even after a white flag was raised in surrender. This was known among Whig partisans as "Tarleton's Quarter," and he became known as "Bloody Tarleton." Further battles occurred at Williamson's plantation at Rocky Mount (of no connection to Hugh Williamson) and at Hanging Rock.[2]

After Lincoln's surrender at Charleston, the nearest Continental regiments were at Hillsborough, North Carolina. Major General Baron Johann de Kalb, recruited by Silas Deane in France, commanded two regiments of Maryland and Delaware regulars in that location. When de Kalb learned of the American defeat at Charleston, he continued to Hillsborough, arriving on June 22. The Continental Congress felt the crisis deserved a more famous general and, against General George Washington's objections, replaced him with the hero of Saratoga, General Horatio Gates.[3]

Washington was not enthusiastic about Gates because of the Conway Cabal, a plot to replace Washington with Gates that had failed. Gates arrived on July 25, but had a small army—only two regiments and a legion of 120 dragoons. There was no food in the camp and morale was poor. Gates decided to march expeditiously to confront the British in the Charleston region, which turned out to be a mistake, since living off the land provided poor rations of unripened peaches and corn. Most of the army became ill. They crossed the Pee Dee River on August 3, north of Camden, South Carolina.

Thomas Sumter appealed to Gates for 400 regimentals to

attack a British supply train headed for Camden. When de Kalb informed Gates that the American army numbered about 3,500 Gates sent Sumter the 400 requested troops. Lord Charles Cornwallis, now in command in Charleston as Clinton had returned to New York, marched to Camden with 1,000 reinforcements. Rather than await Gates's maneuvers, he attempted to intercept him. The armies blundered into each other five miles north of Camden on the evening of August 15, but backed off in preparation to fight in the morning.[4] The battle lines formed with a narrow battlefront because of the swamps along Gum Creek. Gates made a fatal error in placing his battle-tested Continental regulars on the right flank, while defending the center and the left with inexperienced militia. When the British attacked, the Redcoats charged into the American left wing, composed of Virginia and North Carolina militia, and many militiamen turned and retreated without firing a shot. Americans suffered 800 killed and wounded, and another 1,000 captured. Gates basically lost his army, and quickly retreated, riding on to Hillsborough, covering 180 miles in three and a half days.[5] Alexander Hamilton later commented, "Was there ever such an instance of a general running away . . . from his whole army, and was there ever so precipitous a flight?" [6]

The North Carolina militia, when called to duty, had had a number of ill soldiers. Williamson was appointed surgeon general to address the problem. General Caswell wrote Governor

Nash on July 31, 1780: "I have some hopes that our Distresses in some measures will be relived [*sic*] here, especially if I can remain so long as to recruit our men and horces [*sic*] who are much worn down with fatigue, many of the men very ill; but Dr. Williamson is arrived, and I flatter myself he will soon put them on their legs again."[7]

Caswell had given Williamson his commission as head of the North Carolina militia's medical department. When the General Assembly passed an act in April 1780 to send militia to aid General Benjamin Lincoln when he was besieged at Charleston, Williamson joined the troops at Camp Ancrum's Plantation near Anson Court House, on July 31. After its defeat at Camden, the beaten American army, with its many casualties, retreated, and Williamson volunteered to remain with the wounded. An account of the battle notes the number of casualties among the captured troops:

> General [Isaac] Gregory himself was twice wounded by a bayonet in bringing off his men, and several of his brigade, who were made prisoners, had no wounds except from bayonets. Two hundred and ninety American wounded prisoners were carried into Camden, after this action, of this number 206 were continentals, 82 were North-Carolina militia, and 2 were Virginia militia. The resistance made by each corps, may in some degree be estimated from the number of wounded. The Americans lost the whole of their artillery, eight field pieces, upwards of 200 wagons, and the greatest part of their

> baggage; almost all of their officers were separated from their respective commands. The American troops were pursued above twenty miles by Tarleton's legion, and the way was covered with arms, baggage and wagons. Baron de Kalb, the second in command, a brave and experienced officer, was taken prisoner and died on the next day of his wounds. He was actually found on the battlefield by Tarleton. Most likely, the wounding and capture of a General Officer was influential in Williamson's decision to stay with the troops under a flag of truce. The baron, who was a German by birth, had long been in the French service. He had traveled through the British provinces, about the time of the Stamp Act, and is said to have reported to his superiors on his return, "that the colonists were so firmly and universally attached to Great Britain, that nothing could shake their loyalty." The Congress resolved that a monument should be erected to his memory in Annapolis. General Rutherford of North-Carolina, was wounded and taken prisoner.[8]

After the defeat of General Caswell and General Gates at the Battle of Camden on August 16, Williamson requested permission from General Caswell to go under a flag of truce to the British camp to obtain a list of killed, wounded, and captured and to assist the wounded.[9] Caswell wanted to send the regimental surgeons, but a majority had disappeared and the rest were afraid to go. Williamson found 240 men with 700 wounds.

Williamson was frustrated by the lack of assistance he was

able to get from the British officers in providing supplies and medicine for the prisoners and the wounded. Unable to get a satisfactory response, he wrote that the British commissary of prisoners was "one Booth Boots whose Character did not appear to be diversified by a single Virtue, [who] would never do anything that would prove acceptable to us."[10] He wrote to an unknown correspondent, "Sir: The articles you were so kind to order have not been received. Our hospital patients are near 250, many of them dangerously wounded. They are lodged in six small wards, without straw or covering."[11]

Williamson had to deal with smallpox also. Cornwallis had shown displeasure at the inoculation of an officer with a slight wound who was quartered apart from the general prison group. Williamson wrote Cornwallis that confinement of two prisoners with smallpox was to be followed by death as certainly "as immediate execution."[12] Williamson wanted Cornwallis to allow inoculation of prisoners and soldiers as was allowed by the American army. He also wrote Major Richard(?) England of the British Army:

> I presume that Lord Cornwallis is informed that of the N. Carolina prisoners lately sent to Charles Town, who I apprehend are from 3 to 400, hardly a single Man has had the small Pox. There is, I presume, the utmost danger of those Men taking the Disease in the Natural way, unless they are inoculated. Be so kind as to inform me whether Lord Cornwallis is willing

> those Troops should be inoculated, and by whom he wishes it should be done. You will excuse the mention I have made of this subject, but having the chief Medical Care of the Troops of that State, I conceive it is my duty.[13]

He received the following answer from a Major Despond: "I have Lord Cornwallis' order to acquaint you that, with respect to the American prisoners sent to Charles Town being inoculated, his Lordship will give proper orders."[14]

Williamson was allowed to remain to care for the wounded, who, he said, "suffered under great neglect" for eight to ten days after the battle. Williamson lacked medical help without any of the militia surgeons and because Cornwallis did not direct any attention to the wounded. But after the "bitterest Complaint and most urgent importunity" supplies became more available.[15]

Williamson wrote of this experience to Thomas Benbury, speaker of the House in North Carolina:

> It happened that one of the Continental Surgeons fell into the hands of the Enemy. It may be supposed that with his assistance, tho' he was indefatigable, I found it impossible to give the desired help to 240 Men, who Labored under at Least 700 Wounds. After three weeks we were happily reinforced by Dr. Johnson, a Senior Surgeon of great skill & Humanity in the Continental Service. . . . We had the misfortune to lose 5 Privates, who died by their Wounds, 9 by

> the Small Pox, 1 by a Putrid fever, and 4 by the Flux; 2 officers died of by their Wounds and 2 by the Small Pox.[16]

The British had a great deal of respect for Williamson as a physician, and sought his consultation for one of their own general officers who took ill in addition to the surgeons from the British medical department. Furthermore, "He not only treated the prisoners at Camden but also looked after the sick in Caswell's camp at the same time."[17] A possible personal connection for Williamson may have been in Camden in the British camp. Allegedly a member of the Apthorp(e) family was serving with the British Army at Camden. This prominent New York Loyalist family would become Williamson's family by marriage and he is interred in their burial vault in New York City.

Williamson was solicitous and concerned about the hardship that service in the Continental Army or the militia required. He had personal experience of the war's cost, as he recalled in a letter to Richard Bland Lee years later:

> New York 19 May 1810
>
> Sir,
>
> Yours on the 28th would have been attended to sooner but that I was in the country. William L. Davidson the youngest son of George Davidson, my grandfather, was born in Lancaster County, Pennsylvania. His father moved with his

family to Rowan County in N. Carolina, while he was not more than 3 or 4 years old. Two of his sons the heads of families, had settled there before him. William L. Davidson was Director of an academy in Charlotte, the county town. He cultivated a farm that he inherited of his father. He was born about the year 1746. He entered the service of the US when the first N. Carolina troops were raised with the rank (as I think) of Major; he became one with his regiment, early in the spring of 1777. While he served in the Northern main army he obtained the rank of Lieut. Col. In November 1779 the troops in the North Carolina line, were ordered to the Southward, to reinforce Gen. Lincoln. Col. Davidson while his regiment was passing through N. Carolina, obtained leave to visit his family, from which he had been near three years absent. Before he reached Charleston, that city was completely infested by the British troops, and he could not enter. Whence it was that he did not become a prisoner with the troops of the N. Carolina line. Upon the fall of Charleston, the Tories in N. Carolina became very troublesome, they were very numerous in the Western parts of that State. But Davidson, very soon obtained the command of a body of militia who were called out to reduce the Tories. In an action with those people, I think it was at a place called Gatson Mill, near the river Pee Dee, he was seriously wounded, the ball entering at the umbilical region and coming out near the kidney. About 8 weeks from that time in September 1780 he took the field at the head of a corps of militia, with the rank of Brigadier Gen. That he gave the enemy much trouble I had the opportunity of knowing, for I was about this time two months in their camp with a flag. Early in 1781 when Lord Cornwallis was attempting to overtake Gen. Morgan to rescue the troops, lately made prisoners, Gen. Davidson was ordered by Gen. Green to endeavor to retard his march, by guarding the ford of the river Catawba. There were three fords of the river, equally practicable. Lord Cornwallis by the march of his artillery and baggage made a show of intending to cross at the upper ford, but Gen. Davidson suspecting that he intended nothing less, attended in person with the best of his troops at a lower ford. As the Gen. had expected, Lord Cornwallis crossed by that ford, at the dawning of day. The action was very severe for a short time, but Gen. Davidson's fall put an end to the dispute, he was shot through the breast, and his aid who sat near him told one that the general as he conceived did not carry his life to the ground.

He was perfectly in his element when engaged in military service. Congress ordained that he should have a monument. The General left a young family of children. One of his sons, for whom I solicited a commission, has serviced some years in our small army, but he married, and prudently retired.

I am Sir

Your obedient servant,
Hugh Williamson[18]

Davidson was Williamson's uncle, a half-brother to his mother. His family donated land received for service in the Revolutionary War for the founding of Davidson College. Williamson's mother's name was spelled Davison, but the family eventually used the spelling Davidson.

By 1780, the British had taken possession of Norfolk and Portsmouth, Virginia, as well. Under the command of General Isaac Gregory, a militia group from eastern North Carolina was established at Camden, North Carolina, not to be confused with Camden, South Carolina, site of the Cornwallis-Gates battle, on the border of the Great Dismal Swamp. By special request of General Gregory, Williamson was assigned to serve there. He used his own funds to help equip his medical corps. He organized the camp in a structured way and instituted use of sanitary devices that were unique in armies of that period. The result was a remarkable record of health among the troops.

Williamson's six-month time in the Great Dismal Swamp acquainted him with that region. This acquaintanceship undoubtedly was instrumental in his participation later with George Washington, Thomas Jefferson, and others in forming the Dismal Swamp Company in anticipation of the swamp becoming a transportation conduit for the United States. He felt that the drained swamp would be the most valuable land in North Carolina.

Part of Williamson's responsibility as surgeon general for the North Carolina militia was to secure medicine for the militia hospitals, which was very scarce, and to advise the governor about medical personnel. Williamson found it necessary to personally provide instruments, linen, and medical supplies. By the middle of October, the convalescing soldiers wounded at Camden and other actions had no warm clothing, so he purchased it for them from his own money. Williamson carefully attended to the soldiers' sanitation, diet, food, clothing, shelter, and sleeping quarters. These practices were affirmed and his efforts rewarded in that during those six months, with from five hundred to twelve hundred men in camp, only two died from disease and none were sent home due to sickness.[19] Word of Williamson's accomplishments on behalf of the welfare of the Continental Army spread and greatly enhanced his reputation as a patriot.

Williamson's letter of July 5, 1781, to Governor Thomas Burke let the governor know he was withdrawing from his role as surgeon general:

> When I first enter'd the Service of this State 4000 men were expected to take the Field under Major Gen. Caswell. At present there is no considerable body of Militia at any particular Station, and it is more than probable that a regimental Surgeon the only officer not wanted in the medical department. Hitherto I have been obliged to provide Medicines, Instruments, Linen & other necessaries for a Hospital & that too generally at my private Expence. My office has been very Expensive & commonly my duty has been very severe. However, knowing the State of public Finances I make no com-

> plaints. Though I have not sent in my commission I do not consider myself at present as entitled to public Pay, for I am on private Business. Should I find at any Time that my Services can be of particular use to the public I am ready to serve even as a Volunteer.[20]

Williamson was an able administrator as surgeon general for the North Carolina militia. He had a background of a unique nature regarding military medicine. He had trained as a resident pupil in London with the great John Hunter, ironically, surgeon extraordinaire to King George III. He undoubtedly had contact with Sir John Pringle, friend and traveling companion of Benjamin Franklin, who organized and provided a theory for management of the British Army and was regarded as a military genius in England. He had innovative ideas on not just treating soldiers but on preventing illness as well, as is evident in his view of inoculating against smallpox. His training with John Hunter undoubtedly gave him knowledge of this procedure; Hunter's first and most famous student was Edward Jenner, the discoverer of immunity against smallpox by a genetically close virus, the cowpox. The American army was the first one to have inoculation against smallpox. It was a factor in the ultimate success of the war. Williamson wrote:

> From a transient view of our Misfortunes, it is clear that we would save many lives by any kind of Military establishment

> that would admit of the Troops being inoculated before they took the Field.[21]

During his war service, Williamson became well acquainted with William Richardson Davie, who raised a company of cavalry to harass Cornwallis when Charleston was occupied and an invasion of North Carolina was eminent. Davie later became governor of North Carolina, the acknowledged founder of the University of North Carolina, and a delegate appointed by President John Adams to the Hague. His *Revolutionary War Sketches* included a number of details by Dr. Williamson about numbers and logistics of various Revolutionary War battles and troop movements in North Carolina. It is possible that Williamson was gathering material for a third volume of his *History of North Carolina*, as none of the Revolutionary War period is included in the first two volumes, which as noted earlier have been criticized because they do not contain much information about the period and his involvement.[22]

Cornwallis surrendered at Yorktown on October 19, 1781. Major Craig evacuated Wilmington on November 18, thus ending the military phase of the Revolution in North Carolina. The "Tory War" continued until David Fanning, a notorious Loyalist, left the state in May of 1782. The war officially concluded on September 3, 1783, when "His Britannic Majesty" acknowledged the colonies to be free, sovereign, and independent states.

The period from the closure of the war until the adoption of the United States Constitution in 1789 was a critical period for the 350,000 people living in the forty-seven counties in North Carolina. Among the problems were treatment of veterans, release of prisoners, state policy in relationship to Tories, and location of a permanent capital. From 1781 to 1789 considerable factionalism and sectional interest occurred. There were groups loosely called conservatives and radicals that roughly followed the various social classes. Most of the educated, wealthy, and creditor class was in the conservative class, and they had the distinguished leaders Samuel Johnston, James Iredell, Hugh Williamson, William R. Davie, Archibald McLean, William Hooper, Allan Johnson, John Steele, and others. Most of the people in the state were not as well educated or well to do and constituted the so-called radicals, who were small farmers and artisans. Among these were leaders such as Willie Jones, Thomas Person, Samuel Spencer, Mash Viewlock, and Timothy Bloodworth. After the war there were many prisoners of war from North Carolina who were incarcerated at Charleston as a result of the capitulation of that city in May of 1780, some by that point in the British West Indies and off the Florida coast. The legislature authorized Governor Alexander Martin to negotiate a prisoner exchange with the British commanding officer at Charleston, General Alexander Leslie.[23]

After Williamson resigned from the army in July 1781, he returned to Edenton to run his business affairs, in which he became closely associated with the powerful Blount family in Washington, North Carolina. Williamson's extensive business interests and personal connections led to his entry into state politics, as a representative of the merchant class. He immediately began a political career that would lead to service in the first North Carolina legislature, as a North Carolina representative to the Continental Congress, as delegate to the Constitutional Convention, and as representative to the first United States House of Representatives.

Williamson was in attendance as a member of the Continental Congress in Baltimore when General George Washington surrendered his commission, symbolically handed it to the president of the Continental Congress in front of the assembled Congress, and bowed. Congressmen doffed their hats. The gesture, immortalized in the painting by Trumbull (see illustrations), emphasized the primacy of civilian authority over the military. Washington, always with a flair for the dramatic, asked if he could have the commission for his grandchildren. Hugh Williamson advanced the motion in Congress that a gold box be fashioned to hold the commission and that it be presented to Washington. The commission, however, still resides in the National Archives.

Chapter 7

State and National Legislator

> We served together in Congress during the winter of 1783–1784; there I found him a very useful member, of an acute mind, attentive to business, and of a high degree of erudition.
>
> Thomas Jefferson of Hugh Williamson

The thirteen colonies had coalesced in the Second Continental Congress to oppose Great Britain's rule and had, through the genius of George Washington, avoided defeat and won the single, decisive battle of the war at Yorktown, Virginia. Through guerrilla warfare, the colonies had outlasted the British, the most powerful country on earth at the time. The Continental Congresses, following the successful conclusion of hostilities at the peace table in Paris in 1783, were now faced with winning the peace and developing a government. The Articles of Confederation were formed; these articles reflected the desire to prevent the rise of a new tyranny, an unfortunately common outcome following successful revolutions.

After his good works during the Revolutionary War, Surgeon General Hugh Williamson found the transition from war to politics a smooth one. He was to serve in the North Carolina state legislature, the Continental Congress, the Constitutional Convention, and the first two sessions of the United States House of Representatives.

State Legislator

On April 17, 1782, Williamson's hometown of Edenton selected him to represent it in the House of Commons in the North Carolina General Assembly. He took the oath of office the next day.

Williamson at once assumed an active role and, deploring the state of education in North Carolina, presented a bill for promotion of learning in the District of Edenton. Out of passage of this bill, Smith Academy was created. As a member of the North Carolina House of Commons, Williamson introduced eight bills during the session. All of them passed either because of strongly perceived need for them in the state or because of Williamson's exertions on their behalf.[1]

The Continental Congress had chartered the Bank of North America on May 6, 1781. In 1782, Williamson introduced and secured the enactment of a bill into the North Carolina General Assembly to validate the Bank of North Carolina and to punish counterfeiters of its currency. In 1782, a bill was introduced by Williamson that established revenue for North Carolina. A tax of one penny was levied on each pound of taxable property. Every man between twenty and fifty years of age whose taxable property did not equal £100 in value paid a poll tax in lieu of the property tax. Due to their religious exemption from military duty, the Quakers, Moravians, Mennonites, and Dunkards were to pay a higher tax rate.

Two of Williamson's bills related to the war effort, the first defraying war contingencies and supporting the Continental Army for the year 1782. The second was for the relief of Continental soldiers, directing that they be paid their overdue pay plus depreciation from before August 18 for clothing and subsistence, paid in land assigned by the states for cession, often from western lands that were part of territory gained through Indian treaties or from the British (an example of such land was what is now Tennessee and was territory then of North Carolina) and collectible by heirs. Every soldier who remained in the army until the end of the war, or was wounded, was to receive a minimum of 640 acres of land, a settlement that increased in quantity according to rank. Surveyors were appointed for land survey and allocation.

For many years afterward, he continued his efforts for the veterans of the Revolutionary War, including the family of his uncle, General William L. Davidson, for whom Davidson College in North Carolina is named. In a letter to Governor Alexander Martin, he pleaded their cause:

> Philad Novr, 1792.
>
> Sir,
>
> You are probably informed of the Difficulties that have occurred respecting the claims of the late Genl. Davidson's family.
>
> In the year 1785, Provision was made by Law in our State, according to an Act of Congress, for paying widows or children of Continental Officers who dyed in the Services, seven years half pay. . . .
>
> I have lately written to Mrs. Davidson who lives near Nashville on the Cumberland River, advising her to authorize some person by a Power of Attorney to return to the State the money she has received and to take for her use, Generl Davidson Certificates out of the Treasury. I believe Mrs. Davidson might be profited by this measure and the State would lose nothing . . . and I am greatly mistaken if the Legislature of North Carolina will not have a Pleasure in knowing that the Widow and Orphan Children of Genl. Davidson, at this Hour of Distress, when they are in hourly danger from the Indians, have the prospect of some relief by which Life may be supported.

To you, Sir, an apology is not required for my particular application in favour of the Family. I have no Occasion to mention the Services of Genl Davidson; that he fell at the Head of his Brigade in the service of his Country. That having spent his Property in the public service he left his family in a state of Indigence. That his Widow and Children have been obliged to remove to the wilderness where they protract a Life of sufferings; these facts might have served a stranger for an apology, but informed as you are that Genl Davidson was my mother's brother you will admit that in attempting any Relief for that Family, I have only discharged part of the Duty I owe to the suffering Family of my late Unkle.

I have the Honour to be with Sentiments of the most perfect Respect.

Sir,

Your most obedient & very hbble, Servant,

Hu Williamson

His excellency

Alex:Martin[2]

Governor Martin responded in the affirmative. Years later, the land given to the Davidson family for their service in the Revolutionary War was donated toward building Davidson College in Davidson, North Carolina. (Meanwhile, a similar donation of land in 1797, by Major Charles Gerrard, had provided a large donation of land received for his Revolutionary War service, which became the site for the University of North Carolina at Chapel Hill.)

Bills secured by Williamson built a prison in Edenton, created a five-person commission to maintain the structures and streets of Edenton, and built a public market and wharf. He voted in favor of repealing laws that made paper money legal tender in payment of private debts. Since there was little money in circulation, barter was often the only means of exchanging goods and was critical to business survival because in Edenton many citizens made a living selling imported goods, and buying and exporting North Carolina commodities.

Even though his state service was cut short due to entering federal politics, Williamson served on many of the General Assembly's most important committees. He was a member of the Committee on Privileges and Elections, a committee to consider the address of Joseph Hawkins concerning the affairs of North Carolina's boundary line, the Committee on Depreciation of Currency, and many special committees to consider memorials of towns and individuals.

Continental Congress

The success of Williamson's North Carolina legislative career culminated on May 3, 1782, when the General Assembly elected him to be a delegate from North Carolina to the Continental Congress, along with Abner Nash, Benjamin Hawkins, and William Blount, all three also from the eastern part of the state. Williamson's terms of service in the Continental Congress would be the maximum allowed, three consecutive years, to end May 13, 1785.

During his service in the Continental Congress, he again became involved in the management of international affairs. Communicating with ministers of foreign governments was difficult because it depended on lengthy ship travel. On December 15, 1783, a committee of Elbridge Gerry, Thomas Jefferson, and Hugh Williamson recommended that Congress issue a commission that would enable the American ministers abroad to negotiate treaties of amity and commerce with European nations. These recommendations were adopted in May 1784.[3]

While in Congress he also resumed his relationship with Benjamin Franklin, who was serving as an unofficial representative to the French court. Williamson requested of Franklin that he intervene to free two young boys captured by the British.

> Sir Philadelphia, 7 Aug 1782.
>
> When you have a few minutes to spare from the more weighty concerns of late, I wish to interest you in favour of two young men belonging to North Carolina who are now prisoners in England. They sailed from Edenton about the month of August 1780 in the Brig Fair American, Captain Smith, bound for France and were captured on their outward passage. They are twins, and were, if I recollect well, about 14 years old when they left home. They are neither soldier

nor sailor for they never had been at sea before, and on that occasion they through mere whim. The father of those lads, Col. Lockhart, is a worthy and respectable citizen of North Carolina. Having served with him in the Southern Army, in the most perilous times, it is not only my duty but among the first of my wishes that I might render him a service. The Col. apprehends that, considering the age of his boys and other circumstances, the enemy will not make a point of detaining them. They are supposed to be in Fostin . . . Prison. At the first time you may have occasion to inquire concerning any of our people who are prisoners in England will you be so good as cause inquiry to be made concerning these boys. If you should effect their release you will be so good as give them such instructions and assistance may enable them to return to any port in the United States. Any expense you are at, on this account, shall be immediately repaid to your order in Philadelphia where my duty in Congress may detain for the present year. I have the honor to be

With the utmost esteem,
Sir,
Your most obedient
And very humble servant, Hugh Williamson[4]

Earlier, in 1779, Benjamin Franklin had evinced great concern for Americans who commonly became prisoners of the British while sailing on ships commissioned by him while he was in France. Franklin viewed the commissioning of these ships, known as privateers, as a means to capture British sailors to use for prisoner exchanges. Franklin received letters from Fostin Prison at Portsmouth, England, as evidenced in a letter of 1778 complaining of bad faith on Britain's part with regard to prisoner exchange.[5] The privateers Franklin commissioned were predominantly crewed by Irish and French sailors.

The privateer the *Black Prince*, captained by Robert Marchant and Irishman Luke Ryan, captured 35 prizes, the *Black Princess* captured 43 prizes. The *Fearnot* and others brought the total to 114 prizes. The success of Franklin's privateers would only be eclipsed by John Paul Jones's *Bonhomme Richard*.

Unfortunately for Franklin's plans, since privateers usually docked in French ports, the French would parole British seamen instead of capturing them to exchange for American prisoners. Of concern to the French was a British ruling that the seamen captured on privateers would be considered traitors, not prisoners, and potentially punished by death. Instead of a commissioner who dealt with prisoner exchanges, Franklin inadvertently became one who had to rule on disposition of goods seized by privateers. After nine months he was able to resign the obligation.[6]

State Legislator Again

Returning to Edenton on June 15, 1785, after his term in the Continental Congress ended, Hugh Williamson was re-elected to the General Assembly for a second term after the summer's heated political campaign. When the session opened in New Bern on November 19, Williamson's motion to appoint Richard Dobbs Spaight the speaker was unanimously approved. Williamson served on a committee to consider papers submitted by the governor and William Blount regarding residents of Washington County, North Carolina. He was a member of committees that addressed securing a printer for publishing laws and journals, propositions and grievances, claims placating the western counties, and receiving memorials.

During this legislative session Williamson prepared, presented, and seconded a number of bills to protect the interests of merchants and regulate the commerce of North Carolina. To promote commerce, he wrote and presented a bill regulating trade. All import duties previously levied by the General Assembly on goods brought in by water would be payable on goods imported in American ships. An additional 20 percent was levied on goods imported in foreign ships, as long as that duty did not violate a commercial treaty of the United States. Goods manufactured in America would be brought tax free into North Carolina. A tonnage tax was imposed on both domestic and foreign ships. Commissioners were appointed to improve coastal navigation and collect duties. The idea behind this bill was embodied in the first federal revenue act passed by the new Congress under the Constitution in 1789 as advocated by Alexander Hamilton.

Continuing to advocate for the welfare of those who had served in the Continental Army, Williamson proposed legislation to settle with the veterans and provide for their widows and orphans. Williamson introduced an act in accord with a recommendation from Congress that state legislatures carry out the 1778 congressional resolution that promised officers who served to the end of the war half pay for seven years, a right extending to their widows and children. He saw to the appointment of a commission to issue indented certificates to liquidate accounts for services to the army prior to January 1782. Public treasurers were authorized to provide prompt payment. Legislation proposed by a committee on which Williamson served was passed that organized a state militia composed of all men from ages eighteen to fifty. These men were to drill at specified times and provide their own weapons.

Worthy of note, as mentioned earlier, is a bill proposed by Williamson titled "Securing Literary Property" in North Carolina. This bill was an early forerunner to current copyright law. It provided: "The author of every book, map, or chart not then in print, who was a citizen of the United States shall have the sole liberty of printing, publishing and vending the same within the state for the term of fourteen years to commence on the day of publication."[7]

To qualify for this protection, the title of the work had to be recorded with the secretary of state before publication and a copy provided to the state's executive branch. Williamson served on the committee to determine the salary and duties of the state printer and continued to advocate for patents and copyrights. A letter to Williamson from Thomas Jefferson provides a glimpse of the making of legislation in that regard:

> Dear sir, Nov. 13, 1791
>
> On considering the subject of the clause you wished to have introduced in the enclosed bill, I found it more difficult than I had on first views imagined. Will you make the first trial against the patentee conclusive against all others who might be interested to contest His patent? If you do he will have a collusive suit brought it against himself at once or will you give everyone a right to bring actions separately? . . .
>
> I really believe that less evil will follow from leaving him to bring suits against those who invade his right. If, however, you can get over the difficulty and will drop me a line, I will try to prepare a clause, tho I am sure you will put your own ideas into form better than anybody else can.
>
> Yours with sincere esteem
>
> Th Jefferson[8]

During the General Assembly's 1785 November–December session, to Williamson's consternation, a paper money act passed that provided for printing £100,000 in paper money to be applied to part of the foreign debt, to cover part of the current federal government expenses, to repay state government debts, and to redeem certificates issued for interest by the commissioners for Continental loans and due debts. Paper money was to be placed in circulation by the purchase of tobacco that would then be shipped to Europe, the West Indies, and other places per instructions of the Treasury Board. Williamson voted against the bill at each of its three readings. Led by Williamson and Archibald McLean of Wilmington, eight members of the House of Commons on December 27 presented their objections to the bill, pointing to the extensive depreciation that occurred to paper money that had been printed in 1783 and reasoning that printing more would not improve the situation. Williamson was very much opposed to paper money.

> The danger resulting from the circulation of such currency declared by law to be a tender in all payments whatsoever, strikes us with alarming apprehensions for the honor of the state, the security of Commerce and the safety of all ranks of honest men. Depreciated and depreciating even before its existence, the Officers of our civil list . . . must murmur at payment which will necessarily fall short of the provisions intended by the State.
>
> The merchants from whose aid the principal assurance of the credit of any paper money is to be placed cannot give consequence to an emission made against their declared opinion and founded on a revenue which appears inadequate to its redemption; whilst the just creditors will be compelled

> to receive sums nominally equal to the discharge of obligations to them made, but intrinsically of value far inferior; hence the honest and unsuspecting may become the dupes of the artful and designing.[9]

Williamson argued that paper money would not relieve the suffering of the poor because prices would inflate as the money depreciated. Gold and silver would disappear from circulation, which in turn would cause a shortage of paper money. He also found paper money objectionable because it meant that tobacco was being purchased at a price higher than value, which injured North Carolina's credit and directed commerce to other states from North Carolina's ports.

In August of 1787, using the pseudonym "Sylvius," Williamson published in *The American Museum*[10] a series of letters that he had written the year before. These letters, known as the "Essays on Money," had first been published in pamphlet form in New York as *Letters of Sylvius* and were later reproduced by Dr. W. K. Boyd in publications of the Historical Society of Trinity College. In these papers Williamson discussed the scarcity of money, the evils of paper currency, national dress, foreign luxuries, the federal debt, public taxes, the advantages of an excise tax over a land and poll tax, and the promotion of domestic manufacturers. In his *Letters*, Williamson convincingly argued that paper money would hurt the country and that the only means of relieving debt would be by promoting domestic manufacture. He suggested during periods of scarce money that the burden on the poor be reduced by levying an excise tax in place of the poll or land tax. Williamson thought the people had not faced a question of equal importance since the Declaration of Independence. These letters were frequently referenced by advocates of the Constitution and provide valuable insight into the political and economic conditions of the era.

After the Revolution, one of North Carolina's most perplexing problems was the disposition of its transmountain lands, claim of which was based on the Colonial Charter of 1663. As early as 1779, Congress had recommended the cession of all western lands to the Confederation government for the common good of the United States on the grounds that these lands were the common property of all the states, that they would be used for reduction of the public debt, and that ultimately new states would form from this domain. North Carolina was divided on whether to support that position. There was fear that Congress might adopt the proposal of base taxes and calculate representation in Congress from total population. If such a policy should be adopted, it would be to North Carolina's advantage to cede the western lands because the less territory owned and the smaller the population, the less would be the pressure to meet future Continental expenditures. Beyond the mountains, cession was favored. The western area of North Carolina was hostile to domination by the east, and it lacked military protection against the Cherokees, courts, and other governmental services. Westerners figured that it would retard settlement of the area if cession failed to occur and that Spain, which controlled the port of New Orleans, could stop American trade to the sea. Pressure from Congress and the demands of western settlers culminated in the Cession Act of April 1784. The state legislature agreed to cede its western lands to the United States on condition that neither the lands nor the inhabitants of the territory should be used toward estimating North Carolina's share of Revolutionary War expenses. William R. Davie and thirty-six other legislators voted against the act, believing that the land should be used to liquidate the state's Revolutionary debt and that the state had not been given credit for military assistance to other states, notably Virginia and South Carolina.[11]

The Cession Act was sent to Hugh Williamson in Congress in Philadelphia, but was not received until the day Congress adjourned (June 3, 1784), so no action was taken on it. Williamson expressed surprise upon receipt and opposed the act's provisions because they did not give adequate protection to North Carolina. Meanwhile, this impolitic act was causing uneasiness and discontent throughout the state. On the advice of Williamson, Davie and other conservatives of the General Assembly in October 1784 repealed the Cession Act by a great majority. News of the Cession Act, however, had been received happily by the western areas, who now took steps to separate from North Carolina and obtain eventual statehood. The Jonesborough Convention on August 23, 1784, with delegates from all of the Tennessee counties except Davidson, and presided over by John Sevier, charged the North Carolina government with neglect of interest of the people of the Tennessee counties and the delegates petitioned Congress to accept the Cession Act. While the state legislature of North Carolina repealed the law, it did create a judicial district of Washington and a military district with Sevier as brigadier general. A second convention called to draft a constitution for the proposed new state was split between the followers of John Tipton, who opposed separation from North Carolina, and the followers of Sevier, who advocated the creation of a new state, so that the meeting broke up in disorder. At a convention on December 14, 1784, however, the two factions drafted one document that provided for universal suffrage and the popular election of officials for the state of Franklin. Similar to the North Carolina Constitution of 1776, the one championed by Sevier provided for the state of Franklin. A convention of November 1785 adopted the latter constitution and Sevier was chosen governor. The state of Franklin's survival required the support of North Carolina, the cooperation of Virginia, and favor by the Continental Congress. It was unsuccessful on all three counts. Virginia declared attempting such an activity to be an act of high treason. Governor Martin of North Carolina issued a blistering manifesto against it, and the Continental Congress opposed it.[12]

In 1789, though, North Carolina finally ceded its western

lands to the United States. In 1790 a territory south of the Ohio was created, and in 1794 the territory of Tennessee was established. When in 1796 Tennessee was admitted to the Union, its Constitution was written largely by former inhabitants of North Carolina, including Andrew Jackson.

Williamson inserted himself into the center of such state debates regarding the sales, survey, and defense of the western territories. On December 17, 1784, Williamson proposed that a committee of three members be appointed to draft a bill to satisfy the inhabitants of the western counties. Encouraged by the passage of the Ordinance of 1784 by the United States Congress, settlers on the upper Tennessee were aspiring to statehood because they believed the eastern legislators lacked knowledge of conditions that the western counties needed for the passage of suitable laws. This disputed territory happened to coincide almost exactly with one of the states projected in the ordinance.

In a lengthy letter, written by Williamson from Edenton on September 30, 1784, to Governor Alexander Martin and presented by the governor to the legislature, Williamson, who became a major force in the October 1784 rescission, explained his opposition to the Cession Act: "If we should immediately complete the Cession we shall give up the power of making advantageous terms and shall lose the argument which may bring others to adopt federal measures. . . . The situation is critical. Perhaps it is most consistent with prudence and sound policy to make a pause."[13] This letter has since been referred to as "a State paper of the highest value."[14]

Williamson argued that the Cession Act failed to consider the value of the western lands already granted to Revolutionary War soldiers for their services. He also stressed the value of the western lands in properly settling North Carolina's unadjusted debt to the national government. He asserted that due credit had not been given to North Carolina for the state's financial outlays to the Indian expeditions, which he thought to be a federal responsibility. Colonel Davie and Richard Dobbs Spaight supported Williamson in these arguments. "Dr. Williamson knew the situation perhaps better than any of our representatives and did as much as any one in guiding the state's course to a solution of the difficult situation. Some writers claim that the rising state of Franklin hastened the repeal, but it seems more reasonable to infer that the defects pointed out by Williamson and others brought it about."[15]

Before the news of the repeal of the Cession Act in October 1784 had reached the western counties, the settlers had already elected delegates to the first convention to frame the Franklin state constitution. Williamson had advocated suspending cession for a year, but it was 1789 before it was eventually completed. Maryland, in fact, made cession to the central government a condition of ratification of the Constitution.

Williamson attended the North Carolina General Assembly when it met in Tarboro on November 19, 1787. He reported on the 1787 Constitutional Convention in Philadelphia, caught up on the activities of the state legislature, and visited friends and business associates. After serving again in the Continental Congress, he did not enter the General Assembly elections in 1789, though many of his constituents in Edenton and Chowan counties urged him to do so. He relinquished his seat at the end of his term.

HUGH WILLIAMSON, M.D., L.L.D.

1820? Etching by Thomson after John Trumbull. Emmet Collection, Miriam and Ira D. Wallach Division of Art, Prints and Photographs, the New York Public Library, Astor, Lenox and Tilden Foundations

FRANKLIN AT THE COURT OF FRANCE, 1778 BY W. O. GELLER

This nineteenth-century engraving is thought to be imagined. It does show a number of Franklin's associates in France and his understanding of the social setting of the diplomatic milieu of the French court. Louis XVI is seated with Marie Antoinette at his side. Vergennes stands to the right of the woman crowning the popular Franklin with Laurels. *Franklin Collection, Yale University Library.*

GEN. WASHINGTON RESIGNING HIS COMMISSION
to Congress at Annapolis Md. Decemb. 23d 1783

1. Thomas Mifflin, Pennsylvania, President
   Delegate
2. Charles Thompson, Pennsylvania
   Secretary
3. Elbridge Gerry, Massachusetts
   Delegate
4. Hugh Williamson, North Carolina
   Delegate
5. Samuel Osgood, Massachusetts
   Delegate
6. Eleazer McComb, Delaware
   Delegate
7. George Partridge, Massachusetts
   Delegate
8. Edward Lloyd, Maryland
   Delegate
9. Richard D. Spaight, North Carolina
   Delegate
10. Benjamin Hawkins, North Carolina
    Delegate
11. Abiel Foster, New Hampshire
    Delegate
12. Thomas Jefferson, Virginia
    Delegate
13. Arthur Lee, Virginia
    Delegate
14. David Howell, Rhode Island
    Delegate
15. James Monroe, Virginia
    Delegate
16. Jacob Read, South Carolina
    Delegate
17. James Madison, Virginia
    Spectator
18. William Ellery, Rhode Island
    Delegate
19. J. Townley Chase, Maryland
    Delegate
20. Samuel Hardy, Virginia
    Delegate
21. Charles Morris, Pennsylvania
    Delegate
22. General Washington
23. Col. Benjamin Walker
    Aide-de-camp
24. Col. David Humphreys
    Aide-de-camp
25. General Smallwood, Maryland
    Spectator
26. Gen. Otho Holland Williams, Maryland
    Spectator
27. Col. Samuel Smith, Maryland
    Spectator
28. Col. John E. Howard, Maryland
    Spectator
29. Charles Carroll and two daughters,
    Maryland
30. Mrs. Washington and her three grand-
    children
31. Daniel of St. Thomas Jenifer, Maryland
    Spectator

GEORGE WASHINGTON RESIGNING HIS COMMISSION

"On 29 Jan 1784 Hugh Williamson introduced the following resolution: 'Resolved, That his late Commission be returned to General Washington in a neat gold box to be preserved among the archives of his family'" (*Journals of the Continental Congress* 26: 54; the motion is in the DLC:PCC, no. 36, 2). This motion was adopted and referred to committee; however, the commission remains in the National Archives rather than with Washington's family. "George Washington's Resignation as Commander-in-Chief, "*Archives of the Continental Congress*, pp. 408–409. The gesture has great significance, signifying as it does the authority of the civilian government over the military. See attached legends. Shadow outlines identify the participants. Williamson is in the back row. *Courtesy of the Architect of the Capitol*

SCENE AT THE SIGNING OF THE CONSTITUTION OF THE UNITED STATES

1. Washington, George, Va.
2. Franklin, Benjamin, Pa.
3. Madison, James, Va.
4. Hamilton, Alexander, N.Y.
5. Morris, Gouverneur, Pa.
6. Morris, Robert, Pa.
7. Wilson, James, Pa.
8. Pinckney, Chas. Cotesworth, S.C.
9. Pinckney, Chas, S.C.
10. Rutledge, John, S.C.
11. Butler, Pierce, S.C.
12. Sherman, Roger, Conn.
13. Johnson, William Samuel, Conn.
14. McHenry, James, Md.
15. Read, George, Del.
16. Bassett, Richard, Del.
17. Spaight, Richard Dobbs, N.C.
18. Blount, William, N.C.
19. Williamson, Hugh, N.C.
20. Jenifer, Daniel of St. Thomas, Md.
21. King, Rufus, Mass.
22. Gorham, Nathaniel, Mass.
23. Dayton, Jonathan, N.J.
24. Carroll, Daniel, Md.
25. Few, William, Ga.
26. Baldwin, Abraham, Ga.
27. Langdon, John, N.H.
28. Gilman, Nicholas, N.H.
29. Livingston, William, N.J.
30. Paterson, William, N.J.
31. Mifflin, Thomas, Pa.
32. Clymer, George, Pa.
33. FitzSimons, Thomas, Pa.
34. Ingersoll, Jared, Pa.
35. Bedford, Gunning, Jr., Del.
36. Brearley, David, N.J.
37. Dickinson, John, Del.
38. Blair, John, Va.
39. Broom, Jacob, Del.
40. Jackson, William, Secretary

SCENE OF THE SIGNING OF THE CONSTITUTION
BY HOWARD CHANDLER CHRISTY, 1940

There are a number of paintings of the perceived positions of different signers of the constitution. See attached legend with Hugh Williamson, standing and facing George Washington, as Williamson prepares to sign. *Courtesy of the Architect of the Capitol.*

CONSTITUTION CENTER

This statue is in the Signers' Room of the National Constitution Center in Philadelphia. Hugh Williamson is congratulating George Read of Delaware after the signing of the Constitution by thirty-nine of the fifty-five delegates occurred. *Courtesy of National Constitution Center, Philadelphia, PA.*

The CENTINEL. 

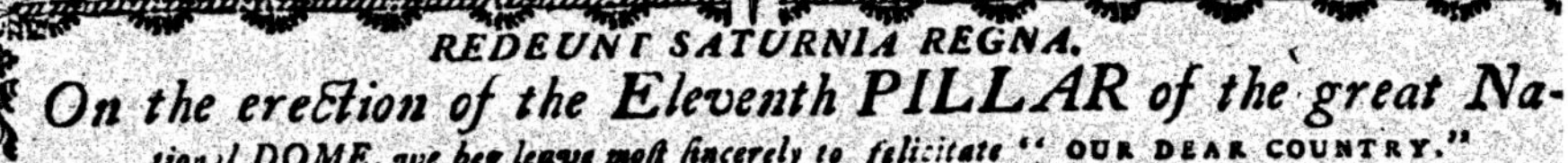

REDEUNT SATURNIA REGNA.

On the erection of the Eleventh **PILLAR** *of the great National* **DOME,** *we beg leave moſt ſincerely to felicitate* "OUR DEAR COUNTRY."

The **FEDERAL EDIFICE.**

ELEVEN STARS, in quick ſucceſſion riſe—
ELEVEN COLUMNS ſtrike our wond'ring eyes,
Soon o'er the *whole*, ſhall ſwell the beauteous DOME,
COLUMBIA's boaſt—and FREEDOM's hallow'd home.
Here ſhall the ARTS in glorious ſplendour ſhine!
And AGRICULTURE give her ſtores divine!
COMMERCE refin'd, diſpenſe us more than gold,
And this new world, teach WISDOM to the old—
RELIGION here ſhall fix her bleſt abode,
Array'd in *mildneſs*, like its parent GOD!
JUSTICE and LAW, ſhall endleſs PEACE maintain,
And *the* "SATURNIAN AGE," *return again.*

ELEVENTH PILLAR—THE FEDERAL EDIFICE,
FROM THE MASSACHUSETTS CENTINEL, AUGUST 2, 1788

Centinel was an Anti-Federalist organization that participated in the state-by-state ratifi debates. This cartoon shows that the required two-thirds of the states, in the order they ra assured the ratification of the Philadelphia constitution as the law of the land, replacing the A of Confederation. Note that North Carolina and Rhode Island failed to ratify during the conventions. *Collections of the New-York Historical Society.*

SAMUEL HOLLYER, APTHORPE MANSION, NEW YORK CITY, 1790, OLD NEW YORK, C.1907

This was the home of the family of Williamson's wife and the place of their marriage ceremony. During the battle for New York, it was occupied briefly by George Washington during his retreat from Long Island. It was subsequently the headquarters of General Cornwallis. Picture Collection, the Branch Libraries, the New York Public Library, Astor, Lenox and Tilden Foundations

HUGH WILLIAMSON, M.D., PLASTER BUST BY WILLIAM JOHN COFFEE, 1816
Williamson was reluctant to sit for portraits and they, in general, are less accurate depictions of his physiognomy than the contemporary lithographs. *The New-York Historical Society.*

Chapter 8

Williamson in the Continental Congress

Williamson had been a citizen of North Carolina for only four years on July 19, 1782, when he took his seat in the Continental Congress. As noted earlier, he was twice a delegate to the Continental Congress from North Carolina, from 1782 to 1785 and from 1788 until the Constitutional Congress convened in March of 1789.

Sectionalism rather than nationalism predominated in the era. North Carolina had been deprived of votes in the Continental Congress during the 1781 and early 1782 sessions due to having only one representative, Benjamin Hawkins. William Blount attended for the first time on July 22, 1782, but served less than a year before resigning on April 30, 1783, to resume his seat in the General Assembly of North Carolina from Craven County. Also from Craven County, Richard Dobbs

Spaight replaced Blount in the Continental Congress. Abner Nash attended for the first time on November 14, 1782.

Hugh Williamson was the oldest member of the state delegation and zealous in participating and keeping North Carolina aware of the central government's activities.

During his time in the Continental Congress, Blount served on only one committee; Nash on six; Hawkins on none; and Williamson on nineteen. Williamson had his most significant impact on Congress through committee participation. Williamson served on five committees with James Madison of Virginia; three with George Clymer of Pennsylvania, John Jay of New York, and John Witherspoon of New Jersey; two with Richard Peters of Pennsylvania, Arthur Lee of Virginia, and John Taylor Gilman of New Hampshire; and one with Samuel Wharton of Delaware.

Since Williamson served in the Continental Congress the full allowable time—three continuous terms, sitting successively at Philadelphia, Princeton, Annapolis, Trenton, and New York—he collaborated with many of the leading men of the time. These included Elbridge Gerry, Nathaniel Gorham, and Rufus King, delegates from Massachusetts; Dr. William S. Johnson, Roger Sherman, and Oliver Ellsworth from Connecticut; Alexander Hamilton, Judge John Lansing, and Gouverneur Morris from New York; William Churchill Houston, from Cabarrus County, North Carolina, who was serving as a commissioner from New Jersey; James Wilson, Thomas Mifflen, George Clymer, Thomas Fitzsimmons, and James Wilson from Pennsylvania; Gunning Bedford from Delaware; James McHenry, Daniel Carroll, and Luther Martin from Maryland; James Madison from Virginia; John Rutledge and Charles Pinckney from South Carolina; and William Few, Abraham Baldwin, and William Houston from Georgia.

Hugh Williamson industriously tackled the issues facing the Continental Congress. He favored the 5 percent impost tax, as did the North Carolina legislature, and he also favored a liquor tax, though this tax was very unpopular in North Carolina, even in his own district. Williamson encouraged the regulation of roads and ferries. He voted in favor of Thomas Jefferson's Land Ordinance of 1784. He served on the committee that developed the ordinance, and he collected maps and the observations of travelers "to estimate the quantity and value of the territory now belonging to the United States on the West of the Ohio."[1] Williamson calculated that the national debt could be halved by selling the fertile 85 million acres between Pennsylvania and the Mississippi River, bordered by forty-two degrees north latitude and the Ohio River, for twenty-five dollars per hundred acres.[2]

Williamson demonstrated considerable talent in settling claims of individuals against the federal government. He was also interested in Indian affairs, particularly Indian trade and treaty negotiations with the southern Indians, mostly the Cherokee. Williamson differed from the Blounts in his stand that Indians should be compensated for land.

Williamson also debated trade agreements, such as the

Definitive Treaty of Peace and Commerce with Great Britain (concluded September 3, 1783); the dismal state of national finances; the prevalence of low estimations of North Carolina's support of the Revolutionary War; the deplorable state of Continental money (some localities were using coonskins and rawhides as currency); and the difficulties inherent in Congress making treaties that it could not enforce. He served on important committees that addressed subjects like the assumption of state debts, the slave trade, the Navigation Acts, and commercial regulations. He was also selected to represent North Carolina on a special committee consisting of one member from each state to consider all remaining matters not covered by a specific assignment like agriculture, fisheries, and so on and to make a report to the Constitutional Convention.

Williamson served on several congressional committees concerned with manufacturing. He thought that New England with its small towns located near waterpower would be particularly suitable to manufacturing. The southern states could provide the raw materials and transport them to New England in fishing boats. Williamson saw it as a sign of patriotism to wear only American-made clothes, and he even recommended a native dress. Because Williamson depended on a widely scattered network of contacts to support his interests in trade, manufacturing, and government, he eagerly promoted a postal service for the country to provide an efficient system of communication to transact personal and political business.

Perhaps deriving his interest from his study of mathematics, Williamson advocated to Congress an orderly survey of the national domain, a perspective he shared with Thomas Jefferson, who called it "an athletic strength of calculation."[3] Williamson designed the system and the procedures used by national surveyors in order to "prevent innumerable frauds and enable us to save millions. The general object is to oblige the Surveyors to account for the land by parallels, dotts, & meridians."[4]

Some authors have claimed that Williamson was responsible for the square shapes of American farms in Ohio and the old Northwest. The Jefferson-Williamson surveying plan is credited by scholars with being the initial fundamental step in the "exertion of national sovereignty in the field of eminent domain."[5] The Ordinance of 1785 included Williamson's grid design for the systematic settlement of 1.3 billion acres in the West. This activity on behalf of systematically ordering settlement of the new nation reflected his compulsive scientific personality:

> Indeed, a preoccupation with particulars and formality was an important component of Williamson's personality. On one level he seemed a restless man, who sought relief from hypochondriasis by plunging into myriad physical, intellectual, and emotional activities. On another level his affectations were those of an ambitious member of rising intelligentsia. Whatever its origins, Williamson's devotion to detail and system was an important aspect of his plans for laying out and governing the territory gained by the War for

Independence. His correspondence, reflecting many of his personal habits, was systematic, inclusive, and witty.[6]

Williamson never owned any slaves. His position on slavery in the territories was revealed during the land-policy debates. According to James Madison, as early as 1783 Williamson declared that "he was principled agst. Slavery; & that he thought slaves were an encumberance to Society instead of increasing its ability to pay taxes."[7] In a 1784 vote to exclude slavery north of the Ohio River, Williamson and Jefferson were the only southern congressmen who voted against their own states' positions. Williamson and Jefferson wanted incorporated into the fundamental instrument of government "that after the year 1800 there shall be neither slavery nor involuntary servitude in any of the said states."[8]

Williamson, however, was also an early practitioner of compromise, which was not a part of governments at that time but rather developed by the American democracy. He recognized the need for compromise as a necessity for obtaining ratification of the constitutional document. So Williamson favored a compromise on the importation of slaves. He explained to Congress that North Carolina did not directly prohibit importation but did have a duty on it. He was fearful that the southern states would not join the Union if slavery was prohibited by the Constitution. He thought it necessary to compromise to get South Carolina and Georgia on those terms rather than to exclude them from the Union.

Also a member of several congressional committees of a diplomatic nature, Williamson was partial to France. When the Continental Congress received a letter being circulated by the British consul that alluded to separating America from her ally France, the North Carolina delegates on April 22, 1783, expressed their congratulations to the minister of France on the birth of the dauphin. This proved to be an important gesture of goodwill. The North Carolina General Assembly endorsed this action by its delegates:

> The General Assembly of North Carolina on May 14, 1783, thanked Hugh Williamson and William Blount for their address to the Minister of France on the auspicious birth of the Dauphin of France. The address was favorably received by the Court of France which assured the inhabitants of North Carolina of the particular interest his Christian Majesty would constantly take in their prosperity. This was some evidence of the state's pride in her independent sovereignty and her enjoyment of the flattery that she received from dipping into a little private diplomacy. On May 24, 1784, the General Assembly also expressed the state's appreciation of faithful services to Dr. Hugh Williamson, and Benjamin Hawkins.[9]

In regard to ambassadorial appointments, the dynamics were quite complicated. Benjamin Franklin, after more than a decade of representing the United States in England and at the

Court of Versailles, was nearly eighty years old and wanting to return home. His most important foreign appointment was at Versailles, where Franklin had understood the French character and methods of foreign policy and had negotiated France's assistance for the United States against the world's greatest military power, England. His assistant in his latter years at Versailles was the prickly John Adams, who never understood the French character or negotiating culture. Williamson and others were concerned that Franklin would be succeeded by Adams and that the influence of the United States in France would become ineffective. Williamson and others felt Jefferson would be superior to Adams at Versailles. Jefferson, accordingly, succeeded Franklin at Versailles, John Jay would represent the United States as ambassador to Spain, and John Adams would be the ambassador to the Court of St. James. Franklin returned to Philadelphia where he was again called to service at the Constitutional Convention.

The Continental Congress was not inclined to think continentally when the Articles of Confederation were written. Williamson's views are apparent in his correspondence with Jefferson on details of proposed legislation. The weakness of government in international affairs under the Articles of Confederation was apparent. Spain, for example, closed the port of New Orleans to American shipping, basically denying access to the ocean from the frontier. The British defied the terms of the Paris peace treaty ending the war by refusing to vacate their

Ohio Valley forts; moreover, the British commanders in these forts encouraged Indian insurrections. The Spanish did the same thing, giving aid to the Choctaw, Creeks, and Cherokees on the southern frontier. The closing of the Mississippi as a result of these actions and the aid to the Indians were of great concern to Williamson, who wrote to Thomas Jefferson from Trenton on December 11, 1784, regarding these and other issues of foreign affairs:

> Dear sir,
>
> You will soon hear many complaints concerning our western Territories, the Spaniards have not only interdicted the navigation of the Mississippi but seem to be making Incroachments and are doubtless taking Pains to exasperate the Indians to the great Terror of our frontier Inhabitants. . . . Should the navigation of the Mississippi continue open, Vast Bodies of People would migrate thither whose mercantile Conneactions could be of No Use to the old states. . . . The business I suppose will cause us to send a minister to the Court of Spain. From the strong representations that have lately been made by Mr. Lawrence who says he is requested by Dr. Franklin to do so I suppose the Doctor will be permitted to return. Should that be the Case I hope you will be his successor at Versailles. In that case to we shall have much difficulty determining who is to go to London. Perhaps Livingston, Jay or Adams, I think the last has Prejudices too strong.[10]

Williamson, like most members of Congress, was struggling with the substantial foreign-policy issues facing the young country, as reflected in this letter to his friend Thomas Jefferson. Williamson and Jefferson were concerned that the navigation of the Mississippi River would be denied to the United States by Spain as in fact was suggested some years later by the Jay Treaty. The Jay Treaty clarified details of the Treaty of 1783 related to the British presence in North America. A number of dispatches were written to John Jay that advocated compliance with the treaty's assurance that legitimate British debts be honored and not abrogated as spoils of war. When in Congress in the first years under the Constitution, Hugh Williamson joined Representatives Carlton, Digby, Peter, and Hamilton in endorsing to President Washington the payments.[11] The Jay Treaty passed by a majority, but it had been negotiated in secrecy mostly and was quite unpopular when it came out because it favored the British. Williamson tried to unmake the Jay Treaty's proposition to yield the navigation of the Mississippi to Spain for a number of years by declaring that the United States had a "clear, absolute and unalienable claim" to free navigation of the Mississippi River. He further claimed that this right was founded on the "great law of nature." The alternative treaty proposed by Williamson to modify the Jay Treaty and to ensure rights to navigation of the Mississippi did not pass. The Jay Treaty was among the most unpopular acts of the Washington administration. John Jay, the chief justice of the Supreme Court, negotiated a treaty highly favorable to England, as opposed to France. Jay would later note that he could travel the Atlantic Coast by the light from burning effigies of his countenance. In fact, it was foresighted in anticipating frienship with Great Britain, the dominant international force in the nineteenth century.

It has been suggested that Madison's purpose in leading opposition to this proposition of the Jay Treaty was to convince Jefferson that the Mississippi was far more important to national interests than the canal system to the west from the Potomac that was under consideration (though Madison also supported the canal system).[12] In a long letter from New York to Jefferson when the latter was president, Williamson wrote of his concerns about the French relationship with Spain and its implications for the Louisiana Purchase. In it Williamson, like Madison, was also hoping to focus Jefferson on waterway transportation via canals, and its implications for the relationship with Spain and the navigation of the Mississippi River. Williamson, as usual, was fascinated by canals as instruments of transportation and commerce.

Williamson and Jefferson conferred on proposed legislation on these issues. Their correspondence on legislation and politics in the issues over the years is illustrated by the following letters:

Hugh Williamson

April 1, 1792

Thomas Jefferson presents his compliments to Doctor Williamson and returns him the draught [draft] of the bill of projects with the alterations he proposes to it. This will certainly put the business into a more steady channel and are [sic] more likely by the establishment of fixed rules, to deal out justice without; [*sic*] partiality of favoritism. Above things he prays to be relieved from it, as being of everything that was imposed on him, that which cuts up his time unto the most useless fragments and give [*sic*] him from time to time the most poignant mortifications. The subjects are such as would require a great deal of time to understand and do justice to them and not having that time to bestow on them, he has been oppressed beyond measure by circumstances under which he has been obliged to give crude and uninformed opinions on rights often valuable, and always deemed so by the authors.[13]

Thomas Jefferson

Sir — New York, 10 May, 1803

I . . . think that East and West Florida had been ceded to France as appendages to Louisiana. It was even asserted that painful presage fellows [*sic*] citizens in Georgia coming in contact with such restless intriguing neighbors. [These events referred to involve conflict over ownership of ceded lands.] . . .

A project suggested to me many years ago by a western gentleman, I deem visionary viz to cut a canal from the great

> bend of the Tennessee [River] to the head of the Mobile [River], we might affect actual access to the sea and . . . could induce the Spaniard to give us West Florida. . . . We would effect actual passage to the sea for our citizens. . . . They would not [as now] arrive at the ocean without passing by a long and narrow river through the possession of France [New Orleans]. [A possible canal from the Mississippi to Florida to access the Gulf of Mexico was what made attractive a war and succession of subsequent acquired territory to the conspirators in the Chisholm Conspiracy (see chapter 12).] I am with the utmost consideration and respect your obedient and very humble servant.
>
> Hugh Williamson
> [to] Thomas Jefferson
> President of the United States[14]

The Confederation could do little to force the British out or deal with the Spanish. (Similar impotence would arise later when President Thomas Jefferson's administration disbanded most of the military, including the navy.) Other international incidents tested the new administration. In 1785 the dey of Algiers seized an American ship and imprisoned its crew. In response, the United States dispatched marines to rescue them. The battle cry of the Marine Corps, "From the Halls of Montezuma to the Shores of Tripoli," originated from this incident, which occurred after the ruler of Tripoli offered to insure safe passage for the price of protection money. So by 1786 that trade route around the Horn of Africa was in doubt. International isolation of the United States to trading, because of both internal problems and the external ones, was a reality.

The morale of the Congress itself was quite poor. The Confederation had sunk into lassitude and paralysis. By the fall of 1785, attendance at congressional sessions was embarrassingly low and absences reached crisis proportions by 1786. Congressmen from every state stayed home rather than be confronted with problems they had no power to solve.[15]

In Paris, London, Madrid, and Amsterdam, American diplomats were unable to negotiate loans. Two plans were advanced in which Hugh Williamson and other leaders were involved. They included the concept of cessions in which Ohio Valley lands that had been ceded to the central government by the states were to be sold to provide revenue to the central government.

Cession was a policy that was a product of Alexander Hamilton's genius. It was one of the key policies that formulated a strong federal government with a financial basis. The plan, as noted earlier, was that western lands of the thirteen colonies would be ceded to the central government. The federal government would use land to pay the Continental Army without debit, soldiers' pay, and other expenses. States such as Virginia and North Carolina that had paid most of their war debts were reluctant to endorse assumption of others'. Income from this sale, through the so-called Northwest Ordinances, provided little income; but it was still an accomplishment in that the division of these lands for sale allowed their eventual progression from territorial status to statehood. In 1785 Congress asked permission to levy an import tax, and all the states said no. Congress's *only* method of obtaining funds was by requisition: it would ask the states to donate funds to the central government; states, however, had the option of doing so or not. Without power to tax for a national government, the central government was weak.[16]

Revenues for the new government were an essential part of the reorganization that occurred later with adoption of the Constitution. In a report to Congress in 1790, Hamilton outlined a fiscal program with five major policies: (1) Old government bonds and securities should be replaced at face value with new federal bonds at a lower rate of interest to fund the national debt; (2) the debts of the states should be assumed at full value by the federal government and similarly funded; (3) national banks should be created to market government bonds and assist in other government fiscal operations; (4) tariffs should be adopted to raise revenue and furnish adequate protection for American manufacturers; and (5) excise taxes on spirituous liquors similarly should be adopted to raise revenue and furnish adequate protection for American manufacturers.

Assumption of states' debts met with violent opposition, particularly by those states, like North Carolina, that had paid their Revolutionary War debts already. Williamson took the view that assumption would increase the burden of taxation in the state, that North Carolina had already taken proper steps to meet its financial obligations, and that no state should be interfered with in the redemption of its paper currency or the liquidation of its securities. He and his Federalist colleagues in the House of the new Congress created by the Constitution voted against assumption, but the policy was adopted by Congress as a result of a political trade by which northern votes were cast to locate the permanent capital at a site on the Potomac River in exchange. In 1791 Congress chartered the Bank of the United States with a capital stock of $10 million. Both North Carolina senators voted for the bank, while the House delegation was divided, Sevier and Steele for, Ashe, Bloodworth, and Williamson against. Those opposed maintained that Congress had no right under the Constitution to establish a fiscal agency. It could create dangerous financial monopolies as a central power, which thus might lead to centralized political power.

Meanwhile, one old matter related to international affairs and finance involved Williamson after the Revolution. Silas Deane had been involved in a complex spy network with Beaumarchais, the French secretary and author of *The Marriage of Figaro*. After the war, Williamson was appointed to a committee of the Continental Congress to investigate the accounts generated by Beaumarchais. Because Beaumarchais's negotiations were secret, however, record keeping was negligible. France was by this time teetering on bankruptcy in part because of its assistance to the United States. The committee was initiated by a memorial to the Continental Congress, after Beaumarchais unsuccessfully asking assistance of Lafayette and Thomas Jefferson on behalf of France. Jefferson noted that "Beaumarchais means to be heard."[17] The president of the Congress, Arthur St. Clair, another physician trained by John Hunter and eventually the first governor of the Ohio Territory, noted: "We will make not reimbursement to M. Beaumarchais, until the accounts are adjusted by us. . . . Hence the Committee of Edward Carrington of Virginia, H. Williamson of N.C., and Abraham Clark of New Jersey. Their investigation was delayed by an agreement drawn up by Vergennes and Franklin."[18]

The informal nature of the great support of the colonies by France had been purposely ill documented because of France's assisting the colonies against England while under treaty obligations to it. So after the war the informality and resulting poor documentation of costs led to difficulties in reimbursement to France from the United States. One result of the French financial assistance was the burden on its economy, which was one of the causes of the French Revolution. When President John and Jacqueline Kennedy visited France in the 1960s as the guests of President Charles De Gaulle, a descendant of Beaumarchais who was a civil servant in the French government showed President Kennedy an unpaid receipt that had been submitted to the new American government. Kennedy, familiar with the issue, asked if he could keep it as a souvenir. M. Beaumarchais, said, of course, there were plenty more where that came from![19]

Chapter 9

The Constitutional Convention

It appears to me, then, little short of a miracle that delegates from so many different states (which states you know are also different from each other), in their manners, circumstances, and prejudices, should unite in forming a system of national government, so little liable to well founded objections.

—Washington to Lafayette, February 7, 1788

I have always regarded that Constitution as the most remarkable work known to me in modern times to have been produced by the human intellect, in a single stroke (so to speak), in its application to political affairs.

—William Ewart Gladstone, "Kin Beyond the Sea"

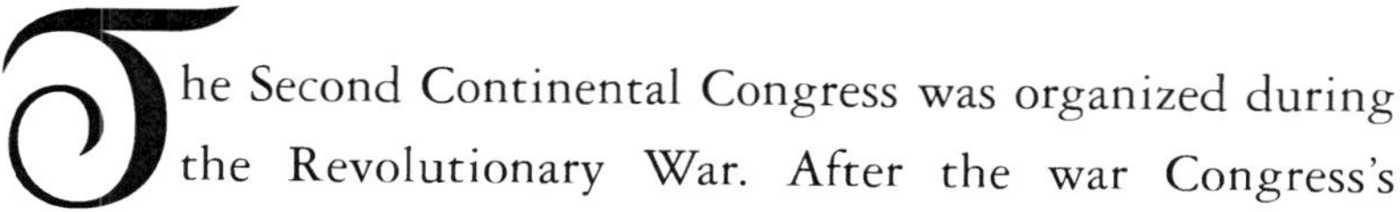

The Second Continental Congress was organized during the Revolutionary War. After the war Congress's authority for governing, the Articles of Confederation was inadequate to implement effective government. The evolution of trade relations, for example, started out with different states negotiating trade agreements one with the other, much like separate countries. The Articles of Confederation lacked a provision for raising revenue. Lacking a tax basis for the central government, its funding was by requisition, an ineffective method by which states would be asked to provide funds.

Government under the Articles of Confederation, however, did have its successes. A Confederation government, 1781–89, concluded the Revolutionary War, negotiated the Treaty of Paris of 1783, established a system for a sale of public lands (the Grayson Land Ordinance of 1785), and established a policy for admission of new states (the Northwest Ordinance of 1787). However, the Articles of Confederation did not have an executive or judiciary, and were too weak to implement federal governance.

Hamilton and influential Virginians, such as Washington, Madison, and Edmund Randolph, attempted to negotiate agreement on the use of rivers. Special agreements between Maryland and Virginia were attempted. Maryland then proposed that a meeting on interstate commerce be held to also include Pennsylvania and Delaware, and the project continued to grow.

On February 23, 1786, Patrick Henry, usually not a friend of the nationalist movement, recommended that states send delegates to a commercial convention in Annapolis that September. After a brief spate of interest, enthusiasm died; when the group met in what has been called the "Annapolis Convention," only five states were represented. Most of the delegates who attended were interested in a strengthening of the central government, which became the primary topic of conversation. "On June 10, 1786, Williamson was elected one of the commissioners to the Annapolis Convention, which had been arranged at Mount Vernon for the purpose of settling the issue of commercial conflicts between the new states."[1] Alexander Hamilton, William Churchill Houston, and James Madison were also commissioners to the Annapolis Convention. Williamson arrived at the convention just as it was adjourning, so he did not participate in its business; he did, however, support its recommendation to call a federal convention.

Williamson, while arriving late to the Annapolis Convention and missing its deliberations, remained in Annapolis for a few days and undoubtedly became familiar with the general themes of the meeting. The group of delegates who attended was not concerned about the poor turnout for the meeting. They called themselves "commissioners" and defined their purpose as being to remedy defects of the federal government. Twelve men (representing New York, New Jersey, Pennsylvania, Delaware, and Virginia) urged legislators of the states to call another meeting, or convention, of the states. This consequently opened the opportunity for what eventually became the Constitutional Convention later held in Philadelphia. The group's Annapolis Report framed the issue as transcending commerce to issues beyond.[2]

The delegates to Philadelphia in 1787 were to "take into consideration the situation of the United States, to devise such further provisions as shall appear to them necessary, to render the Constitution of the federal government adequate to the exigencies of the Union."[3] Clearly, the charge was to develop a federal system.

The first phase of this movement toward centralization of the newly independent states had been the Annapolis Convention, which had been intended to reform trade agreements but when it failed to achieve a caucus concluded with the proposal to call a convention to strengthen the central government.

Meanwhile, external pressures provided impetus toward a more centralist and federal system. As the Annapolis Convention was meeting, 600 farmers were storming the courthouse in Springfield, Massachusetts, protesting economic depression in the western counties of the state, having watched their property taxes rise and their profits decline. Shays's Rebellion (1786–1787), led by Daniel Shays and farmers in western Massachusetts, objected to the taxation of whiskey, likening it to the taxes that had led to the Revolutionary War. Washington and others noted that a difference existed, as their own country was levying the tax, as opposed to that of a "foreign" government, England. Taking matters into their own hands, the farmers denied loyalty to any government. The revolt spread through many of the towns of western Massachusetts, but the heart of the rebellion was in Springfield. A thirty-nine-year-old veteran of the Battle of Saratoga, Shays led 1,500 people in an assault on the courthouse dressed in their Continental Army uniforms. Washington was persuaded to lead the federal force to suppress the rebellion and went to Massachusetts with an army of 16,000, larger than the army he led in the Revolutionary War! In addition, the governor of Massachusetts called up a force, led by General Benjamin Lincoln, also a veteran of Saratoga, who routed the farmers. Shays and some followers were tried and convicted, but John Hancock, then governor of Massachusetts, pardoned them and declared a general amnesty.[4] This event further demonstrated the weakness of the Continental Congress.*

The Confederation Congress had not endorsed the Annapolis Report for a national convention, but while the impact of Shays's Rebellion was still being felt, Virginia and New Jersey announced their intention to send delegates to Philadelphia. Pennsylvania, North Carolina, Delaware, and Georgia soon followed suit. Clearly, the lack of a central government contributed to instability.

The Second Continental Congress, meeting at the time, had little choice but to go along, and on February 21, 1787, the Confederation issued the following resolve: "In the opinion of

*Shays's Rebellion is not to be confused with the Whiskey Rebellion (1794), which was the first use of the Militia Law of 1792. Washington called out a militia of 13,000 troops, the same size as he commanded to defeat the British.

Congress, it is expedient, on the second Monday in May next a convention of delegates who shall have been appointed by the several States be held in Philadelphia for the sole and express purpose of revising the Articles of Confederation."[5] All states sent representatives to Philadelphia except Rhode Island.

The second phase in developing an authoritative federal state was the Constitutional Convention. This was Hamilton's hope—that a convention moving on beyond the tentative one focused on trade at Annapolis would be able to develop a federal system. On January 6, 1787, in a joint ballot of both houses, the North Carolina General Assembly elected Richard Caswell, Alexander Martin, William R. Davie, Richard Dobbs Spaight, and Willie Jones to attend the Constitutional Convention to be held on May 4, 1787. Willie Jones declined to serve; so in Kinston on April 3, Governor Caswell appointed Hugh Williamson to serve in his place. Poor health precluded Richard Caswell's attendance, and the governor appointed William Blount as Caswell's replacement. Williamson became the dominant, and most consistent, member of the North Carolina delegation.

The average age of the delegates was a little less than forty, ranging from Davie's age thirty to Williamson's age fifty-one. Davie, Martin, and Williamson were all college graduates and all five had served in the Revolutionary War. Davie was a prominent attorney and planter, owner of thirty-six slaves; Blount, a merchant, planter, businessman, owner of thirty slaves; Martin, a lawyer and planter, owner of forty-seven slaves;

Spaight, a wealthy planter, owner of seventy-one slaves; and Williamson, a physician, merchant, and businessman, but not a slave owner. All but Martin had served in the Congress of the Confederation and Martin had been governor and judge. None of the five had experience in Constitution making. Blount was a silent and inactive member. The same was true of Martin, whose participation is recorded as seconding three motions of minor importance. Williamson wrote sarcastically of Martin that his "great exertions of political wisdom as governor had so exhausted his fund, that time must be required to enable [him] again to exert his abilities to the advantage of the nation."[6] Davie made five speeches, seconded two motions, and served as a member of the important grand committee that finally effected the Great Compromise of the Convention, which was creation of a Senate based on equality of states and a House of Representatives based on population. William Pearce, a Georgia delegate, noted that Davie was silent in the convention, but his opinion was always respected. Spaight's activity consisted of four brief speeches, nine motions, and three seconds. Two provisions of the Constitution were first proposed by him: the election of senators by the state legislatures and the power of the president to make recess appointments. He differed from the rest of his colleagues in his opposition to the Great Compromise. Williamson was, by far, the most active, valuable, and influential North Carolina delegate. He made seventy-three speeches, offered twenty-three motions and seconded thirteen, and served on five committees. He was usually the spokesman for the delegation.

Spaight was the first North Carolina delegate to arrive in Philadelphia. By May 22 he was joined by Davie, making North Carolina the fifth state represented at the convention. To assemble the delegation, Alexander Martin and Hugh Williamson had arrived by the time the convention began on Friday, May 25. Williamson and Martin stayed at the Indian Queen Tavern, elegant but relatively inexpensive lodging. Others staying there including Caleb Strong and Nathaniel Gorham of Massachusetts, James Madison and George Mason of Virginia, John Rutledge of South Carolina, and Alexander Hamilton of New York.[7]

As the convention got under way, among the rules adopted were that seven states would constitute a quorum and decisions would be made by a majority of the delegations possessing their own quorums. Nothing spoken was to be printed or communicated without permission in order to assure freedom of discussion. The convention met every day, six days a week. Guards were posted outside the building to preserve the secrecy of the deliberations.

Some of the first questions in the Constitutional Convention were articulated by Governor Edmund Randolph of Virginia, who reiterated the failures of the Articles of Confederation, which, among many, included inadequacy of the requisition system, threat of social anarchy, the embarrassment of unpaid foreign debts, violations of treaties by foreign nations and even by some of the states, and the havoc produced by paper money.[8] Randolph offered fifteen resolutions that amounted to a constitutional revolution but were voiced in the sense of correcting and enlarging the Articles of Confederation. On Wednesday, May 30, at the urging of Gouverneur Morris, Randolph proposed a postponement of debate on the corrected and enlarged resolution. He offered, instead, a bolder resolution, which was "that a national government ought to be established consisting of a supreme legislative, executive and judiciary." Morris, sometimes called one of the fathers of the convention, bluntly asked the question, "Do we want a confederation or a nation?"[9] Debate continued over various proposals. One outcome was the Connecticut Compromise of July 5 on representation in the House (see below), in which basically New Jersey, Virginia, and Connecticut compromised. The Great Compromise refers to the vote on July 16 that ushered in a new spirit in the convention. Assignment of responsibility and tasks were to one or the other legislative branch of government. The Great Compromise provided that all bills of appropriation would originate in the lower chamber, the House, where the large states would dominate; but as a gesture of goodwill to the southern states, the population calculation for slaves would be changed to a proportion of three to five to free persons. The convention also voted Congresses power to veto state laws. On July 31, Jefferson wrote to Adams from Paris expressing concern about some of the leading principles that seemed to trend toward the centralization of government.[10]

The delegates were in dispute over the executive branch. Some strange alliances emerged: Elbridge Gerry with George Mason, for example, and Luther Martin with Gouverneur Morris. Other Virginia delegates aired their differences openly with Mason and Randolph, edging closer to their final refusal to sign the constitution.[11] Some newcomers to national politics, such as John Mercer from Maryland, aggressively waded in on the issue.

William Paterson, author of the New Jersey Plan, actually went home for most of the month of August. On July 10, George Washington wrote Alexander Hamilton, who also had left, a note saying, "I am sorry you went away; I wish you were back."[12] A variety of issues were on the table. Hugh Williamson and Benjamin Franklin favored rotating a tripartite presidency from an executive committee. Issues of how long the president would serve were also brought forward.

Williamson, like his fellow North Carolina delegates and those from the majority of the states, voted in favor of establishing a national government with three branches: executive, judicial, and legislative. He voted with the majority in favor of the election of the lower house of the federal government by the people. Williamson preferred a small senate, but wanted it to include at least one senator from every state. He suggested twenty-five. He approved voting per capita. He favored proportional representation, as states treated their own counties that way.

Williamson was against giving power to the federal government that could restrain the states from regulating their internal police. He was against a federal veto of state legislation.[13] Williamson favored a six-year term for senators and moved that they be compensated for their service. Franklin and Pinckney had advocated not paying senators so that the office could be held only by men of wealth, but Williamson's motion carried.[14] A primary area of contention among the states represented in Philadelphia was that of representation in the two houses of the legislature. Williamson served on the grand committee to apportion representation in the lower house.

Williamson was strongly opposed to a single executive. He favored a three-part executive branch that would accord the northern, middle, and southern interests equal powers. In the case of one executive, he advocated a six-year term with ineligibility for succession. The three-executive suggestion was opposed by Madison and others who cited the example of the conflicts that occurred among the Roman triumvirate when that executive arrangement was attempted in antiquity. Williamson favored longer terms in the executive branch to prevent the expensive burden of frequent elections driving away the best men, thus leaving the office to those of inferior and thus corruptible character. With regard to re-election of the president, Williamson argued that the election of the president by the people would open the doors to foreign influence. He thought that the legislative branch of the government should elect the executive. The creation of the electoral college was in part the result of Williamson's concern over clandestine foreign intervention in the American electoral process.[15]

Williamson supported impeachment. In the discussion on June 2, 1787, that aimed to characterize the offenses for which impeachment would be warranted, Williamson coined the operative words "mal-practice or neglect of duty" when he moved that there be inserted in the emerging text the provision "be removable on impeachment and conviction of mal-practice or neglect of duty."[16] He drew this language from North Carolina's state constitution. Ironically, the first person impeached under the new constitution was Senator William Blount, his friend and fellow member of the Constitutional Convention from North Carolina and later senator and governor of Tennessee. Blount was accused of colluding with the British against the interests of the United States.

Although Williamson was in favor of the veto power of the president, he resisted investing too much power in the office. In September he moved to have the three-fourths majority in both houses required to override the president's veto changed to two-thirds, as the former put too much power in the president's hands.

Williamson feared not too few but rather too many laws. He was concerned that the repeal of bad laws would be rendered too difficult by requiring the three-fourths majority to overrule the president's dissent.[17]

Williamson argued to restrict solely to the president the power to appoint members of the judiciary. Also in regard to judicial issues, it was not acceptable to him that no provisions had been made for a jury to hear civil cases. He argued that juries are essential to civil trials for justice to be served.

The convention also took up the issue of a national capital. Earlier, in 1783, when the Continental Congress had been considering a location for the federal seat of government, Williamson argued for a southern location. He had expressed to the governor of North Carolina his preference for the falls of the Potomac, near where Washington, D.C., is now located.

> The seat of government, it was urged, must not be in the same city with a state government. Jurisdictional disputes might arise, and besides, it would give a provincial tincture to the national deliberations. Yet New York and Philadelphia both had expectations of being the national capital; it would not do to make enemies of these cities. Williamson of North Carolina reminded delegates how deeply the passions of men were agitated by this matter.[18]

Williamson, from personal experience, had an accurate and varied knowledge about trade, and he let his views be known at the convention. As a member of the Grand Committee for Trade, he played a role in its declaration that all duties, imposts, excises, prohibitions, and restraints made by United

States legislators be uniform and equal throughout the country. Some states, notably Virginia, objected to the constitutional ban on taxes by the states on exports from other states, but Williamson found the federal monopoly on export taxes a sound enough idea if any were to be taxed. However, he was opposed to placing any tax on most exports; he believed such a tax would bear heavily on the southern states that produced staples. He also realized the threat that would be posed by states reaching across state lines to extract taxes—Virginia, for example, could tax exports of North Carolina tobacco. In a speech in Edenton on November 8, 1787, Williamson spoke out against taxation: "By such means our citizens are taxed more than $100,000 every year, but the state does not receive credit for a shilling of that money. Like a patient that is bleeding at both arms, North Carolina must soon expire under such wasteful operations."[19]

With the southern states in mind, he favored requiring two-thirds instead of a simple majority vote to pass laws pertaining to navigation. Influenced by the strong objections of North Carolina to the proposed treaty with Spain, Williamson and Spaight moved that no treaty of peace affecting territorial rights should be made without consent of two-thirds of the members of the Senate present.[20] Williamson remarked that treaties should be made in the branch of government where there could be a majority of states without a necessary majority of people.

Williamson was uneasy that arguments over prohibiting

slave trade could keep the southern states from joining the Union. Strategically he was against forcing anything disagreeable that was not absolutely necessary.[21] In order that South Carolina and Georgia would not be lost to the Union over slavery, Williamson crafted a compromise that would postpone the prohibition against slave importation until 1808 and concede legislative control of commerce. Though very much opposed to slavery, Williamson favored extending the bounds of slavery importation because he thought it better to risk the concession than to lose the Constitution. His long legislative experience had taught him that compromise was sometimes necessary to effect legislation.

One of Williamson's most notable contributions was his position that representation in the House of Representatives of the new national government be based on the slave as well as the free population. This concept evolved into the so-called Three-fifths Compromise, in which slaves would be counted as three-fifths of a person in determining representation and taxes. Williamson likewise was one of the first to propose voting representation for three-fifths of the slaves, as in the Virginia plan as amended, the New Jersey plan, and the Compromise Committee plan.

Williamson was actively involved in almost all of the main issues addressed at the convention. He was usually the selected representative whenever the convention elected a special committee composed of a deputy from each state committee on postponed affairs. The only exception was when Colonel Davie represented North Carolina on the grand committee to settle the dispute over representation in the legislative branch. Even in this case, however, the convention when organizing the committee to reconsider that part of the grand committee's report addressing proportional representation in the House of Representatives elected Williamson to participate in the reconsideration.

During the dispute about legislative representation, Williamson was the first to move for a national census to be taken of the new nation during the first year and periodically thereafter. His proposal grew out of his opposition to reducing the number of representatives from New Hampshire from three to two in favor of more representatives from Rhode Island and Providence Plantations. Williamson thereby introduced the modern view that a state's representation could be increased or decreased in accordance with census returns.[22] It is of note that the representation of North Carolina was doubled after the first census, disclosing North Carolina's rank as third in population among the original thirteen states.

"It is said that Dr. Williamson was the first to assert that the Constitution would be the supreme law of the land. This can be substantiated in Article VI of the Constitution where the wording states: 'This Constitution, and the Laws of the United States which shall be made in pursuance thereof . . . shall be the supreme Law of the Land.'"[23] Williamson made certain that national legislative acts would only be valid when passed in accordance with the Constitution.

Regarding the legislative branch, Williamson preferred a small number of senators, believing that such a system would preserve state powers. He opposed any power that would restrain the states from regulating their own internal policies, such as the veto of state laws. He joined the debate over the oath of office by contending that oaths should be reciprocal between state and national officers. Williamson addressed the election, pay, and term of office for senators. He expressed concern that if a majority of the legislature should happen to be "composed of any particular description of men, of lawyers for example . . . the future elections might be secured to their own body."[24]

Regarding representation in the legislative branch, Williamson urged compromise, recommending that a subcommittee be formed to more objectively study the issue. "He and Col. Davie were the only delegates from North Carolina who were outspoken in the convention on the Connecticut Compromise, which provided for equal representation [of states] in the Senate and proportional representation in the House of Representatives. No doubt he aided in switching North Carolina to the small states, giving these states the necessary controlling vote to carry their point and save the Convention and the Constitution."[25] Jefferson, Franklin's successor to the court of France, kept up with the progress of the Constitutional Convention by correspondence with Madison. Jefferson's immediate reaction to the new constitution, when it reached him in Paris, was negative. He said that its far reaching proportions "stagger all my dispositions to subscribe to it."[26] He was critical of its provisions that assigned authority to a central government. It is possible had Jefferson been in attendance at the Constitutional Convention, the proposed constitution might not have passed. He was eventually persuaded to support it by Madison.

Williamson eventually complained that North Carolina had been betrayed by the small states when it was agreed that money bills would be confined to the House of Representatives in return for equality of votes in the Senate. Williamson opposed paying state representatives from the national treasury. He believed that congressional members should be ineligible for any offices created by the Congress, "stating that he had scarcely seen a single corrupt measure in the legislature of North Carolina that could not be traced to office-hunting."[27]

Williamson confronted most of the controversial issues of the day. He addressed the capitation tax,* the standing army, and the vice presidency. As in his earlier legislative career, Williamson favored an excise tax over a land or poll tax, he supported the promotion of domestic manufactures, and he spoke of the evil of paper money. When, after an especially trying week of argument, Ben Franklin proposed prayer, Williamson bluntly opposed it, explaining that the convention lacked money to pay a chaplain. Hamilton opposed hiring a chaplain

---

*An assigned tax on citizens.

on the grounds that it would bring in "*outside consultation*" (italics added).

> Franklin, apparently believing that passions needed to be cooled, proposed that the daily sessions be opened with prayers offered by a local clergyman. Sherman seconded the motion, but Hamilton opposed it. Hamilton sarcastically noted that to ask for divine help would be asking for outside or foreign assistance. The latter feared the presence of a minister might cause the public to believe the Convention was torn with dissension. Others argued that reason—not heavenly help—was what was needed. In any case, Franklin's proposal died after Williamson raised the embarrassing question of where the money would be obtained to pay the clergyman.[28]

After Williamson pointed out the lack of funds for a chaplain, Edmund Randolph offered an amendment to hire a preacher to offer prayer on July 4. Franklin accepted the amendment.[29]

Williamson argued forcefully for stringent requirements to admit western states to the Union. He was outspoken in advocating that equality of representation should not be accorded until the new state's population and wealth justified it. His reasoning was twofold: new states would be relatively poorer than the old ones and thus unable to contribute to the nation's treasury; and the interests of new states would differ from those of the older ones.[30]

Hugh Williamson

William R. Davie had to leave the Philadelphia convention around the first of August to fulfill his obligations to the North Carolina superior circuit court; and, short of cash, Alexander Martin returned with him. That left Williamson the dominant, experienced member of the state delegation.

Williamson was a strong promoter of the new constitution that was signed by the convention delegates on September 17, 1787, and from North Carolina by Hugh Williamson, William Blount, and Richard Dobbs Spaight. Williamson was anxious for North Carolina to come into the Union. He described his views in the *State Gazette of North Carolina*:

> It seems to be generally admitted, that the system of government which has been proposed by the late convention, is well calculated to relieve us from many of the grievances under which we have been laboring. If I might express my particular sentiments on this subject, I should describe it as more free and more perfect than any form of government that has ever been adopted by any nation; but I would not say it has no faults. Imperfection is inseparable from every device. Several objections were made to this system by two or three very respectable characters in the convention, which have been the subject of much conversation.
>
> When you refer the proposed system to the particular circumstances of North Carolina, and consider how she is to be affected by this plan, you must find the utmost reason to rejoice in the prospect of better times. This is a sentiment

> that I have ventured with the greater confidence, because it is the general opinion of my late honorable colleagues, and I have the utmost reliance in their superior abilities. But if our constituents shall discover faults where we could not see any—or if they shall suppose that a plan is formed for abridging their liberties, when we imagined that we had been securing both liberty and property on a more stable foundation—if they perceive that they are to suffer a loss, where thought they must rise from a misfortune, —they will at least do us the justice to charge those errors to the head and not to the heart.[31]

On September 18, 1787, the three North Carolina delegates, Hugh Williamson, Richard Dobbs Spaight, and William Blount, mailed the governor a copy of the Constitution, accompanied by a letter which he was to present to the General Assembly. They called his attention to the fact that North Carolina would have five delegates in the national legislature and compose one-thirteenth of the entire House of Representatives, and that counting in the census would be the whole number of white and three-fifths of the black inhabitants. The delegates believed that the state's population was actually greater than one-thirteenth of the union, but chose not to argue since it would have had the effect of increasing the state's taxes. On November 8, 1787, Williamson met with a considerable number of inhabitants of Chowan County and Edenton at the courthouse in Edenton, where he gave an extensive address on the proposed system of the federal government under the Constitution.

The issue of unchecked legislative power was a concern in the discussion of the Constitution that followed. The concern was that foreign intrigue would occur through the legislatures. So the compromise that gave the states the Senate stronghold was to be countered by the executive branch. There was concern as to how the executive branch president would be elected. The legislatures would not choose the president. The other alternatives were by the people or through electors, the latter of which was eventually accepted. Issues of how much trust to give to the people versus how much to the legislatures as indirectly representing the people were a recurring theme. In addition to how the president reached office and how many presidents there would be, the powers they were to enjoy were deeply debated. Most people were concerned with their experience with the British that there would be too much power invested in the presidency. Additionally, if the judiciary were given the veto process to check legislation, the concern was that the judges would dominate the executive. The idea eventually arose, as put forth by James Madison, that the executive was the people's last line of defense against shortsightedness or worse of the legislature, and that the Senate was a stronghold of the states. It was decided that if the legislature selected the executive, it would have too much power; if the electors were chosen by the people, the concern was that they would be uninformed. There were also concerns that large states would have advantage over the small and the northern states, where most of the population who were eligible to vote would have an advantage over the South.

Popular election of the executive was of concern. One of the problems was that there was no national communication network by which to make a national candidate known. George Washington's war fame was what made him well known. There was concern that there would be twenty to thirty candidates. The executive, though, was eventually decided to be a single person rather than a triumvirate. At the convention, the Committee of Detail had labored hours over organizing the finalization of those issues. A few flourishes were added to the executive as to what the person was to be called. It was decided he was to be called "Your Excellency." That sobriquet would be argued in the first congress with John Adams pressing for flowery titles and others advocating a simple, democratic salutation, i.e., "the President."

During the last five weeks of the convention, most of the details were picked apart and the group coalesced around devising a completed document. There were some last-minute details. One of the issues was from the Committee on Postponed Affairs, which was an important committee because it clarified and solidified issues that had been debated but not resolved.[32] Hugh Williamson was one of the individuals who had that challenge, along with Nicholas Gilman of New Hampshire, Rufus King of Massachusetts, Roger Sherman of Connecticut, David Brearly of New Jersey, Gouverneur Morris of Pennsylvania, John Dickinson of Delaware, Daniel Carroll of Maryland, James Madison of Virginia, Pierce Butler of South Carolina, and Abraham Baldwin of Georgia. This was one of the most important committees in the Constitutional Convention. It was a committee that was voted upon and was composed of one individual from each state chosen by ballot. It was, in effect, a convention in miniature. This group would be the one to basically put the debates in focus into articles. The chairman, Abraham Baldwin of Georgia, was the leader of the delegation and Hugh Williamson, North Carolina's best debater, was the most active participant. Committee people were chosen for their ability to compromise and work with others. The committee met for almost a week, well aware of pressures on it, and made a number of recommendations, including a direct election of the president, a process for impeachment, and the president's treaty-making power.[33] As the Committee on Postponed Affairs began to focus on the Constitution, a variety of small, but significant, changes began to emerge. Where the preamble once listed all of the states, it was simplified to say "We, the people of the United States." The goal was put forward in the purpose mentioned in the preamble: "In order to form a more perfect union, to establish justice, insure domestic tranquility, provide for the common defense, promote the general welfare and secure the blessings of liberty to ourself and to our posterity." The listing of national goals corrected many of the flaws of the Articles of Confederation.[34]

Chapter 10

The Struggle for Ratification of the Constitution

> I believe there is now little or no reason to doubt the success of the question [ratification] in North Carolina. The Honorable Mr. Williamson has lately arrived from that state and assures that he has not been able to inform himself from what quarter the opposition to come and that he entertains no doubt of the ratification by their Conventions.
>
> —James Madison

Ratification was the third phase of the evolution to a centralized government. The ratification debate receives inadequate attention by scholars of the period. The delegates left Philadelphia with a constitution that, to be adopted, required approval by the states. What followed was a spirited debate lasting from September 1787 to July 1788. The extensive debate, much of it articulated in *The Federalist Papers*, explained the rationale for and against the federal system embodied in the Constitution, written in Philadelphia in 1789.

For the product of the Philadelphia convention to replace the Articles of Confederation and become the law of the land, two-thirds of the states were required to ratify. That requirement was from the tradition of the Continental Congress, which had established a two-thirds requirement for the Articles of Confederation. Some of the delegates at the convention were concerned that signing the document would imply acceptance by their state. In fact, the document was signed without affirming recommendations for its acceptance. So the convention found a way to dissemble on that issue. The endorsement was carefully worded by Gouverneur Morris, who called for consent of the states at the convention rather than the delegates so that a few dissenters would not jeopardize the appearance of unanimity. The vote was on the statement "Done in Convention by the unanimous consent of the States present, the 17th of September and witnessed where we inscribed our names."[1] The New Hampshire delegates were the first to sign. Of the fifty-five delegates to the Philadelphia convention, only thirty-nine delegates signed the concluding document. The politicians of the Committee on Style anticipated some problems, also. One was that these articles would supersede the Articles of Confederation at a time when some of the delegates to the Constitutional Convention were actually serving in the Congress, which was meeting at that time in New York. A letter, along with the

Constitution, was addressed to the Confederation Congress that was intended to gain the sympathy of constituents back home anticipating ratification debates. This was written in Gouverneur Morris's hand and discussed the Lockean social contract and union of the states. A proposal to add canal building to the letter was defeated; it was an issue, as noted earlier, in which Washington and Williamson had a keen interest. Some of the Virginia delegation, specifically Edmund Randolph and George Mason, declined to sign the Constitution. Elbridge Gerry objected to it. Some others proposed a second convention.

The summation, at the adjournment, was expressed by Benjamin Franklin who, upon moving to the heart of the matter said: "I agree to this Constitution with all its faults, if there are such," he said, "because I think a general government necessary for us and there is no form of government but what may be a blessing to the people if well administered."[2] He went on to say that he hoped that this would be unanimously signed and endorsed by all the people, something, of course, that did not happen. He asked that people like himself who objected to part of the Constitution might doubt a little of their own infallibility and still put their name to it, and he moved that this be done with a motion that the Constitution be signed by everyone present (some delegates were away at this point). Franklin would further comment, "I consent, Sir, to this Constitution because I expect no better."[3] He commented that in noting a design on the back of Washington's chair, of the sun, he was uncertain if it were a rising sun or a setting sun and he added, "I have the happiness to know that it is a rising and not a setting sun."[4]

Each state seemed to have its problem with some details in the Constitution.[5] The North Carolina delegation was irreconcilably opposed to the plan finally adopted for the national executive, that of a single executive. They objected to the admission of new states on the same basis of equality with original states, although the North Carolina delegates voted with the majority to give Congress authority to admit new states. On September 15 the completed Constitution, a "bundle of compromises," was unanimously adopted and ready to be signed on the 17th.[6] Among the thirty-nine signers from the delegates were three North Carolinians: Blount, Williamson, and Spaight. Davie and Martin had been absent for several weeks and did not sign. Blount declared at first that he would not sign, but he did so after Franklin signed the document. As they adjourned, most delegates anticipated a second political battle, the battle for ratification, was going to occur. Most of the individuals who adjourned from the convention went home while others took their seats in the Confederation Congress. Washington wrote his old friend Henry Knox and noted that the Constitution is now "before the judgment seat."[7]

The Federalist Papers articulated the philosophy of the Union and were a media blitz of advocacy for the Constitution, with similar lobbying by the Anti-Federalist advocates. There were eighty-five Federalist and Anti-Federalist papers. Alexander

Hamilton was the leader of *The Federalist Papers*; Williamson was among the supporters of ratification. Williamson delivered a speech titled "Remarks on the New Plan of Government" in three installments over February 25, 26, and 27, 1788, in which he advocated ratification. His remarks were published in the *State Gazette of North Carolina* in New Bern, as well as in Pennsylvania, South Carolina, and Massachusetts. His speech is part of *The Federalist Papers* for June 12, 1788 (see appendix).

Opposition to the Constitution in North Carolina was intense. Concerns voiced by Anti-Federalists included that too much power had been delegated to the central government; the commerce clause would enable the states to the north and south of North Carolina to impede the state's commerce; the treaty-making powers of the Senate would cripple North Carolina's control of the western lands and interfere with the state's outlet to the Mississippi River and the sea; and that personal security and personal liberty were not sufficiently incorporated. North Carolina refused to ratify the Constitution at the Hillsborough Convention in 1788, and as in other parts of the evolving country, a realignment of conservatives and radicals began to occur. The conservatives were now called Federalists. A new North Carolina legislature was formed, and as early as July of 1787, Williamson and a few other Federalist leaders urged North Carolina voters to choose capable men for it in the August election. Anti-Federalists were also active, and a bitter campaign occurred. There were charges of irregularities and fraud.

William Hooper, a signer of the United States Declaration of Independence, had his eye blackened by an Anti-Federalist. On October 4, 1788, the publication of the Constitution in full, for the first time in North Carolina, in the *State Gazette of North Carolina*, intensified the struggle for ratification. When New Hampshire ratified, the two-thirds requirement was met. Virginia watched the position of New York, as there was some small possibility for a northeastern pullout and formation of a separate government. When New York ratified, Virginia was well on the way and soon did so, too (see "Eleventh Pillar" illustration).

In Edenton on November 8, Williamson declared that the Constitution was far from perfect but was superior to the Articles of Confederation. He said there was a need for strong central government with power to enforce laws over states and individuals, protect property rights, guarantee a stable and sound national currency, stimulate foreign trade, and support the dignity and rights of the United States in formal foreign relations. An able defense of the Constitution in North Carolina was also made by James Iredell.[8] He argued that the disordered and distracted state of the country with public debts unpaid and other issues could be remedied only by united vigorous government. He praised the character and ability of the members of the Philadelphia convention and asserted that local interest ought to give way to the general good. He pointed out the popular representation in the document, and that union was the watchword of American liberty and safety. The Anti-Federalists criticized the Constitution in the belief that it would destroy state rights and remove government from popular control, that capital and industry would be promoted at the expense of agriculture, and that the omission of a Bill of Rights would be disastrous. Thomas Person, an Anti-Federalist, insisted that the Philadelphia Constitution would be impractical and dangerous, and thought that most of North Carolina was against it. The legislature convened at Tarboro on November 19, 1787, and Person attempted to block every move toward ratification. He tried unsuccessfully to prevent the call of a convention to consider ratification.

The convention met at Hillsborough on July 21, 1788, and elected Governor Samuel Johnston as president. When the convention began its deliberations, the Constitution had already been adopted by ratification of one more than the requisite of nine states. Five days later, the eleventh state, Virginia, ratified in order to influence the Bill of Rights and other amendments under discussion. North Carolina is thought to have followed Virginia's initial delaying lead during the debate and which would have wound up with Virginia and North Carolina *out* of the Union. Virginia, as noted, ratified after the requisite two-thirds requirement had assured acceptance of the Philadelphia constitution. By an extraconstitutional procedure, however, the old constitution of the United States—the Articles of Confederation—had been nullified, so now North Carolina was left outside, a sovereign and independent state, in company with only a somewhat unsavory other former colony, Rhode Island. At the Hillsborough convention, the Anti-Federalists permitted a long, one-sided discussion, and after eleven days of debate, on August 4, 1788, by a vote of 184 to 83, they carried a resolution neither rejecting nor ratifying the Constitution—a sweeping Anti-Federalist victory that meant North Carolina officially declined unconditional ratification. The convention also declared that a bill of rights asserting and securing from encroachment the great principles of civil and religious liberty and the unalienable rights of the people together with amendment ought to be laid before Congress and a second federal convention before North Carolina could ratify the Constitution. The convention proposed a bill of rights consisting of twenty parts, and also twenty-six amendments.[9] Williamson wrote an apology for North Carolina that appeared in the *New York Advertiser* on September 17, 1788, and immediately thereafter in the *State Gazette of North Carolina* in Edenton. In this article he concluded that North Carolina would eventually support the Union.[10]

The most persuasive and brilliant minds of the period—John Jay, Alexander Hamilton, and James Madison—defended the Constitution through *The Federalist Papers*, under the pseudonym "Publius." The Anti-Federalists suffered from a bad misnomer—"anti." What they shared was a pervasive suspicion that the Constitution was an end product of a cabal of ambitious men. The ten months of argument and discussion that followed the introduction of the Constitution debated these concerns, which resulted in the eventual ratification. As a member of the Continental Congress and a North Carolina delegate to the federal convention, Williamson was an informed participant in the debate. He wrote to James Iredell, July 26, 1788, after the Constitution had been ratified by eleven states, commenting on a celebratory procession and reception in New York, which, since North Carolina had not ratified, the North Carolina delegates did not attend. He noted, "We conceived it was respect we owed the State, not to celebrate an event in our public characters which the State we represent has not hitherto sanctioned by her approbation."[11] Williamson sarcastically added:

> Dear Sir, By letters from sundry correspondence, it appears that North Carolina has at length thrown herself out of the Union, but she is happily not alone: the large upright and respectable State of Rhode Island is her associate. The circumstances, however, I hope does [*sic*] not, render it necessary that the delegates from North Carolina should profess a particular affection for the delegates from Rhode Island. That state was some days ago represented by a Mr. Arnold who keeps a little tavern ten miles out of Providence; and Mr. Hazard, the illiterate "quondam" skipper of a small coasting vessel, who now, the very leader of Know Ye justices, officiates at county courts, and receives small fees, not as a lawyers, but agenda for suitors.[12]

Williamson was upset and embarrassed that North Carolina was not among the initial states ratifying a document he had worked so hard to develop. He noted that the new government was to be formed in March, and that Virginia and Kentucky (the latter soon to be a state) would not have their delegations formed, and advantages would accrue to the states in the Northeast, as the new government would be sited in New York. He noted that had North Carolina been in the Union, her five members could have helped position the new Congress in a more favorable southern position.

The North Carolina delegates wrote Governor Johnston of New York's adoption as capital. The new government was to be put in place by July 1789 and attention became directed toward its permanent site. New York and Philadelphia were leading candidates and the North Carolina delegation favored Philadelphia as the seat of government.

In the interim period, when the Constitution was ratified, but North Carolina was not among the states ratifying, Williamson occupied a tenuous position. He was not part of the celebratory politicians from Congress and the convention with whom he had worked to write the document. He was asked by Governor Martin to remain in New York to monitor the activities as a confidential servant of North Carolina. He even lost his franking privileges as he no longer was officially part of the Congress. He was allowed, though, to contribute to the discussion in Congress.

The two states not in the new Union, North Carolina and Rhode Island were potentially subject to tariffs by the other eleven states. However, Williamson's views were valued by the members of the Congress, as it became apparent that he was leading his state to eventual joining with the Union, and he was able to persuade them to exclude tariffs on North Carolina ports until 1790. He also pressed for a bill of rights, an important consideration for North Carolina ratification. The House of Representatives accepted seventeen of his proposals, and Congress submitted twelve to the states for ratification. Williamson, Governor Johnston, and the other North Carolina Federalists were delighted because this action countered Anti-Federalist claims that promises of a bill of rights would be forgotten once the Constitution had been ratified.[13]

It was generally accepted that North Carolina would ratify when the delegates gathered for a second convention at Fayetteville on November 16, 1789. Willie Jones, who had led the opposition at Hillsborough, did not participate. Other Anti-Federalists changed their votes and some sought to delay action until the Bill of Rights actually became a part of the Constitution.

By a close vote in the new legislature in August 1789, a second convention was scheduled to meet at Fayetteville on November 16 to consider ratification. The Anti-Federalist minority tried to postpone ratification, but by a vote of 195 to 77, the Federalists secured ratification on November 21. Twenty-four counties and twenty-four delegates had shifted to the Federalist position since the Hillsborough convention. The vote showed that the Federalists controlled the entire state except for Sullivan County, west of the mountains; Wilkes County; and three separated groups of counties in the New Hanover, Anson, Granville, and Guilford areas, where local Anti-Federalist leaders were particularly influential.

In November 1789, in fact, two prestigious bodies met simultaneously in Fayetteville: the General Assembly met in annual session to discuss postwar rehabilitation, and the North Carolina ratification Constitutional Convention met to reconsider the state's previous refusal to ratify the Constitution. Led by William Richardson Davie, the same men constituted the majority in both bodies. With supreme statesmanship, the convention ratified the Constitution of the United States and the General Assembly established and endowed the University of North Carolina. Dr. Kemp P. Battle, the first historian of the University of North Carolina, pointed out these two measures as "forming part of a comprehensive plan" for developing the state of North Carolina.[14] Williamson, elected from Tyrrell County, attended this Fayetteville convention of 1789 and voted for ratification of the Constitution.

> Due credit has never been given to Dr. Hugh Williamson for his intense interest in the ratification of the Federal Constitution. None of our local historians, so far as has been observed, has ever credited him with moving the resolution

of adoption. After an appropriate preamble which among other things set forth the language of the Constitution, and which on his motion, seconded by Mr. Blount, had been read before the Convention, he resolved as follows:

Resolved. That this Convention, in behalf of the freemen, citizens, and inhabitants of the State of North Carolina, do adopt and ratify the said Constitution and form of government.

This motion was referred to a Committee of the whole house and several days were consumed before the Committee reported. On the 20th, the Committee reported a resolution concurring with the Williamson preamble and resolution. It was ordered that the resolution be tabled until the 21st. On that day, after several amendments were proposed and rejected, Mr. Davie moved that the Convention concur with this Committee resolution, which was in the same language as the original Williamson preamble and resolution. On the yeas and nays being called, the motion carried in the affirmative by a vote of 195 to 77. So the Constitution of the United States, in reality, was adopted on the resolution of Williamson, though the final motion on his resolution as concurred in by the Committee of the whole House, was made by Davie. [15]

On March 4, 1789, the first Congress, under the new Constitution, submitted twelve amendments, ten of which were soon adopted by the requisite number of states. It was after their submission and ratification by Congress on September 25, 1789, that North Carolina now re-assured by the Bill of Rights, ratified the Constitution on November 21,

> 1789, and became the twelfth member of the Union. Shortly after, Washington conveyed his appreciation and thanks to the State.[16]

Several influences accounted for the reversal of position. Association with the smallest state, Rhode Island, and one which had a reputation for radicalism and paper money, was a factor. Iredell and Davie published and distributed the debates of the Hillsborough Convention. The public read endorsements by Washington and received favorable reports, and the need for increased southern influence with Congress was urged. There was a growing consciousness of the need for greater protection from Indians, Spain, and Great Britain. James Madison, influenced by pressure from Virginia and other states, had recommended amendments in Congress. The desire to secure the ratification of North Carolina and Rhode Island led to twelve amendments, a bill of rights. North Carolina Federalists welcomed them and freely predicted their adoption. The Fayetteville Convention ratified the Constitution before it was known that any state had ratified any of the amendments. Undoubtedly, North Carolina's refusal to ratify the Constitution at Hillsborough was one of the factors behind the Bill of Rights. Though North Carolina did not like the Constitution, the state did not desire to remain independent.[17] As to the issue of North Carolina ratifying, Madison is quoted as saying: "I believe there is now little or no reason to doubt the success of the question in North Carolina. The Honorable Mr. Williamson has lately arrived from that state and assures that he not been able to inform himself from what quarter the opposition to come and that he entertains no doubt of the ratification by their Conventions."[18]

At the same location, Fayetteville, the North Carolina Constitutional Convention of 1789 ratified the Constitution, the North Carolina state legislature, which contained 109 members, also voted for ratification and had ceded the state's western lands to the United States. The legisltature also chartered the University of North Carolina, and elected two United States senators, Samuel Johnston and Benjamin Hawkins, both of whom were Federalists. The governor, Alexander Martin, though not a Federalist, was a moderate. In the first election for the national House of Representatives, the electorate of the state chose three Federalists, Hugh Williamson, John Steele, and John Sevier, and two Anti-Federalists, John B. Ashe and Timothy Bloodworth. In 1792, the same representatives were re-elected, but in 1794, Martin, now an avowed Republican, was chosen senator, and nine of the ten seats in Congress went to Republicans, the party of Jefferson.

The state government and the central government moved quickly to make North Carolina a full partner with the other states. The legislature chose senators, provided for the election of representatives, and ratified the Bill of Rights amendments. Lands west of the mountains were once more ceded to the

United States, and this time the cession was accepted by Congress. President Washington welcomed the state to the Union. He sought "first Characters" (people of quality) to serve as appointments on the United States Supreme Court and appointed Robert Harrison, a jurist from Maryland, to serve, but he declined because of his health. Accordingly, Washington offered a founding position on the Supreme Court to James Iredell of North Carolina, who at age thirty-eight remains one of the youngest persons to serve on the bench.[19] Williamson described Iredell as *"one of the best men, as well as best lawyers in America"* (italics added).[20] On December 22, 1789, North Carolina was one of the four states to vote approval of all twelve amendments. Elected from the Edenton district as the first representative of five to qualify from North Carolina, Williamson took his seat in the second session of the Congress of the United States of America on March 19, 1790.[21]

One of the primary issues in these years was Hamilton's proposed spirituous tax; opponents in the state emphasized that distant markets made money scarce in North Carolina and that farmers in the Piedmont and mountain counties needed to manufacture whiskey as a stable crop, in which the federal government had no right to interfere. The excise tax became law in 1791, but it was reduced from the original proposal, and small distilleries were exempted. North Carolina thus escaped an uprising similar to the Pennsylvania Whiskey Rebellion of 1794, which was suppressed by federal forces.

The Federalists controlled the national government for the first twelve years during the administrations of George Washington and John Adams. In North Carolina, however, of the governors during that time—Alexander Martin (1789–1792), Richard Dobbs Spaight (1792–1795), Samuel Ashe (1795–1798), William R. Davie (1798–1799), and Benjamin Williams (1799–1802)—only Spaight and Davie were Federalists, and Spaight later became a Republican. The General Assembly was predominantly Republican. There was a small Federalist majority in the House of Representatives from 1789 to 1793, when Williamson and Steele retired. All the state's representatives from 1793 to 1796, except W. B. Grove, were Republicans. All were agrarians, except Grove, Thomas Blount, and Nathaniel Macon, the state's most popular representative, who entered Congress in 1791. In 1796, the general unpopularity of Federalist policies and dislike of the Jay Treaty led the state to give eleven electoral votes to Jefferson and one to Adams. When Washington retired from the presidency, the General Assembly voted a warm address in his honor. However, Washington was not very popular with the North Carolina congressional delegation. In Congress Thomas Blount openly criticized Washington's last message, and criticized the legislature's resolution on the grounds that it was too adulatory.[22]

The fourth phase toward a central government was the first session of Congress under the new Constitution, March–September 1789. Williamson, involved in all phases of its evolution, from the Articles of Confederation to writing and ratifying the Constitution, and participating in its initial legislative deliberations, was a member of the first two sessions of the House of Representatives.

Chapter 11

Educator

> Civil liberty has always been supported by learning. . . . Ignorance in the Subjects and despotism in the ruler go hand in hand; . . . there never has been a nation who preserved the semblance of freedom without being enlightened by the rays of science.
>
> —Hugh Williamson, *History of North Carolina*

As one of the Founders with a formal education, Williamson valued the need for the development of institutions of higher learning. Indigenous education was often available through academies sponsored by religious and other philanthropic groups, which competed for charters and funds from the English king. Americans who had the means frequently followed their academy education with higher education in England or Europe. Successful academies sometimes evolved into colleges or universities if they could secure funding. The successful academies often had presiding Scottish educators. Examples are what became the University of Pennsylvania, Harvard, William and Mary, Princeton, and Columbia. By 1800, there were sixteen universities in America.

George Washington had a dream of a secular, nonparochial, national university, a hope he mentioned in an inaugural address and in his will.[1] Publicly funded universities, however, eventually evolved out of state rather than national government. The University of Georgia and the University of North Carolina were the two founded in the eighteenth century.

As a youth, Williamson like many others had studied with an influential Scot, Frances Alison, in his Philadelphia academy. After graduating from the College of Philadelphia, obtaining a master's degree, and joining the faculty as a professor of mathematics, when eventually Williamson changed his career goal to medicine, he followed a well-defined path toward medical education among colonial scholars. He received the preeminent medical education of Georgian times, at the University of Edinburgh, where 20.9 percent of MD degrees were obtained by North Americans.[2] Though Williamson attended the university, he did not obtain his MD degree at Edinburgh; he received it from the educational precursor to Edinburgh, Leiden, where the famous educator Herman Boerhaave had developed a system of medical physiology. Then, as described earlier, he also studied as a resident pupil with the preeminent surgical scientist of the eighteenth century, John Hunter.

After securing his European medical degree, Williamson returned to Philadelphia. His nine years of medical practice were not very satisfactory to him; he was much more interested in science, the activities of the American Philosophical Society, and education. He eventually followed his mentor, Francis Alison, to Delaware where the Newark Academy was evolving into what became the University of Delaware. He also was appointed to the faculty of Princeton: on October 1, 1767, it was announced that Dr. Hugh Williamson of Philadelphia was appointed professor of mathematics and natural philosophy at the College of New Jersey at Princetown, the precursor of Princeton University.[3]

Other Scottish Presbyterians were appointed as presidents of nascent American universities. John Witherspoon, a New Side Presbyterian, became president of Princeton. After accepting the position, he had second thoughts and was prepared to decline. Had he done so, the likely president of Princeton would have been Williamson's mentor, Francis Alison. An Old Side Presbyterian, Benjamin Rush of Philadelphia, in medical school in Edinburgh at the time, persuaded Witherspoon to take the Princeton presidency. Witherspoon became one of the most outstanding clerical spokesmen in America. He organized the Presbyterian Church in America and was a purveyor of the Scottish Enlightenment. He also signed the Declaration of Independence.[4]

After following Alison to Newark, Williamson was named

a trustee of the academy. Other trustees were Chief Justice of Delaware William Allen, Vice Provost Francis Alison, the Reverend John Ewing, Professor Charles Thompson, and Andrew Allen, all except Alison graduates of the academy and of the College of Philadelphia. The trustees appointed Ewing and Williamson as fund-raisers, and they traveled to the West Indies and London on several successful fund-raising missions. Over the years, the academy developed a reputation for fine learning, which propelled it into its various stages as Newark College in 1834, Delaware College in 1843, and the University of Delaware in 1921.[5]

Fund-raising included production of documents and flyers describing the need for a university in Newark that were distributed to potential donors; they noted the increase in population in Delaware and western Pennsylvania and the need for educational resources to produce an educated citizenry. These flyers were prepared for distribution in London, the West Indies, and elsewhere.[6]

One of Williamson's most successful fund-raising efforts was his trip during 1772 to Jamaica, West Indies, where he secured considerable funding for the academy in spite of stiff competition from another physician, Dr. John Morgan, who was also in Jamaica soliciting funds for the College of Philadelphia. Hugh Williamson and John Morgan had been classmates in the first graduating class of the College of Philadelphia, and John Morgan later became a founder of the first school of medicine in America, at the University of Pennsylvania. Williamson refused compensation for his work for the academy. His detailed expense accounts are available, and show meals, clothing, servants, horses, and so on provided for this activity.[7]

While still in the West Indies, Williamson made plans to tour Great Britain, Scotland, and Ireland on behalf of the academy. In the fall of 1773, Dr. Williamson sailed for London, along with Professor Ewing, to solicit funds for the School of Liberal Arts and Sciences of Newark. His fund-raising enjoyed limited success in England, due to the growing tensions between England and the colonies, though as noted earlier, he did manage to secure a liberal contribution from King George III, despite the king's growing displeasure with the American colonies. When he moved to North Carolina, Williamson made many efforts to enhance the quality of education in the state. He was active in the founding of the Dobbs Academy in Kinston, the Pitt Academy at Greenville, and the New Bern Academy. The Greenville Academy was chartered January 6, 1787, with Hugh Williamson, William Blount, Reading Blount, and Richard Caswell as trustees. (The name of the town was changed later from Martinborough to Greenville.)[8] He was instrumental in the founding of the Smith Academy in Edenton and served by appointment of the state legislature in 1785 to its board, as well as to that of the Davidson Academy.[9] That academy, six miles from Nashville, Tennessee, became Cumberland College and was later renamed the University of Nashville.[10]

Williamson was always seeking learned individuals to teach in these academies. He wrote to John Gray Blount about a man named Marcus George and attested to his morals and learning in mathematics and science. He was concerned that the trustees at Greenville were not ready to employ George but, through Blount, he secured a position in the Warrenton Academy, where George eventually became principal.[11]

When North Carolina ratified the Constitution on November 21, 1789, the general assembly's concurrent legislation included the founding of a state university—a radical departure from the existing practice of having private or denominational colleges. William R. Davie is considered the founder of the University of North Carolina. Among his other accomplishments, Davie became governor of North Carolina and had served as emissary to the negotiations in Paris for the peace treaty ending the Revolutionary War.

Davie and the Reverend Samuel E. McCorkle, a preacher and teacher from Rowan County, were leaders of the university, but they proposed sharply different curricula for it. The Reverend McCorkle favored the classics and a student regimen of piety. Davie gave the sciences and history equal footing with the classics. Although McCorkle left Chapel Hill, Davie's ambitious curriculum never materialized in those early years.

In December of 1789, when the charter of the University of North Carolina was ratified by the state's General Assembly, Hugh Williamson was one of the original trustees appointed to oversee the university. The primary responsibility of the trustees of the University of North Carolina, according to the charter, was to handle all "monies, goods, and chattels . . . and Land, Rents, and Hereditaments for the Use and Purposes of establishing and endowing the University."[12]

The duties and structure of the UNC Board of Trustees remained essentially the same as North Carolina grew, though the method of selecting the trustees varied somewhat as the board increased its membership due to university growth. Until 1868 appointments to the UNC Board of Trustees were for life. One of the first actions taken by the University of North Carolina's Board of Trustees was the appointment of a secretary. On November 24, 1790, James Taylor was chosen by his fellow trustees to hold the position. The bylaws of the University were written by McCorkle. After amendment by the trustees, they were adopted on February 6, 1795.

Hugh Williamson served as secretary of the UNC Board of Trustees from February 6, 1795, to December 4, 1798. He did not receive compensation for his services. His responsibilities included keeping minutes of meetings, handling correspondence, compiling agendas, and mailing notices of the meetings to board members. Williamson's volunteer services as secretary of the UNC board did not go unrecognized. During the Board of Trustees meeting on Friday, December 4, 1798, the trustees voted: "On Motion, Resolved, that the Board have a proper and a thankful sense of the Services of Doctor Hugh Williamson, during the time he acted as their Secretary, the many Services incident to that appointment having become laborious and troublesome; the Board can no longer wish to impose them on the Doctor, but have Resolved that a Secretary to the Board of Trustees be appointed who will receive compensation for his Services."[13]

There was little formal committee structure to the UNC Board of Trustees at that time. Much of the business that would later be handled in the forum of a committee was carried on during the general meetings of the board. Such duties included the selection and manufacture of the seal of the University of North Carolina: "At a meeting of the Trustees of the University of North Carolina by adjournment, at Fayetteville the 24th: November 1790. . . . On Motion of Mr. Hay, that a committee shall be appointed to form a device for the common seal of the University, the folly. Gentlemen were appointed on that Committee. . . . And that a majority of them shall be sufficient to determine on the device and have the seal made."[14] In regard to the seal and its makeup, Battle explained the rationale:

> July—20. 1791—The committee on the University seal, consisting of James Hogg, Alfred Moore, and John Haywood, appointed by the Board of Trustees, July 20, 1791, was given plenary power to "cause a seal to be made, with such device thereon as to them may appear to be proper." Of their design, Dr. Battle says: "They chose the face of Apollo, the God of Eloquence, and his emblem, the rising sun, as expressive of the dawn of higher education in our State."[15]

Hugh Williamson referenced the seal in his letter to Governor Alexander Martin of February 17, 1792, which also conveys his concern about land the university owned that it was in danger of losing:

> Dear Sir,
>
> There are three Engravers in this City each of them very capable of engraving Seals and there is in New York at least one Engraver who is very capable of cutting Seals on Metal to great Advantage. As to the Seal of the University, The Things I mentioned may doubtless be executed, but I shall not contend for it, on the contrary if it shall be proposed to take the small Cow and large Ear of Corn from the present Seal of the State, provided any Person shall engage that the Ear of Corn shall be properly supported so as not be in Danger of falling on the Cow to destroy her, I shall with great resignation submit to the Project.
>
> I am very solicitous that Learning be promoted in our State and that the most useful Kinds of Learning shall be more attended to than has generally been done in much older Colleges. The Clerks of the Assembly with their usual want of Attention to Duty have neglected to send us the Copy of the Petition of the Claimants of Land under Warrants issued from Armstrongs Office. They indeed have sent us the Vote of the Legislature on that Head and they have sent us the Petition of the Trustees respecting their Claim for 20,000

> A[cre]s of Land and the Petition of the Survivors of Rd Henderson & Co for about 100 Thousd A[cre]s: but the Petition of the great Body of Complainants is not forwarded. Patience itself would be provoked at such execrable Neglect of Duty by which so many People may be injured. I am Dr sir With great Truth and Sincerity, Your obed Servt, Hu Williamson[16]

Williamson attended trustee meetings on a regular basis. He took an active role in developing the university into a sound and nationally competitive institution:

> July—20. 1791—The Board met according to Adjournment—present as yesterday. . . . On Motion resolved, that Mr. M. Corkle, Mr. Hawkins and Mr. Williamson, be requested to procure and transmit to the Secretary, such Information as may be in their power respecting the laws, Regulations and Buildings of the different Universities and Colleges within the United States and elsewhere; together with an account of their revenues and expenditures, and an Estimate of the Expence or Cost of the necessary Buildings. [Note: Dr. Battle thought that by their appointment of this committee, the trustees 'made a mainly implied confession of ignorance on the subject of the great task resting on their shoulders and displayed a proper carefulness to perform their duties intelligently.'] McCorkle and Hawkins had received their college education at Princeton, Williamson at the Universities of Pennsylvania, Edinburgh, and Utrecht, and,

therefore, were supposed to know more about the matters entrusted to them than their colleagues.)[17]

At the December 4, 1792, meeting of the trustees at New Bern, Williamson was appointed to a committee to develop an education plan. He, Dr. McCorkle, and David Stone from Bertie were the only trustees at that time who had completed a college education. The committee recommended that the instruction include the study of languages, especially of English, ancient and modern history, mathematics, belles lettres, natural philosophy, botany and the theory and practice of agriculture that would be best suited to North Carolina, and the principles of architecture. The committee recommended procuring a set of globes, a barometer, thermometer, telescope, quadrant, prismatic glass, air pump, and an electrical machine for experimental philosophy and astronomy. These recommendations, probably due to Williamson's University of Pennsylvania influence, were ahead of their time because they emphasized science and practical studies. McCorkle and Stone were graduates of Princeton, which unlike Pennsylvania was a seat of the older-style curriculum.[18]

The trustees allocated Dr. Hugh Williamson, also by then UNC professor of humanities, $200 to use to purchase "such Grammar, Classical and other books as in his opinion will be first needed."[19] He was to sell the books to students at cost. Charles W. Harris wrote April 10, 1795: "At present we find much difficulty in procuring books. The trustees have ordered 200 Dol. to be expended for that purpose; but it is very uncertain when the Books will arrive; Dr. Williamson is commissioned to purchase and he is so totally engaged about his own book [*History of North Carolina*] which he is preparing for the press, that he may forget others of less importance."[20]

Money, like books, was scarce in Williamson's day. Williamson, it seems, rightly estimated the slight enrollment to be expected in the more advanced Greek classes. The most expensive prices recorded in the table of his purchases shown here point to the scarcity of demand for both Latin and Greek: $2.50 for Xenophon, $3.75 for Homer, $2.25 for Cicero, Virgil, and Horace.

Books Purchased by Hugh Williamson with $200 Entrusted to Him by the Trustees of the University of North Carolina

Title	Quantity and Cost of Each
Ruddiman's *Rudiments*	48 @ $0.28
Whittenhall's *Greek Grammar*	24 @$0.375
Webster's *Grammar*	48 @ $.333
Scot's *Dictionary*	6 @ $1.00
Corderii	36 @ $0.28

Erasmus	24 @ $0.47
Clark's *Nepos*	2 @ $1.33
Sallust	10 @ $0.875
Cicero *Delphini*	6 @ $2.00
Virgil *Delphini*	6 @ $2.25
Horace *Delphini*	6 @ $2.25
Young's *Dictionary*	6 @ $2.25
Schrevelius's *Lexicon*	6 @ $0.25
Greek Testaments	6 @ $1.67
Lucian	4 @ $.90
Xenophon	3 @ $2.50
Nicholson's *Philosophy* (Natural)	6 @ $2.67
Homer	4 @ $3.75
Epictetus	6 @ $0.31

Source: Kemp P. Battle, *History of the University of North Carolina*, volume 1 (Raleigh, NC: Author, 1907).

As a trustee of the University of North Carolina, Congressman Williamson looked after the university's interests in the General Assembly. In 1792 he supported a petition on behalf of the university and other claimants and became irritated by state bureaucracy: "I suppose the stupid Clerks of the Assembly have carry'd off the Petition and we shall hear nothing of it. The patience of Job could hardly prevent him from swearing at such Jack Asses."[21] Williamson was incensed as he estimated that the trustees controlled 20,000 acres that could be lost to Indian claims from the Chickasaw and Cherokee tribes. The university gained little redress in this matter from either state or federal legislatures.

Hugh Williamson continued to serve on the University of North Carolina Board of Trustees in retirement. He served from Edenton on the Committee of Visitation with Willie Jones (Halifax district), John Williams (Hillsborough), William Polk (Salisbury), William Porter (Morgan), Robert Sneed (Wilmington), John Willis (Fayetteville), and Benjamin Williams (New Bern). In 1796 he served on a committee to select university faculty. Williamson sought individuals with a commanding style.[22] At the Monday, December 9, 1799, meeting of the board, Hugh Williamson was appointed to the Committee of Appointment along with David Stone, Thomas Blount, William Polk, and John Haywood.

More than a century after Williamson's death in 1819, the North Carolina General Assembly passed the Act of Consolidation on March 27, 1931. The act created the Consolidated University of North Carolina, a system comprising three previously separate institutions—the University of North Carolina, North Carolina State College of Agriculture and Engineering, and the North Carolina College for Women. It also appointed a new board of trustees of one hundred members, at least ten of whom were to be women, to serve as the governing body of the new system effective July 1, 1932. The pre-Consolidation boards of trustees of the individual institutions were discontinued.

Though many of the members of the consolidated board had previously served as a trustee of their constituent school, their purpose was now to promote the interests of the entire university system.

As noted earlier, Williamson had a connection to another fine North Carolina academic institution, Davidson College, named for his uncle, Brigadier General William Lee Davidson, half brother to Williamson's mother. Davidson was a founder of the Committee of Safety and involved in the evolving revolutionary movement in Mecklenburg County. As noted earlier, on July 21, 1780, he was shot over the kidney as his two hundred men tried to stop Cornwallis's troops after the Battle of Camden, recovered, but was subsequently shot and killed on February 1, 1781, at Cowan's Ford near the Catawba River in North Carolina. His son, William Lee Davidson II, provided the initial land for the college, which was from land awarded to Davidson by the federal government to veterans of the Revolution.

Chapter 12
Entrepreneur

I have ever had the Commercial Interest of the State much at heart, and shall never Shun any opportunity on which it may seem probable that my service may be of any use to the state.

—Hugh Williamson on accepting the commission from Governor Caswell to the Annapolis Convention

Williamson's spectacular public career occurred in North Carolina between 1777 and 1793. During much of that period, he was in New York, Philadelphia, or Baltimore as a North Carolina representative to the Continental Congress, the Constitutional Convention, or the House of Representatives in the new Congress. After the Constitutional Convention, and during the ratification debate, he remained in New York at Governor Martin's request, representing North Carolina to Congress. When North Carolina did not ratify the

Constitution at the Hillsborough Convention in 1788, Williamson's position became anomalous. After ratification of the Constitution, without North Carolina included, he functioned as a sort of North Carolina ambassador to the Congress in New York. At this time he was made the state's agent for settling North Carolina claims with the Union. He drew praise by being called "our worthy citizen" after North Carolina joined the Union. Williamson served two terms in Congress, which met in New York prior to Washington, D.C., being established as the capitol.[1]

Williamson was heavily involved in the economics of the colonial and post–Revolutionary War period when the Hamiltonian and Jeffersonian views of the new nation influenced a chaotic, formative financial era. Williamson's economic career is divided into three periods. The *first* began when he graduated from college, before the Revolution, when he administered his father's estate (chapter 1), and extended through the years he studied medicine in Europe and practiced medicine in Philadelphia. The *second period* was when he completed fund-raising for the Academy of Newark and was in England when the Revolutionary War began, through his return to America in 1777; his partnership with his brother, John, in shipbuilding and commerce; and eventually his association with the powerful mercantile Blount family. During this period he was heavily involved in land speculation and mercantile enterprises. The *third period* was when he permanently located to New York and administered the extensive Bloomingdale holdings of the Apthorp family.

The Post-Revolutionary War Period

Most entrepreneurs and capitalists understood the value of western lands and their dependency on and need for involvement of a strong federal government. Charles A. Beard in his study of the economy of the period and the influence of capitalists and speculators described the chaotic financial times in which Williamson, Blount, Hamilton, and others shaped the national domain.[2] The Blount family's land speculation in the western lands of North Carolina, which became Tennessee after North Carolina ceded it to the federal government, was based on military warrants and grants made to Revolutionary War veterans.

After Williamson settled in Edenton, he became friends with many prominent supporters of the Revolution. After the war concluded, he developed an extensive business involvement with the Blount family, one of the most prominent commercial families in America. They had mercantile businesses of an extensive nature, which included merchandising, shipping, saw and grist mills, currency speculation, and land speculation.

There were three Blount brothers. William Blount, as noted earlier, was active in politics and, like Williamson a member of the Constitutional Convention. In 1790 Blount was appointed by George Washington to be governor of the new territory of the United States south of the Ohio River, on Williamson's recommendation. When William Blount moved to the southwest territory of North Carolina, he was accompanied by his younger brother, John Gray Blount, as secretary. John Gray Blount had been with Daniel Boone on the expedition to found Boonesboro, Kentucky. Williamson offered to buy the Greenville home of William Blount when he left for the southwest territory, the western trans-Appalachian portion of North Carolina. Blount led Tennessee to statehood in 1795. Thomas Blount, active in commerce and North Carolina politics, served with Williamson as a trustee of the University of North Carolina until his death in 1812.[3]

Entrepreneurs such as the Blounts were heavily involved in land speculation. Veterans of the Revolutionary War, including Williamson, were awarded ceded western lands in the Ohio Valley as land script. These land scripts were often bought by speculators, who then held the land, anticipating a rise in value. The frontier economy was further confused by Spanish land grants, treaties with Indian tribes, and a weak central government. Land ownership was further complicated by Spain holding land in Louisiana, Mississippi, and Florida, and the British presence in the frontier forts yet to be vacated according to the terms of the Treaty of Paris of 1783.

With the French Revolution in full swing, public sympathies shifted from Jefferson's view of the French as good allies to the Federalist view that favored England. When Spain eventually changed allies from France to England in 1793, the situation became even more volatile.

Although Williamson initially opposed cession of western land of North Carolina (Tennessee) to the federal government, after a convention in Nashville asked North Carolina to formally cede the western lands to the federal government, he changed his position.[4] Williamson, as a member of Congress, supported the Blounts' view that Spanish ownership of territory in the Southwest was problematic because it denied use of the Mississippi to New Orleans and the rivers to the Gulf of Mexico at Mobile, Alabama.

In 1795 Thomas Pinckney negotiated the Treaty of San Lorenzo between the Spanish government and the United States. This treaty was subsequent to the Louisiana Purchase and established the boundary between Florida and the United States. It also gave America full access to the Mississippi River. Limited access to the waterway had been an unpopular feature of the Jay Treaty and carried with it the potential to serve as an excuse or justification for a war with Spain, which some of the "filibusters" such as Blount, Aaron Burr, Doctor Romayne, and others had as a central feature of their ambition for an independent country evolving out of the Louisiana Purchase.

After the Treaty of San Lorenzo had been ratified, thereby establishing the federal government's claim to the land, the states of Georgia and Alabama asserted similar claims. Those state claims were referred to as Yazoo Grants and induced a number of so-called Yazoo speculators. This led to the Yazoo Land Fraud, whereby tracts of the Louisiana Purchase were purchased by the members of the Georgia legislature. These men then sold and deeded nine million acres of Yazoo land to New York speculators. Similar speculators from other states, such as Virginia, bought land from the Georgia legislators-speculators. Georgia Senator James Jackson, who was firmly opposed to these activities, was even offered a sizable bribe if he would offer his support. These land grants of questionable legality were now under the control of the federal government as a result of the Treaty of San Lorenzo. The territory encompassing the Louisiana Purchase now belonged to the federal government, which had previously signed the Treaty of Hopewell (1786) with the Choctaws, Chickasaw, and Creek Indians the provisions of which covered some of this land. Moreover, President George Washington's initial Indian Policy was liberal and supportive of Native Americans' land claims and was supported by Williamson. So the choice was to continue to validate the Hopewell Treaty with the Native Americans or support the Yazoo speculators. The Georgia legislature declared the Yazoo speculations invalid and burned the offending pages of the state journal. President Washington sent congress a resolution of condemnation of the Yazoo purchases. The Supreme Court ruled against the speculators. Senator Jackson, who had opposed the Yazoo speculators, was involved in several duels over the issue and was eventually killed in one of them in June 1806.[5]

The instability of the southwestern frontier and the frontiersmen's isolation from the eastern government led to an environment of conspiracy. Most conspiracies centered on evicting the Spanish and establishing independent states. Ambitious conspiracies would have liberated Spanish land in Georgia, Mississippi, and Florida. Another "filibuster" (a term used for land conspiracy at the time) extended the conflict with the Spanish to annexation of Mexico. The number and details of the plots will never be known because of their secret nature. The plots, or at least the discussion of them, involved the brother of John Morgan, a classmate of Williamson's at the University of Pennsylvania; George Rogers Clark; Elijah Clark; and Brigadier General James Wilkinson, the ranking general of the United States Army, who was on the Spanish payroll as an informant. The most famous plot was the Burr Conspiracy, lead by the vice president of the United States, Aaron Burr, who was tried for treason and acquitted.[6]

Some of the plotters were acquainted, and there was somewhat of an overlap in different schemes. Stephen Genet, a French friend of Jefferson's, schemed to seize Spanish lands for the Revolutionary French government. The Chisholm-Romayne Scheme involved a Spanish-hating, former British soldier of fortune, John Chisholm, who was denied United States citizenship, and who served his client William Blount as

Indian agent (though he was never trusted by Blount), and Dr. Nicholas Romayne, a founder of Columbia University Medical School and the University of New Jersey Medical School, and like Blount a friend of Hugh Williamson. The Chisholm-Romayne scheme was aimed at Spanish Florida. Blount combined foreign intrigue, domestic treachery, and land speculation in another conspiracy to evict Spain from her North American possessions. Blount and Romayne planned to seize Spanish Louisiana, not Florida, and establish British sovereignty over it in 1797. Romayne wrote in correspondence that year with Blount that "I have spoken to Col. Burr about a land scheme between you and me,"[7] but it is not known if Burr was involved in that specific plot. The British minister, John Liston, who contemplated an attack on Spain in the New World, was interested in Blount's scheme but never committed to it.[8] Moreover, as discussed later, Blount, a sitting senator, was exposed as a "filibuster" in a letter read to the US Senate by Vice President Thomas Jefferson. He was then expelled, and later impeached, by the Senate.

Meanwhile, everything changed in the year 1797: a financial panic occurred; speculation, credit, and land prices fell; and money disappeared. Speculators such as Blount faced bankruptcy. Blount escaped creditors' arrest warrants by citing senatorial privilege. Several letters in 1795 to the Blounts indicate growing concern for the financial climate. One correspondent, David Allison, noted that "the Doctor [Williamson] is paid his generous loan—one other bill is paid—I will attend when in Cash to Stuarts note, I can't do it sooner."[9] Williamson wrote John Gray Blount about this matter and similar ones later:

New York, 2nd Febr, 1797

Dear Sir

Your Draft of 26th Octr for Dlrs 1550 on David Allison by him accepted was protested the 28th Decr. for non payment. The Holder of the Bill Jac Joné came to this City with your Brother William six Days ago. Your Brother it seems had promised by some means or other to get him the Money, and being disappointed in raising it here by the means he expected, he explained the Embarrassment to me two Days ago. I had no Cash in Hand except what was proper for necessary & contingent Expences, but it was clear that the Money must be had. Joné seemed to be greatly distressed and alledged that no Damages he could expect would compensate his Disappointment. It became necessary to borrow, which is a bad Business at all Times and at this breaking season is almost a hopeless one [this alludes to the beginning of the Panic of 1797]. . . .

Your Brother prayd'd me to relieve him from the French Man who haunted him like a ghost. He is paid and the Bill and Protest are in my Hands. I would not deposit them for security, for I wished to prevent them from being hawked about as such Incidents to mercantile Men are never agreeable. [William Blount's financial affairs were evolving to bankruptcy as discovery of his conspiracy became known.] . . .

Though you will naturally be desirous to make an early remittance that Subject to myself may prove very interesting. Some advances that I have made to your Brother and others that will probably be necessary, to prevent a Loss to him of a very large Property may render it extremely inconvenient for me to pay the Amount of that Bill at a short Notice should it be demanded.

I most sincerely hope that before this time my good friend Mrs Blount has fully recovered her Health. I am

Dr Sir With great Respect
Your obed Servt
Hu Williamson

Addressed John G Blount Esqr
Washington
N: C[10]

The desperation of the Blounts about William Blount's financial and political problems very much involved Williamson. The impending impeachment and the financial strains are noted in another letter from Williamson to John Gray Blount.

Dear Sir, Philad[a] : 6 July, 1797

Your brother William having occasion for money last Winter drew on W[m] Murdock of London for £500 S[tg] [sterling] which you had authorised him to use. I indorsed his Bills upon the assurance that the Money was on Hand & that he was authorised to draw for it. Your Letter of advice did not arrive in Time and the Bills are come back protested. Without being prepared with cash I must absolutely take them up in six or eight Days at whatever sacrifice of Property it may be done. The amo[t] with 20 P Cent Damages is about 2666 Dlrs. After I had indorsed those Bills, your Brother having a very urgent Demand for money, I lent him 2000 Dlrs and took up a Draft for 1550 Dlrs that he should have paid. Those last advances have cut so deep on my Cash Accot. that I am now in a situation, by no means pleasant. It is really humiliating to make application to Jews and Infidels on such Occasions for a supply of Cash. Your Brother, on the Return of the Bills, promised to draw again, or rather you would draw in his favour or mine & I promised to send over the Bills so that they should not be subject to Damages if again protested; but his present Disasters I fear will prevent him from writing to you on the Subject. I have therefore to request that you would for immediate Relief send me inclosed a Set of Bills on M[r] Murdock for £500 S[tg] with Duplicates of Letter of Advice. I shall be at New York where my attendance for some Time is necessary occasion'd by the late Death of Mr Apthorp[e] my father in Law. I know nothing of the means you may have of repayment, in case of money advanced to your Brother, but if he has drawn without your approbation for this money, I have to request that you would send me the Bills for that money to be passed to any acco^{t} you shall prefer. I could so manage the Bills as to relieve myself in a good measure from this most distressing Predicament.

I can imagine from my own feelings what your's must be, occasioned by the late misfortunes of your Brother, I need not say that I condole with you. Not to think at all about it seems to be the only Remedy.

I am Dr Sir, with much Respect

Your obed Servt.
Hu Williamson[11]

John G: Blount Esqr
Addressed: John G Blount Esqr
Washington
N: C

In a letter from John Gray Blount to Hugh Williamson dated Washington, August 17, 1797, Blount noted that "I am much pleased to see Doct Romayne publication for many reason and one is that he says of Old Tim [Pickering] what I have long thought."[12] Both Blount and Romayne were enemies of Timothy Pickering, then secretary of state under President John Adams.

Widespread gossip concerning the Blount filibuster occurred. A letter of April 21, 1797, to James Carey from

Blount documenting his involvement in efforts to forestall France's claim to Spanish Mississippi was given by Carey to a federal official. It was read to the Senate by its presiding officer, Vice President Thomas Jefferson, who directly asked Blount, who was in attendance serving as one of the first senators from Tennessee, if he had written it, to which he admitted. The letter disparaged former president George Washington and revealed details of the plot. The letter documenting his foreign intrigues was also seen by Washington, discrediting Blount with the government. Washington felt the Blounts were using their political roles to enhance their land speculations.

William Blount was expelled from the Senate and was subsequently impeached but not convicted, due to a technicality.[13] Blount was served the papers of impeachment in Tennessee, but the local authorities refused to arrest him, and he declined to go to Philadelphia for the trial. As he had been expelled from the Senate, he technically could not be convicted or impeached. A popular figure and eventually governor of Tennessee as a state, Blount was elected to the Senate of Tennessee while under investigation for impeachment by the US Senate from which he had just been expelled! The president of the Senate resigned in favor of Blount to further immunize him from federal prosecution. Blount did not appear for his impeachment trial in the US Senate and the issue became moot.

There is no evidence that Williamson was involved in the conspiracies, but he certainly was involved in the mercantile and land speculation of the Blounts. Their relationship with Williamson was such that in 1795 the state of Tennessee, led by William Blount, honored Hugh Williamson by changing the name of Davidson County to Williamson County, in the tradition of naming its counties for distinguished people (military heroes, American statesmen, European noblemen, Indian tribes, etc.). The county seat is Franklin. When the boundaries of the western ceded land were eventually worked out, some of the bordering area of what was then Tennessee was allocated to Illinois. A county in Illinois is also named Williamson. Williamson expressed the view in a letter to Madison that "for myself, I conceive that my opinions are not biased by private Interests, but having claims to a considerable Quantity of Land in the Western country, I am fully persuaded that the value of those Lands must be increased by an efficient federal government."[14] He rationalized patriotism in his speculation. The Blounts and Williamson were not alone as land speculators; most of Congress, as well as George Washington and Benjamin Franklin, had a considerable amount of land in the new national domain.

Williamson was known as the "old gladiator" of the Blounts,[15] and he served almost as a lobbyist for the Blounts in letting them know about various federal acts and treaties that might affect their land holdings. In one land deal involving the Blounts, Williamson alerted his friend John Gray Blount, who also owned real estate along the Obion River, that "The Court of Spain has lately by its minister here [Philadelphia], for the first Time avowed its Intention to support the Claim of the Creek Indians *its friends and allies* Against our Claims to certain Land *fraudulently* taken from those Indians at the Treaty at New York made with McGillivry & Co."[16] No known records exist that indicate Williamson completed the sale.

Williamson was active in settling war claims with land. As an officer in the Revolutionary War, he claimed bounties for military service that amounted to 4,800 acres, which were granted August 2, 1784. In September 1784, Williamson attempted to buy 20,000 acres in the western country, financed by depreciated loan certificates bought at a fairly reasonable sum. He wrote John Gray Blount years later, "You are not to wonder that a man in my situation, whose estate is not large, should prefer a small certainty to anything that possibly during the next century may accrue from these lands." Williamson's relationship with the Blounts eventually cooled as he felt they were reckless in their schemes. He distanced himself from their projects after William Blount's filibuster and subsequent disgrace occurred.[17]

Williamson's interest in land speculation continued during retirement from public life. He attempted to sell land that he owned along the Obion River, a tributary of the Mississippi River in northwestern Tennessee. Williamson wanted to sell this land before westward expansion ended, because he feared that the Spanish would limit future settlement and land purchases by restricting navigation of the Mississippi and by supporting the land claims of the Creek Indians.

The intrigues and land speculation involving the Louisiana Purchase were the beginnings of the Manifest Destiny Movement. The intrigues of William Blount, Aaron Burr, General James Wilkinson, Dr. Nicholas Romayne, and others were designed to evict Spain from American possessions obtained through the Louisiana Purchase. As noted earlier, Brigadier General James Wilkinson was actually on the payroll of the Spanish government; he swore loyalty to the Spanish government, was identified as "agent #13," and communicated in cipher to the Spanish government via the Marquis of Casa Calvo, who was still in New Orleans even though the territory had been transferred to France and was then part of the Louisiana Purchase.[18]

Williamson was sensitive to sectionalism and its potential problems. In the passage of the Land Ordinance of 1784, designed to dispose of the national domain, Jefferson and Williamson produced the ordinance, and they collected maps and travelers' observations to estimate the quantity of the territory belonging to the United States west of the Mississippi River. Williamson estimated there were 85 million acres bordered by the line of latitude north of the Ohio at forty degrees and speculated that land would sell for $25 per hundred acres and pay off the national debt. He had a prospect, with Jefferson, that was intended to develop an orderly survey of the national land domain.[19] The intent was to follow some of the organizational concepts of English land grids. It did not emulate them, but this new system, known as the Williamson-Jefferson Plan, created the sections, miles, and acres that were the pattern for land sales and land grants under Manifest Destiny. As a mathematician and surveyor, Williamson was disposed to formalize land parcels and devised the grid system used in the Williamson-Jefferson Plan to settle western lands based on a group pattern. With the cession of the states' western claims, however, Williamson reversed his position and recognized that the organization of land claims was being subjected to congressional maneuvering. Williamson also was continuously supporting Indian claims and separated with the Blounts over his belief that the Indians must be compensated for land protected for them by treaty, as American settlers illegally took up residence.

Williamson's talents extended to the design of maps. In 1790 he used his scientific and mathematical knowledge to compile a map of the trans-Appalachian region. The map was sold for a nominal fee to assist "the proprietors of large Tracts in Our Western Country to agree on some plan of Settling Their Lands."[20] Tennessee largely benefited from this work in that Williamson hoped that his maps would help to divert Tennessee settlers who were planning to move to Kentucky.[21] Additional maps by Williamson were published in Matthew Carey's *General Atlas* in 1795.

The Ordinance of 1784 has even been labeled the Williamson-Jefferson Plan.[22] His influence continued after his political career concluded. The Land Act of 1796 originated in a bill introduced four years earlier by Williamson. The act sustained the policies of the land ordinances of 1784–1785, especially that of the six-mile-square township.

In 1811 Williamson's work on climate and the effect of climatic changes on prevailing diseases of the time, titled *Observations on the Climate in Different Parts of America, Compared with the Climate in Corresponding parts of the Other Continents,* was published in the *Transactions of the American Philosophical Society.* Europeans had belittled America as having a climate that fostered colonization and so spacious as to be difficult to govern. Williamson's writings reflected his aggressive nationalism and his career as a public servant, and in part the book was written to refute European claims about the connection of climate and government. He wrote:

> The habits and manners of every nation take their form and impression from the spirit of the government under which they live, or from the administration of that government. . . . The very consciousness of being free, excites a spirit of enterprise, and gives a spring to the intellectual faculties. . . . But in all governments, where the tenure of property is uncertain, the rewards of diligence are counted as a dream. It follows, that the increase of science in every government, has been proportioned in a considerable degree, to personal liberty, and the safety of property.[23]

This publication was the first American work on the subject. It was largely Williamson's answer to the negative aspersions by foreign writers about the climate of North America.

Williamson considered *Observations on the Climate* an introduction to his book *History of North Carolina*, which he published in 1812. Williamson put a great deal of work into writing the history, but its potential was compromised from the beginning due to the unavailability of historical records. The history did receive wide circulation because of Williamson's highly acclaimed reputation. The notes in Davie's journals suggesting that Williamson may have intended to write a book about the Revolution but that it never was completed indicates that he was gathering information for a detailed and scholarly account, which perhaps would include the Revolutionary War period and the Constitutional Convention.[24]

Hugh Williamson continued to be a philanthropist during his twenty-six years in New York and he was generous in his support of community charities. His activities in New York constituted a substantial amount of public service. He did not practice medicine, but he served on hospital boards and engaged in related activities. This is the period when he was in close contact with Dr. David Hosack, the surgeon who attended Hamilton after he was fatally shot in the Burr-Hamilton duel. Hosack wrote the lengthy memorial obituary of Williamson.

Williamson is listed as an assistant dean of Columbia University, but little record of significant activity in that sphere exists. He functioned almost as an attorney and served as administrator of estates for friends and family members. The Orphan Asylum, the Society for the Relief of Poor Widows with Small Children, the Humane Society, and the City Dispensary of the New York City Hospital were among the beneficiaries of his generosity and attention. He was a trustee of the College of Physicians and Surgeons of the University of the State of New York, to which he liberally contributed his time and money. Williamson was one of the founders of the Literary and Philosophical Society of New York, and was a prominent member of the New York Historical Society. He was elected a governor of the society of the New York Hospital.[25] He made donations to the Assistance Society.[26] He served as vice president of the Humane Society.[27] He served as a trustee of the City Dispensary.[28] He donated funds to the New York Bible Society through an acquaintance, Dr. Nicholas Romayne, the roguish founder of New York medical schools and a western land conspirator with William Blount.

Williamson remained in contact with his Federalist friends, such as Alexander Hamilton and DeWitt Clinton, the last Federalist Party candidate for president of the United States. Williamson was an important advisor to Clinton on the first large public-private federal project of the new country, the Erie Canal. Williamson had supported building a canal to connect the waters of Lake Erie with the Hudson River in order to enhance the commercial potential of New York City. This project was eventually completed as the Erie Canal in 1823 and had substantial impact on national growth. Williamson's time in Holland gave him a lifelong interest in canal systems as a mode of transportation. With Jefferson, Washington, and others, as noted earlier, Williamson was involved in the Dismal Canal project to link Virginia and North Carolina and the new capital, Washington, D.C. It was planned as the locus of a transportation system now roughly known as the inland waterway. With steam power becoming a practical water and land power source for transportation by 1820, railroads became the instrument of western expansion.

While a member of Congress, Williamson married Maria Apthorp, daughter of Charles Ward Apthorp and Mary McEvers. The wedding occurred in January 1789 at the Apthorp mansion of Elmwood (see illustration), located at Bloomingdale, near New York City. The couple was married by the Right Reverend Dr. Provost, bishop of the Episcopal Church and one of the chaplains of Congress.[29] Charles Ward Apthorp, an attorney, was the eldest son of Charles Apthorp of Boston, a scion of a Tory family. The younger Mr. Apthorp moved to New York and was appointed to the Governor's Council and King's Council throughout the Revolutionary War. He purchased land that encompassed much of the central part of today's New York City. His holdings were part of a Dutch plantation named Bloomingdale and bordered on the west side of the city from Seventy-seventh Street and the

Hudson River. It encompassed fifty square blocks from Central Park to the Hudson River between Eighty-ninth and Ninety-eighth Streets. The household was located between Ninetieth Street, Ninety-first Street, and Columbus Avenue. He also held land in Maine, Boston, and areas near Boston. Part of his holdings, the Bloomingdale right of way, eventually resulted in litigation over property lines that involved the Astors, Schuylers, Hamiltons, and other famous New York families. In 1790 Williamson bought a claim of one of the Apthorp heirs that had been foreclosed by the sheriff. Litigation involving the estate, which included the sorting of over forty deeds, including ones with names like Astor, encompassed the years 1790–1910.[30]

Following the Treaty of Paris in 1783, Americans who were loyal to King George III were subject, against the terms of the treaty, to severe treatment that included land confiscation. Moreover, in New York, their names were published under the New York State Statute of Confiscation in 1779 (other states had similar statutes). Apthorp does not appear in the New York lists. He was charged, though, with activities of a treasonous nature, and a case was brought before a Canadian settlement court for arbitration. He had commissioned privateers to fight against the rebels. His son, Captain Apthorp, served as an active officer under Cornwallis. Although acquitted and allowed to live in New York, Charles Ward Apthorp lost property. His lands in the area of Boston, elsewhere in Massachusetts, and Maine were confiscated under those states' postwar statutes relating to Loyalists.

New York was occupied by the British during the Revolutionary War, after George Washington's abortive attempt to expel them. In Washington's retreat, he stayed in the Apthorp home for a few days after the Battle of Long Island. The house was subsequently occupied as headquarters by Lord Howe, General Clinton, Lord Cornwallis, and General Carleton. The British did not physically leave New York until after the Treaty of Paris in 1783. New York was perhaps more tolerant to the Tories than other states since it was a British and Loyalist site throughout the war. Apthorp was a powerful man in the city and the Statute of Confiscation would not have applied to his ten children. Williamson became a manager of the Apthorp estates and fortunes left by Charles Ward Apthorp at his death in 1797. His real property encompassed over two hundred acres.[31] One of the daughters of Charles Ward Apthorp, Charlotte Augusta, became the wife of John Cornelius van den Heuvel, a wealthy Dutch gentleman. The van den Heuvels were a neighboring family, and Williamson managed many of their real-estate transactions and businesses. Maria Eliza, daughter of Charlotte Augusta van den Heuvel, married John C. Hamilton, son of Alexander Hamilton. Maria van den Heuvel Hamilton was a namesake and niece to Williamson's wife, Maria, and was Hugh Williamson's favorite niece. She was with Williamson when he died. He left his estate to her, as she apparently reminded him of his wife. Williamson effectively intervened in the seizure of a ship owned by Mr. J. C. van den Heuvel that was seized by a frigate of Lord St. Vincent's fleet and condemned in Gibraltar as Spanish property.[32] There are frequent notices in contemporary newspapers of Williamson's involvement in land and other real-estate sales. He seems to have speculated some in real estate with notices of homes and farms for sale.

Williamson's retirement from public life, and his long career in New York after leaving his last public office as a member of the House of Representatives, lasted twenty-six years. A number of his legislative ideas about national expansion and development did not come to fruition until after he left public life.

Chapter 13

Williamson the Man

People contending for liberty have never been subdued . . . the Americans say the Lord hath helped them.

—Hugh Williamson, *The Plea of the Colonies on Charges Brought against them by Lord Mansfield and Others*

It is the pleasure and frustration of biographers to always incompletely know their subject. Williamson's contemporaries provide insight into how he was perceived. Thomas Jefferson, who served with him in the Continental Congress at Annapolis, described Williamson as "a very useful member of the Congress of the Confederation, of an acute mind and of a high degree of erudition."[1] His colleague, William Pierce, referred to Williamson as "a gentleman of education and talents with a great deal of humor and pleasantry in his character."[2] In his eulogy of Williamson, David Hosack, a faculty member at Columbia, referred to him as "the American Cato":

Hugh Williamson

In person, Dr. Williamson was considerably taller than the general standard; he was of a large, well proportioned frame, but was not fleshy. He carried himself erect even in the decline of life. His forehead was high and open; his cheek bones were elevated. His eyes were dark gray, penetrating, and steady. His nose was aquiline; his chin was long and prominent. . . . In his conversation, Dr. Williamson was pleasant, facetious, and animated; occasionally indulging in wit and satire; always remarkable for the strength of his expression, and an emphatic manner of utterance, accompanied with a peculiarity of gesticulation, originality in part ascribable to the impulse of an active mind, but early in life had become an established habit. . . . As might be expected because of his trade and education his manners, though in some respects eccentric, were generally those of a polite gentleman. Occasionally, however, when he met with persons who either displayed great ignorance, want of moral character, or a disregard to religious truth, he expressed his feelings in such a manner, as distinctly to show that they had no claim to his respect. . . . The steadiness of his private attachments ought not to be passed over in silence. Dr. Williamson was slow in forming his friendships, but when formed, as the writer of this memorial of his worth can testify, it was immovable, and not to be changed by time or distance.

David Hosack, M.D., LL.D.

Personal friend of Hugh Williamson[3]

Winthrop Jordan, historian, noted: "He brought to his work the assumptions of a Protestant Christian, a Pennsylvanian who lived in the south, a Jeffersonian intellectual, a gentlemanly go-getter and an American nationalist. It would be difficult to find a more representative man."[4] One author refers to him as the "Southern Franklin" because of his broad interests in science, government, politics, and so on.[5] Unlike Franklin, Williamson had a formal education, while Franklin's doctorate was an honorary one from the University of St. Andrews in Scotland.

Carolinians joked about Williamson's abilities as an elocutionist and his aristocratic pretensions but they did acknowledge that he was loyal to and diligent for his adoptive state. At the Constitutional Convention he was described by Otto, the French chargé d'affaires, as a doctor, a professor of astronomy, and a man who was hard to understand. He described Williamson's speech in Congress as a florid harangue. Otto described Williamson as "very odd, magnetic in speech, always speaking with spirit. It is very difficult to picture his character. It is always possible he doesn't have one but his activity for a long time has given him a great influence in Congress."[6] A caustic critic, Archibald McLean, labeled him "the all knowing Dr. Williamson who would have made a pretty good pettifogging attorney rather than a legislator."[7] He had inordinate attention to detail. He seemed to be hypochondriacal and complained about his health. This dimension of his personality suggests that stress from his many pursuits often led to depression.

Dr. James Thacher, physician and historian, heard Williamson preach at Plymouth before he studied medicine and recalled that "his oratory was grotesque," and Rufus King later noted that his oratory in Congress provoked laughter.[8] Thacher notes that Williamson was asked to sit for a bust by Ceracchi, who did busts of Washington, John Adams, John Jay, George Clinton, Alexander Hamilton, and others. Ceracchi also referred to Williamson as the American Cato, but Williamson thought Ceracchi was employing flattery to obtain permission for a bust and refused.[9] An accurate, if flattering, statue of Williamson is in Philadelphia at the Constitution Center, opened on July 4, 2003, where a room designated as "Signers' Hall" has statues of the thirty-nine signers of the Constitution, including Williamson, along with the three dissenters (see photo insert).

Williamson's relationship with Benjamin Franklin is interesting and our knowledge of it tantalizingly incomplete. Williamson's entry into colonial politics occurred in the context of the Great Awakening, the eighteenth-century religious phenomenon that evolved more broadly into patriotic leanings toward independence. He became a supporter of the proprietary government of Pennsylvania in the government's belief that Franklin was not supporting the colonial position on taxation. In Williamson's pamphlet *What Is Sauce for a Goose Is Also Sauce for a Gander*, as we saw earlier, Franklin, "the Great Man," was indirectly accused of abetting passage of the Stamp Act, and he responded by labeling Williamson "one of the detestable skunks in human society."

Franklin held a grudge and deprecated Williamson's scientific contributions to the American Philosophical Society. Jefferson, however, judged Williamson's publication on comets, "remarkable, ingenious sound and satisfactory."[10] Franklin and Williamson seemed to become friends when Williamson was serving as courier between Franklin and the Continental Congress, and Dr. Williamson brought Franklin and then the British Privy Council the first news of the Boston Tea Party. As noted in chapter 3, Williamson was considered by some, probably incorrectly, to be associated with Franklin in the Hutchinson-Oliver Affair.

After the Declaration of Independence, Williamson and James Hutchinson, another young physician who had been studying in England, were nearly captured by the British off the coast of Delaware while bringing dispatches from Franklin to the Continental Congress. When Williamson returned from Europe six months after the Declaration of Independence, he expected to obtain a commission in the medical department of the Continental Army, but his arrival in Philadelphia was preceded by Silas Deane's first report to the Continental Congress as emissary to France, suggesting that Williamson was disloyal. Williamson was totally exonerated after the war.[11] Franklin signed, but did not write, the dispatch questioning Williamson's loyalty.

Franklin and Williamson's friendly relationship in England in 1774 included their collaboration on electrical experiments with the electric eel, and it expanded Franklin's electricity discovery. Their associate investigator, the famous surgeon-biologist John Hunter, Williamson's teacher and Franklin's doctor, was among the greatest minds of the eighteenth century.

Williamson was associated with Franklin again when they both served as delegates to the Constitutional Convention in 1787. During tense negotiations over some details of the constitution, after Franklin suggested that a prayer be offered at the opening of the sessions to move the discussion to another level, Williamson challenged the idea on budgetary grounds, and Hamilton objected, noting that the delegates had agreed not to seek outside help in the debates, a compromise, out of deference to Franklin, was to intermittently ask for a prayer if it was deemed necessary.

Williamson's associates in the Continental Congress in New York included Thomas Jefferson, with whom he shared an interest in all things scientific, including the bones of prehistoric animals. Jefferson hoped that a mammoth or some of the other animals, which we now know as part of the dinosaur family, might still be living in the western part of the United States and seen by the voyage of discovery led by Lewis and Clark in 1802. Williamson procured some specimens for Jefferson. Williamson wrote Jefferson in 1801 requesting that he meet Captain John Williamson, Hugh Williamson's brother, at the White House. In addition to serving as a merchant, seaman, and shipbuilder, he had been a captain in the Continental Navy.

Williamson the Man

Sir, New York, September, 1801

This will be handed you by my brother John Williamson who now for the first Time has expressed a desire of being introduced to the President of the United States, for it is but a short Time since a system of government has been abdicated which for many years he has zealously opposed. Not that he is a bad citizen or pleased with controversy but he served his native country in arms during the revolution war and he does not forget that he had an Enemy who since the war has given too many proofs of hollow friendship.

My brother settled as a merchant in Charleston, South Carolina, at the End of the war. That city as you know had been some years in the Possession of the Enemy and its commerce after the war was chiefly managed by British agents. Their first representative in congress was little Wm Smith himself warm from England & warmly supported by British influence. The Treaty called Jay's, was uniformly supported by the same influence and the same men. Parties were soon formed in Charleston; They were government or anti-government men; Treaty or anti-treaty men. Capt[n] Williamson chanced to be one of the very few American merchants in Charleston whose commercial capital placed him above the necessity of seeking British credit. He spoke and acted with perfect freedom. As he could not be suspected of sinister or selfish views and was by all who knew him of blameless Integrity, his influence at elections was the greater, for he had embraced many opportunities of serving his fellow Citizens. He has now the satisfaction to find that a great and decided majority through the State have embraced the same political opinions with himself.

If there is any individual in Charleston of whose integrity or political opinions you may wish to be informed I think my brother will tell you what he knows of him or them with truth and sincerity.

I have the honor to be
With the utmost consideration & respect
Your most obedient and
very humble servant,
Hu Williamson[12]

Charleston was remote from the Revolutionary War until the Southern Strategy was implemented in the last three years. Charleston, in fact, was officially neutral for part of the war and continued commerce with England. After the war, many of the previous commercial arrangement were re-established. Washington's policy invoked bitter criticism in North Carolina when Jay's Treaty with England was negotiated in 1794 and ratified in 1795.The state fought this treaty from the beginning; both senators voted against it and voted against John Jay as a peace commissioner; both voted against ratification, and meetings were held at Warrenton, New Bern, Wilmington, Charlotte, Edenton, Chapel Hill, and other places to protest provisions of the treaty. Since the treaty called for an appropriation of money, it had to come before the North Carolina House of Representatives. Moreover the Jay Treaty, a fairly secret treaty when revealed to Congress and the public, unleashed the greatest criticism of Washington's administration as it gave many concessions to the English.

Williamson's association with George Washington was mostly limited to the legislative and political arena, with the exception of their work on the Dismal Swamp project. He was the congressional contact for Washington about land issues. Williamson was immortalized in the portrait in the National Gallery in the Trumbull painting of Washington surrendering his commission to Congress in Annapolis, Maryland, where the Congress was meeting (see illustration). The symbolism is important; it demonstrates Washington's acknowledgment of the authority of an elected legislature over the military. Williamson's estimation of Washington can be gauged from his action after Washington submitted his commission and resignation to the Congress and suggested his family might like to have the commission for posterity; Williamson was the one who proposed that the commission be returned to Washington in a gold box in gratitude for his service (though as noted earlier, it was not).

With the Blounts, Williamson was among the early people to see personal advancement and national greatness as coinciding. He and others set the stage for the policy of westward expansion, later labeled "Manifest Destiny." Blount and Williamson, because of a formula that evolved, as described in an earlier chapter, devised a method for ceding land claims in the back country to the federal government as they placed more confidence in the federal government than in states. This was one way of having the public debt retired for the states. It was Hamilton's plan to fund the budget of the federal government. As a speculator and a legislator, Williamson played an important role in shaping the national domain; he saw no conflict of interest in mingling national and personal interests.

His practical bent can be seen in his participation, after his move to New York, with Governor DeWitt Clinton in the development of the Erie Canal. Their plan, of course, was superseded by the early and rapid growth of railroads, which began with steam engines after 1820. Williamson's interest in land and its speculation resulted in his publishing maps, and he continued through his life to publish essays and articles about land and climate in the American Philosophical Society's and other journals. He continued his land speculation after political retirement. He sold land he owned along the Mississippi in northwest Tennessee, sales of which were controlled by Spain at the time.

He supported the land claims of the Creek Indians, as did President George Washington, and alerted John Gray Blount that Spain had avowed its intention to support the claim of the Creek Indians against claims for certain land that Spain believed had been fraudulently taken in a treaty at New York made with Creek Indian leader Alexander McGillvray, and a large delegation of Indian chiefs. He let Blount know that he was trying to sell the claims to Spain in order to recoup his losses but there is no record that the sale was ever completed.

Williamson's position on slavery was revealed in the context of his involvement in land policy. According to James Madison, in 1783 Williamson declared that he was "principled against slavery as he thought slaves were an encumbrance to society instead of increasing its ability to pay taxes."[13] In the 1784 vote to exclude slavery north of the Ohio River, Williamson and Jefferson were the only southern congressmen who voted against their sections' interests.

In the heat of the financial panic of 1797, when Williamson was assisting William Blount to avoid bankruptcy, he seemed to reveal an anti-Semitic bias, in that he refers to "Money changers" and expressed concern at leaving "my note in the Hands of a Levite."[14]

Williamson was involved in the development of the Great Compromise at the Constitutional Convention, which determined how the states would be represented in the new national government, and in the decision terminating the foreign slave trade. He contributed the suggestion that representation in the House be based on both slave and free population, the so-called Three-fifths Compromise, which counted slaves as three-fifths of a person. His attitude toward the Constitution is reflected in this compromise, in which he said, much like Franklin, that he did not think a better plan was to be expected and would have no problem signing it.

Williamson, as others, was alert to the possibility of special interests in the East making excessive concessions to Spain. This issue was problematic in the wake of the Jay Treaty, an unpopular treaty with England that did not guarantee access to the Mississippi River from Spanish-held land. The economic basis of westward expansion was dependent on access to the Mississippi River and control by Spain was worrisome to westward-looking speculators and settlers. His concern mounted when President Jefferson did not appear concerned about the possibility of conflict with Spain.

In the mid 1790s Williamson switched his land speculative focus from the west to the project with George Washington and Thomas Jefferson. The plan was to develop the northeastern counties of North Carolina that bordered Virginia, land that was referred to as the Great Dismal Swamp. The Dismal Swamp Company had a coterie of personnel, many of them slaves, drain the swamp lands and exploit the reclaimed soil. A canal system was envisioned, which today forms part of the modern inland waterway. To a degree, this was part of the fallout from the compromise, which located the seat of the government in Washington, D.C., at the mouth of the Potomac River. There are remnants of the canals in Foggy Bottom, Washington D.C., which was envisioned to be the center of a canal-based transportation system.

During Williamson's years in New York he remained interested in land speculation and real estate. Under two pseudonyms he boosted the idea of building a canal to connect the waters of Lake Erie with the Hudson River, a project that was consummated in 1823.

In the *French Observer*, Archibald McLean reported that Williamson was sometimes abrupt and rude to those who did not command his respect.[15] One of Williamson's most awkward assignments was serving as a delegate, or ambassador without portfolio, to the Continental Congress. When the new constitution was put in place, North Carolina had not signed it. Governor Johnston wrote to Williamson on February 19, 1789, "I shall not withstanding hope that you will still consider yourself a confidential servant of the State, that you will occasionally communicate to me every matter of public nature which you may consider this State to be interested in which may come to your attention."[16] Williamson did stay but the situation became problematic when George Washington was inaugurated on April 30, 1789, an inauguration that Williamson attended.

The two states that had not ratified the Constitution, Rhode Island and North Carolina, technically could have imported goods and been taxed by the eleven states that had ratified the Constitution. Williamson did the arithmetic and showed how deleterious that would be to North Carolina. North Carolina did join the Union but not in time to attend the first Congress. When North Carolina ratified the Constitution, Williamson was in the first House of Representatives attending the second session. Hamilton saw the need to get a southern leader on his side for dealing with the cession issue, which he had proposed. While Williamson served in Congress, the bill fixing the seat of government in what was called Washington City passed on July 16 and the funding and assumption bill on August 4, 1790. Williamson supported Hamilton's American policy when the excise tax for raising revenue was presented. A tax on whiskey was also put forward, which eventually led to the Whiskey Rebellion in Pennsylvania in 1794.

Williamson's travel and peripatetic movement and involvement in many activities precluded developing romantic attachments. When he and the Rev. Ewing were in England soliciting funds for the Newark Academy, Ewing returned to the colonies and Williamson stayed on in England to woo the wealthy widow in Scotland. At the time when the Congress met in Annapolis, Maryland, Williams wrote William Blount,

> The Acco^{t} given of the beauties of this City was not exaggerated. There really are several lovely girls here, a younger man perhaps would call them Angels, and to their faces I believe I may have said as much; but when a man commits it to Paper, more familiar Epithets may express his Ideas. In fact I have seen no women in Philad^{a} near so pretty.
>
> (Letter Hugh Williamson to William Blount, Annapolis 5th Decr 1783)[17]

At the age of fifty-three, while a representative in Congress from North Carolina, Hugh Williamson married Maria Apthorp, daughter of the Honorable Charles Ward Apthorp, a wealthy New York attorney and landowner. Their wedding was described as one that "adds to the gayeties of New York Society"[18]; Williamson's colleagues, however, viewed the union with a bit of humor. John Dawson, a Virginia congressman, noted in a letter, "Williamson from North Carolina was married a few days since to a Miss Aptho[r]p, a beautiful girl about twenty two. She appears much pleased with her bargain—may she never repent."[19] Williamson's family is mentioned in correspondence to John Gray Blount in Washington from A. C. Thomas from New York dated October 19, 1789. In the letter, which is concerned primarily with financial matters, is the statement that "Doctor W. is [a father] as you may See by the inclosed." The enclosed note by Hugh Williamson to Colonel Thomas says that on "Sunday Morning at 11 O'Clock: Mrs. Williamson has about an Hour ago brought me a Son. She is in good spirits & the Child perfectly well."[20] A second son was born in October 1789.

Williamson's anticipated retirement from public life to the enjoyment of family life was not to be. Maria Apthorp Williamson died October 20, 1790, shortly after the birth of their second child.[21] In a letter to James McEvers from Philadelphia July 23, 1791, Williamson, contemplating a picture likeness of his wife, wrote, "I could make a strong likeness of her in my minds eye" and in discussing his son noted that "only a mother could have cherished him more than the aunts that were now raising him."[22]

He was to outlive both of his sons. Charles Apthorp Williamson, age twenty-one years and four months, died in 1811. A law student, living at 160 Greenwich Street, he had an eight-day fever. Complaining of pain in the legs, he took a bath to relieve his discomfort and was found dead in the bathtub by Dr. Williamson.[23] The second son, John, died on November 19, 1815, after an illness of about eight days.[24] Williamson tried to assuage some of his grief through pursuits in literature and philosophy but attained, at best, only partial relief.

Williamson's intellectual faculties remained sharp and vigorous to the end of his life. On May 22, 1819, at the age of eighty-three, he died suddenly while riding in a carriage with Maria van den Heuvel Hamilton, his wife's niece and namesake, and the wife of John C. Hamilton, son of Alexander Hamilton. Williamson had been particularly fond of this niece, who looked like his wife, and he willed his property to her. His funeral was held at the home of John Cornelius van den Heuvel at 229 Broadway. Considered a member of the Apthorp family, he was buried in their vault in New York City's Trinity Church Graveyard in Manhattan, near the remains of Alexander Hamilton, with whom he had collaborated in framing the federal Constitution.

Delbert Gilpatrick, in the *North Carolina Historical Review*, noted:

Williamson the Man

Few men in their lifetime have had as many different occupations as Williamson. He appears in the roles of Presbyterian minister, professor of mathematics, physician, writer on scientific, literary, and historical subjects, legislator and constitution maker, merchant, active patron of education, and advocate of internal improvement. About him in almost all of these capacities are to be found comments, friendly or unfriendly, by contemporaries.[25]

Perhaps the best epilogue for Williamson is the concluding paragraph from his address to the freemen of Edenton and County of Chowan, North Carolina, which resembles Benjamin Franklin's observation at the conclusion of the Constitutional Convention, on the product created by the convention:

> But it is a government, unless I am greatly mistaken, that gives the fairest promise of being firm and honourable; safe from foreign invasion or domestick sedition: A government, by which our commerce must be protected and enlarged; the value of our produce and of our lands must be increased; the labourer and mechanick must be encouraged and supported. It is a form of government that is perfectly fitted for protecting liberty and property, and for cherishing the good citizen and the honest man.[26]

Appendix A

"Remarks on the New Plan of Government"

Hugh Williamson

Hugh Williamson was a member of the Continental Congress and North Carolina delegate to the Federal Convention; he served in the House of Representatives from 1789 to 1793. This speech was printed in three installments over 25, 26, and 27 February 1788. During 1788 a version of the "Remarks" was also published in the *State Gazette of North Carolina*, New Bern, as well as in Pennsylvania, South Carolina, and Massachusetts.

Daily Advertiser, New York, 25–27 February 1788

Appendix A

The following Remarks on the New Plan of Government are handed us as the substance of Doctor WILLIAMSON*'s Address to the Freemen of Edenton and the County of Chowan, in North-Carolina, when assembled to instruct their Representatives.*

Though I am conscious that a subject of the greatest magnitude must suffer in the hands of such an advocate, I cannot refuse, at the request of my fellow-citizens, to make some observations on the new Plan of Government.

It seems to be generally admitted, that the system of Government which has been proposed by the late Convention, is well calculated to relieve us from many of the grievances under which we have been laboring. If I might express my particular sentiments on this subject, I should describe it as more free and more perfect than any form of government that ever has been adopted by any nation; but I would not say it has no faults. Imperfection is inseparable from every human device. Several objections were made to this system by two or three very respectable characters in the Convention, which have been the subject of much conversation;[1] and other objections, by citizens of this State, have lately reached our ears. It is proper that you should consider of these objections. They are of two kinds; they respect the things that are in the system, and the things that are not in it. We are told that there should have been a section for securing a Trial by Jury in Civil cases, and the Liberty of the Press: that there should also have been a declaration of rights.

In the new system it is provided, that "*The Trial of all crimes*, except in cases of Impeachment," *shall be by Jury*, but this provision could not possibly be extended to all *Civil* cases. For it is well known that the Trial by Jury is not general and uniform throughout the United States, either in cases of Admiralty or of Chancery; hence it became necessary to submit the question to the General Legislature, who might accommodate their laws on this occasion to the desires and habits of the nation. Surely there is no prohibition in a case that is untouched.

We have been told that the Liberty of the Press is not secured by the New Constitution. Be pleased to examine the plan, and you will find that the Liberty of the Press and the laws of Mahomet are equally affected by it. The New Government is to have the power of protecting literary property; the very power which you have by a special act delegated to the present Congress. There was a time in England, when neither book, pamphlet, nor paper could be published without a licence from Government. That restraint was finally removed in the year 1694 and by such removal, their press became perfectly free, for it is not under the restraint of any licence. Certainly the new Government can have no power to impose restraints. The citizens of the United States have no more occasion for a second Declaration of Rights, than they have for a section in favor of the press. Their rights, in the several States, have long since been explained and secured by particular declarations, which make a part of their several Constitutions. It is granted, and perfectly understood, that under the Government of the Assemblies of the States, and under the Government of the congress, every right it reserved to the individual, which he has not expressly delegated to this, or that Legislature. The other objections that have been made to the new plan of Government, are: That it absorbs the power of the several States: That the national Judiciary is too extensive: That a standing army is permitted: That Congress is allowed to regulate trade: That the several States are prevented from taxing exports, for their own benefit.

When Gentlemen are pleased to complain, that little power is left in the hands of the separate States; they should be advised to cast an eye upon the large code of laws, which have passed in this State since the peace. Let them consider how few of those laws have been framed, for the general benefit of the Nation. Nine out of ten of them, are domestic; calculated for the sole use of this State, or of particular citizens. There must still be use for such laws, though you should enable the Congress to collect a revenue for National purposes, and the collection of that revenue includes the chief of the new powers, which are now to be committed to the Congress.

Hitherto you have delegated certain powers to the Congress, and other powers to the Assemblies of the States. The portion that you have delegated to Congress is found to have been useless, because it is too small, and the powers that are committed to the assemblies of the several States, are also found to be absolutely ineffectual for national purposes, because they can never be so managed as to operate in concert. Of what use is that small portion of reserved power? It neither makes you respectable nor powerful. The consequence of such reservation is national contempt abroad, and a state of dangerous weakness at home. What avails the claim of power, which appears to be nothing better than the empty whistling of a name? The Congress will be chosen by yourselves, as your Members of Assembly are. They will be creatures of your hands, and subject to your advice. Protected and cherished by the small addition of power which you shall put into their hands, you may become a great and respectable nation.

It is complained that the powers of the national Judiciary are too extensive.[2] This objection appears to have the greatest weight in the eyes of gentlemen who have not carefully compared the powers which are to be delegated with those that had been formerly delegated to Congress. The powers that are now to be committed to the national Legislature, as they are detailed in the 8th section of the first article, have already been chiefly delegated to the Congress under one form or another, except those which are contained in the first paragraph of that section. And the objects that are now to be submitted to the Supreme Judiciary, or to the Inferior Courts, are those which naturally arise from the constitutional laws of Congress. If there is a single new case that can be exceptionable, it is that between a foreigner and a citizen, or that between the citizens of different

States. These cases may come up by appeal. It is provided in this system that there shall be no fraudulent tender in the payments of debts. Foreigners, with whom we have treaties, will trust our citizens on the faith of this engagement. And the citizens of different States will do the same. If the Congress had a negative on the laws of the several States, they would certainly prevent all such laws as might endanger the honor or peace of the nation, by making a tender of base money; but they have no such power, and it is at least possible that some State may be found in this Union, disposed to break the Constitution, and abolish private debts by such tenders. In these cases the Courts of the offending States would probably decide according to its own laws. The foreigner would complain; and the nation might be involved in war for the support of such dishonest measures. Is it not better to have a Court of Appeals in which the Judges can only be determined by the laws of the nation? This Court is equally to be desired by the citizens of different States. But we are told that justice will be delayed, and the poor will be drawn away by the rich to a distant Court. The authors of this remark have not fully considered the question, else they must have recollected that the poor of this country have little to do with foreigners, or with the citizens of distant States. They do not consider that there may be an Inferior Court in every State; nor have they recollected that the appeals being *with such exceptions*, and *under such regulations* as Congress shall make, will never be permitted for trifling sums, or under trivial pretences, unless we can suppose that the national Legislature shall be composed of knaves and fools. The line that separates the powers of the national Legislature from those of the several States is clearly drawn. The several States reserve every power that can be exercised for the particular use and comfort of the State. They do not yield a single power which is not purely of a national concern; nor do they yield a single power which is not absolutely necessary to the safety and prosperity of the nation, nor one that could be employed to any effect in the hands of particular States. The powers of Judiciary naturally arise from those of the Legislature. Questions that are of a national concern, and those cases which are determinable by the general laws of the nation, are to be referred to the national Judiciary, but they have not any thing to do with a single case either civil or criminal, which respects the private and particular concerns of a State or its citizens.

The possibility of keeping regular troops in the public service has been urged as another objection against the new Constitution. It is very remarkable that the same objection has not been made against the original Confederation, in which the same grievance obtained without the same guards. It is now provided, that no appropriation of money for the use of the army shall be for a longer time than two years. Provision is also made for having a powerful militia, in which case there never can be occasion for many regular troops. It has been objected in some of the Southern States, that the Congress, by a majority of votes, is to have the power to regulate trade. It is universally admitted that Congress ought to have this power, else our commerce, which is nearly ruined, can never be restored; but some gentlemen think that the concurrence of two thirds of the votes in Congress should have been required. By the sundry regulations of commerce, it will be in the power of Government not only to collect a vast revenue for the general benefit of the nation, but to secure the carrying trade in the hands of citizens in preference to strangers. It has been alledged that there are few ships belonging to the Southern States, and that the price of freight must rise in consequence of our excluding many foreign vessels: but when we have not vessels of our own, it is certainly proper that we should hire those of citizens in preference to strangers; for our revenue is promoted and the nation is strengthened by the profits that remain in the hands of citizens; we are injured by throwing it into the hands of strangers; and though the price of freight should rise for two or three years, this advantage is fully due to our brethren in the Eastern and middle States, who, with great and exemplary candor, have given us equal advantages in return. A small encrease in the price of freight would operate greatly in favor of the Southern States: it would promote the spirit of ship building; it would promote a nursery for native seamen, and would afford support to the poor who live near the sea coast; it would encrease the value of their lands, and at the same time it would reduce their taxes. It has finally been objected that the several States are not permitted to tax their exports for the benefit of their particular Treasuries. This strange objection has been occasionally repeated by citizens of this State. They must have transplanted it from another State, for it could not have been the growth of North-Carolina. Such have been the objections against the new Constitution.

Whilst the honest patriot, who guards with a jealous eye the liberties of his country, and apprehends danger under every form: the placeman in every State, who fears lest his office should pass into other hands; the idle, the factious, and the dishonest, who live by plunder or speculation on the miseries of their country; while these, assisted by a numerous body of secret enemies, who never have been reconciled to our Independence, are seeking for objections to this Constitution; it is a remarkable circumstance, and a very high encomium on the plan, that nothing more plausible has been offered against it; for it is an easy matter to find faults.

Let us turn our eyes to a more fruitful subject; let us consider the present condition of the United States, and the particular benefits that North Carolina must reap by the proposed form of Government. Without money, no Government can be supported; and Congress can raise no money under the present Constitution: They have not the power to make commercial treaties, because they cannot preserve them when made. Hence it is, that we are the prey of every nation: We are indulged in such foreign commerce, as must be hurtful to us: We are prohibited from that which might be profitable, and we are accordingly told, that on the last two years, the Thirteen States have hardly paid into the Treasury, as much as should have been paid by a single State. Intestine commotions in some of the States: Paper Money in others, a want of inclination in some, and a general suspicion throughout the Union, that the burthen is unequally laid; added to the general loss of trade have produced a general bankruptcy, and loss of honor. We have borrowed money of Spain—she demands the principal, but we cannot pay the interest. It is a circumstance perfectly humiliating, that we should remain under obligations to that nation: We are Considerably indebted to France but she is too generous to insist upon what she knows we cannot pay, either the principal or interest. In the hour of our distress, we borrowed money in Holland; not from the Government, but from private citizens. Those who are called the Patriots were our friends, and they are oppressed in their turn by hosts of enemies: They will soon have need of money: At this hour we are not able to pay the interests of their loan. What is to be done? Will you borrow money again from other citizens of that oppressed Republic, to pay the interest of what you borrowed from their brethren? This would be a painful expedient, but our want of Government may render it necessary. You have two or three Ministers abroad; they must soon return home, for they cannot be supported. You have four or five hundred troops scattered along the Ohio to protect the frontier inhabitants, and give some value to your lands; those troops are ill paid, and in a fair way for being disbanded. There is hardly a circumstance remaining; hardly one external mark by which you can deserve to be called a nation. You are not in a condition to resist the most contemptible enemy. What is there to prevent an Algerine Pirate from landing on your coast, and carrying your citizens into slavery? You have not a single sloop of war. Does one of the States attempt to raise a little money by imposts or other commercial regulations.—A neighboring State immediately alters her laws and defeats the revenue, by throwing the trade into a different channel. Instead of supporting or assisting, we are uniformly taking the advantage of one another. Such an assemblage of people are not a nation. Like a dark cloud, without cohesion or firmness, we are ready to be torn asunder and scattered abroad by every breeze of external violence, or internal commotion.

Is there a man in this State who believes it possible for us to continue under such a Government?—Let us suppose but for a minute, that such a measure should be attempted.—Let us suppose that the several States shall be required and obliged to pay their several quotas according to the original plan. You know that North-Carolina, on the last four years, has not paid one dollar into the Treasury for eight dollars that she ought to have paid. We must encrease our taxes exceedingly, and those taxes must be of the most grievous kind; they must be taxes on lands and heads; taxes that cannot fail to grind the face of the poor; for it is clear that we can raise little by imports and exports. Some foreign goods are imported by water from the Northern States, such goods pay a duty for the benefit of those States, which is seldom drawn back; this operates as a tax upon our citizens. On this side, Virginia promotes her revenue to the amount of 25,000 dollars every year, by a tax on our tobacco that she exports: South-Carolina on the other side, may avail herself of similar opportunities. Two thirds of the foreign goods that are consumed in this State are imported by land from Virginia or South-Carolina; such goods pay a certain impost for the benefit of the importing States, but our Treasury is not profited by this commerce. By such means our citizens are taxed more than one hundred thousand dollars every year, but the State does not receive credit for a shilling of that money. Like a patient that is bleeding at both arms, North-Carolina must soon expire under such wasteful operations. Unless I am greatly mistaken, we have seen enough of the State of the Union, and of North-Carolina in particular, to be assured that another form of Government is become necessary. Is the form now proposed well calculated to give relief? To this, we must answer in the affirmative. All foreign goods that shall be imported into these States, are to pay a duty for the use of the nation. All the States will be on a footing, whether they have bad ports or good ones. No duties will be laid on exports; hence the planter will receive the true value of his produce, wherever it may be shipped. If excises are laid on wine, spirits, or other luxuries, they must be uniform throughout the States. By a careful management of imposts and excises, the national expences may be discharged without any other species of tax; but if a poll-tax, or land-tax shall ever become necessary, the weight must press equally on every part of the Union. For in all cases, such taxes must be according to the number of inhabitants. Is it not a pleasing consideration that North-Carolina, under all her natural disadvantages, must have the same facility of paying her share of the public debt as the most favored, or the most fortunate State? She gains no advantage by this plan, but she recovers from her misfortunes. She stands on the same footing with her sister States, and they are too generous to desire that she should stand on lower ground. When you consider those parts of the new System which are of the greatest import—those which respect the general question of liberty and safety, you will recollect that the States in Convention were unanimous; and you must remember that some of the members of that body have risqued their lives in defence of liberty; but the system does not require the help of such arguments; it will bear the most scrupulous examination.

When you refer the proposed system to the particular circumstances of North-Carolina, and consider how she is to be affected by this plan; you must find the utmost reason to rejoice in the prospect of better times—this is a sentiment that I have ventured with the greater confidence, because it is the general opinion of my late Honorable Colleagues, and I have the utmost reliance in their superior abilities. But if our constituents shall discover faults where we could not see any, or if they shall suppose that a plan is formed for abridging their liberties when we imagined that we had been securing both liberty and property on a more stable foundation; if they perceive that they are to suffer a loss where we thought they must rise from a misfortune; they will at least do us the justice to charge those errors to the head, and not to the heart.

The proposed system is now in your hands, and with it the fate of your country. We have a common interest, for we are embarked in the same vessel. At present she is in a sea of troubles, without sails, oars, or pilot; ready to be dashed into pieces by every flaw of wind. You may secure a port, unless you think it better to remain at sea. If there is any man among you that wishes for troubled times and fluctuating measures, that he may live by speculations, and thrive by the calamities of the State; this Government is not for him.

And if there is any man who has never been reconciled to our Independence, who wishes to see us degraded and insulted abroad, oppressed by anarchy at home, and torn into pieces by factions; incapable of resistance and ready to become a prey to the first invader; this Government is not for him.

But it is a Government, unless I am greatly mistaken, that gives the fairest promise of being firm and honorable; safe from Foreign Invasion or Domestic Sedition. A Government by which our commerce must be protected and enlarged; the value of our produce and of our lands must be encreased; the labourer and the mechanic must be encouraged and supported. It is a form of Government that is perfectly fitted for protecting Liberty and Property, and for cherishing the good Citizen and the Honest Man.

Notes

1. This is apparently a reference to Elbridge Gerry, George Mason, and Edmund Randolph. See Storing [Herbert J. Storing, *The Complete Anti-Federalist* (Chicago: University of Chicago Press, 1981)], 2:1, 2:2, and 2:5. The objections of Mason and Gerry are also in Allen [W. B. Allen, *The Essential Anti-Federalist* (Lanham, MD: University Press of America, 1985)], 11–13 and 20–22, respectively.

2. See especially the criticisms by Brutus, Storing, 2:9, 130–96, and the Federal Farmer, Storing, 2:8, 183–95. For more on Brutus, see *Friends*, 182 n. 5. The exact identity of Federal Farmer, one of the ablest of the Anti-Federalists and quite popular, is unsettled. While Richard Henry Lee is generally thought to be the author, Storing is unconvinced. See the introduction to Storing, 2:8. Essays I, III, IV, V, XI, XII, and XV of Brutus are in Allen, 102–17, 201–23, and 269–74. Letters I, II, III, VII, VIII, IX, XII, and XVII of Federal Farmer are in Allen, 75–93, 177–201, and 261–69.

Appendix B

Publications by Hugh Williamson in the New York Historical Society

1. "Essays on the Constitution of the United States," 1865–1902, ed. Paul Leicester Ford, Brooklyn, New York Historical Printing Club.

2. "Remarks on the Importance of the Contemplated Grand Canal Between Lake Erie and the Hudson River."

3. *The Plea of the Colonies on the Charges Brought Against Them by Lord Mansfield and Others in a Letter to His Lordship*. Philadelphia, 1776; reprint, Robert Bell, 1777.

4. *The History of North Carolina* (microfilm). Philadelphia, Thomas Dobson; reprint, Philadelphia: Frye and Cammer, 1812.

5. *Observations on the Climate in Different Parts of America, Compared with the Climate in Corresponding Parts of the Other Continent: To Which Are Added, Remarks on the Different Complexions of the Human Race, with Some Account of the Aborigines of America,*

Being an Introductory Discourse to the History of North Carolina. 1794; New York: T & J Swords, 1811.

6. "Discourse on the Benefits of Civil History" (microfilm). Address delivered to the New York Historical Society, December 6, 1810.

7. *The Plain Dealer or Remarks upon Quaker-Politics and Their Attempts to Change the Government of Pennsylvania.* Nos.1–3. April 12, 1764, Philadelphia (copy in the American Philosophical Society Library).

8. "Of the Fascination of Serpents." Presentation to the American Philosophical Society. *American Medical Repository, and Review of American Publication on Surgery and the Auxiliary Branches* 10 (1807).

9. "An Attempt to Account for the Change of climate which has been Observed in the Middle Colonies of North America." *Transactions of the American Philosophical Society*. Vol 1 (1769–77), Appendix 1. Read August 17, 1770 before the society.

10. "An Essay on the Use of Comets and Their Luminous Appearances, with Some Conjecture Concerning the Origin of Heat." *Transactions of the American Philosophical Society*. Vol. 1 (1769–77). Read November 16, 1770.

11. "Experiments and Observations on the Gymnotiuc electicus or the Electric Eel." With Benjamin Franklin and John Hunter. *The Philosophical Transactions of the Royal Society of London*. Vol. 22 (1775).

12. "Letters of Sylvius." *Historical Papers of Trinity College* (1911).

13. "A Plea of the Colonies on Charges Brought against them by Lord Mansfield in a Letter to His Lordship." 1775, London.

Notes

Preface

1. George Sheldon and Mary Jane Kagarise, "John Hunter and the American School of Surgery," *Journal of Trauma, Injury, Infection and Critical Care* 44 (1998): 13–40.

2. Hugh Williamson, *The History of North Carolina*, 2 vols. (Philadelphia: Thomas Dobson, 1812).

3. A. Roger Ekirch, *Poor Carolina: Politics and Society in Colonial North Carolina, 1729–1776* (Chapel Hill: University of North Carolina Press, 1981), xviii–xix.

4. Harold Holzer, *Lincoln at Cooper Union: The Speech That Made Abraham Lincoln President* (New York: Simon & Schuster, 2004).

Prologue: "He Was No Ordinary Man"

1. John Washington Neal, "Life and Public Services of Hugh Williamson," *Historical Papers of the Trinity College Historical Society* 13 (1919): 111.

Chapter 1: Early Years

1. Hugh F. Rankin, *North Carolina in the American Revolution* (Raleigh: North Carolina Division of Archives and History, 1959), 22–23.

2. David Hosack, *Biographical Memoir of Hugh Williamson, M.D., LL.D.* (New York: New York Historical Society, 1820), 20.

3. *Pennsylvania Gazette*, November 24, 1743.

4. Hosack, *Biographical Memoir*, 17.

5. John Washington Neal, "Life and Public Services of Hugh Williamson," *Historical Papers of the Trinity College Historical Society* 13 (1919): 62.

6. Archives of University of Pennsylvania, Philadelphia, http://aechives.upenn.edu/histy/features/1700s/students1757.html (accessed March 19, 2009).

7. Register of Wills and Clerk of the Orphans Court, County of Cumberland, Pennsylvania, Will Book A, 43–44.

8. Hosack, *Biographical Memoir*, 18–19.

9. Ibid., 20.

10. Hosack, *Biographical Memoir*, 21.

11. Ibid., 22.

12. Louis Potts, "The Poor Man's Franklin and the National Domain," *North Carolina Historical Review* 64, no. 4 (1987): 374.

13. Carl Bridenbaugh and Jessica Bridenbaugh, *Rebels and Gentlemen: Philadelphia in the Age of Franklin* (New York: Oxford University Press, 1968), 122–23.

14. Ibid., 121.

15. Ibid., 117.

Chapter 2: Scientist

1. Robert G. Ferris, ed., *Signers of the Constitution* (Washington, DC: United States Department of the Interior National Park Service, 1976), 219.

2. Hugh F. Rankin, *North Carolina in the American Revolution* (Raleigh: North Carolina Division of Archives and History, 1959), 23.

3. Brooke Hindle, *The Pursuit of Science in Revolutionary America, 1735–1789* (Chapel Hill: University of North Carolina Press, 1956), 91.

4. Ibid., 189.

5. Ibid., 153.

6. Carl Bridenbaugh and Jessica Bridenbaugh, *Rebels and Gentlemen: Philadelphia in the Age of Franklin* (New York: Oxford University Press, 1968), 343.

7. Ibid., 355.

8. Hindle, *The Pursuit of Science*, 172–73.

9. David Hosack, *Biographical Memoir of Hugh Williamson, M.D., LL.D.* (New York: New York Historical Society, 1820), 41–42.

10. Peter L. Bernstein, *Wedding of the Waters: The Erie Canal and the Making of a Great Nation* (New York: W. W. Norton, 2005), 203–10.

11. Charles Royster, *The Fabulous History of the Dismal Swamp Company: A Story of George Washington's Times* (New York: Alfred A. Knopf, 1999), 299–302.

12. Hindle, *The Pursuit of Science,* 372.

13. Hugh Williamson to American Philosophical Society, Annapolis, May 24, 1784, library 7, American Philosophical Society, Philadelphia (quoted with permission).

14. Royster, *The Fabulous History of the Dismal Swamp Company*, 299–301.

15. Ibid., 299–301.

16. J. W. Francis, *Old New York: A Reminiscence of the Past Sixty Years* (New York: W. T. Middleton, 1868), 98; Bernstein, *Wedding of the Waters*, 109.

17. *Early Proceedings of the American Philosophical Society*, vol. 81, archives, American Philosophical Society, Philadelphia.

18. Williamson to Jefferson, New York, May 10, 1803, *Papers of Thomas Jefferson*, Library of Congress.

19. Louis W. Potts, "The Poor Man's Franklin and the National Domain," *North Carolina Historical Review* 64, no. 4 (1987): 392–93.

20. Hindle, *The Pursuit of Science,* 208–209.

21. Ibid., 181.

22. Martin Brian Schiffer, *Draw the Lightning Down: Benjamin*

Franklin and Electrical Technology in the Age of Enlightenment (Berkeley: University of California Press, 2003), 50–51.

23. Wendy Moore, *The Knife Man* (New York: Transworld Publishers, 2005), 260–61.

24. Ibid., 260.

25. 65: 94–101, cited in Hindle, *The Pursuit of Science,* 300.

26. "Of the Fascination of Serpents," *American Medical Repository, and Review of American Publication on Surgery and the Auxiliary Branches*, 10 (February–April 1807): 341–48.

27. Minutes of the North Carolina House of Commons, *The Colonial and State Records of North Carolina*, ed. William Saunders and Walter Clark, 26 vols. (Raleigh: State of North Carolina, 1895– 1907), 17: 280, 24: 747–48, Documenting the American South, University Library, University of North Carolina at Chapel Hill, 2007, http://docsouth.unc.edu/csr/index.html/document/csr01-0061.

28. Bernstein, *Wedding of the Waters,* 47.

29. Charles A. Miller, *Jefferson and Nature* (Baltimore: Johns Hopkins University Press, 1993), 50–52.

Chapter 3: Revolutionary War Spy

1. Stephen F. Knott, *Secret and Sanctioned: Covert Operations and the American Presidency* (New York: Oxford University Press, 1996), 21.

2. Burton Craige, *The Federal Convention of 1787: North Carolina in the Great Crisis* (Richmond, VA: Archibald Craige), 1987, 133.

3. H. W. Brands, *The First American: The Life and Times of Benjamin Franklin* (New York: Anchor Books, 2000), 452–55.

4. Samuel Adams, *The Writings of Samuel Adams*, 1773–1777, ed. Harry Alonzo Cushing (New York: G. P. Putnam's Sons, 1907), 45–46.

5. Benjamin Franklin, *The Papers of Benjamin Franklin*, 39 vols., ed. Leonard Woods Labaree, Whitfield J. Bell Jr., William Bradford Willcox, et al. (New Haven: Yale University Press, 1959–), 1: 125.

6. Adams, *The Writings of Samuel Adams*, 76.

7. Craige, *The Federal Convention of 1787,* 133.

8. *The Evening Post*, July 24, 1821, p. 2; David Hosack, *Biographical Memoir of Hugh Williamson, M.D., LL. D.* (New York: New York Historical Society, 1820), 125.

9. Hosack, *Biographical Memoir*, 50–51.

10. Louis W. Potts, "The Poor Man's Franklin and the National Domain," *North Carolina Historical Review* 64, no. 4 (1987): 375.

11. Adams, *The Writings of Samuel Adams,* 40–41.

12. Carl Van Doren, *Benjamin Franklin* (New York: Viking Press, 1938), 312.

13. David T. Morgan, *The Devious Dr. Franklin, Colonial Agent: Benjamin Franklin's Years in London* (Macon, GA: Mercer University Press, 1996), 218.

14. John Washington Neal, "Life and Public Services of Hugh Williamson," *Historical Papers of the Trinity College Historical Society* 13 (1919): 65.

15. Ibid., 66.

16. Helen Jenkins, "The Versatile Dr. Hugh Williamson" (master's thesis, University of North Carolina, 1950), 32, 37.

17. Beverly McAnear, "The Raising of Funds by the Colonial Colleges," *Mississippi Valley Historical Review* 38, no. 4 (1952): 591–611.

18. Ibid.

19. Lucy E. Lee Ewing, *Dr. John Ewing and Some of His Noted Connections* (Philadelphia: Allen, Lane and Scott, 1924), 8.

20. Ibid., 22.

21. J. M. Flavell, "Lord North's Conciliatory Proposal and the Patriots in London," *English Historical Review*, April 1992: 302–22.

22. Ibid., 302–22.

23. Ibid., 310.

24. Franklin, *Papers*, 23: 23.

Chapter 4: Continental Congress and Secret Committees

1. Stephen F. Knott, *Secret and Sanctioned: Covert Operations and the American Presidency* (New York: Oxford University Press, 1996), 14–15.

2. Ibid., 120; Alexander Rose, *Washington's Spies: The Story of America's First Spy Ring* (New York: Bantam Dell, 2006), 25.

3. Burton Craige, *The Federal Convention of 1787: North Carolina in the Great Crisis* (Richmond, VA: Archibald Craige, 1987), 135; David T. Morgan, *The Devious Dr. Franklin, Colonial Agent: Benjamin Franklin's Years in London,* 218; David Hosack, *Biographical Memoir of Hugh Williamson, M.D., LL. D.* (New York: New York Historical Society, 1820), 39.

4. Stacey Schiff, *A Great Improvisation: Franklin, France, and the Birth of America* (New York: Henry Holt, 2005), 171.

5. John Jay, *John Jay: Unpublished Papers*, ed. Richard B. Morris (New York: Harper & Row, 1975), vol. 1, *The Making of a Revolutionary, 1745–1780*, 195

6. Ibid., 325–30.

7. Julian P. Boyd, "Silas Deane: Death by a Kindly Teacher of Treason," part 1, *William and Mary Quarterly*, 3rd series, 16 (1959): 165–87.

8. Ibid., 186.

9. Benjamin Franklin, *The Papers of Benjamin Franklin*, 39 vols., ed. Leonard Woods Labaree, Whitfield J. Bell Jr., William Bradford Willcox, et al. (New Haven, CT: Yale University Press, 1959–), 23: 50.

10. H. W. Brands, *The First American: The Life and Times of Benjamin Franklin* (New York: Anchor Books, 2000), 522.

11. Ibid., 609.

12. Boyd, "Silas Deane,"186.

13. Ibid., 186.

14. Franklin, *Papers*, 23: 50.

15. Letter to the Committee on Secret Correspondence to the Americans, cited in Franklin, *Papers*, 23: 50.

16. Franklin, *Papers*, 23: 50.

17. John Fothergill, *Chain of Friendship: Selected Letters of Dr. John Fothergill of London, 1735–1780* (Cambridge, MA: Belknap Press, 1971), 472.

18. Ibid., 472.

19. Quoted from Charles Francis Adams, *Life and Works of John Adams*, in John Washington Neal, "Life and Public Services of Hugh Williamson," *Historical Papers of the Trinity College Historical Society* 13 (1919): 67.

20. Letter to John Mease, February 11, 1778, cited in Neal, "Life and Public Services,"112.

Chapter 5: The War for Independence in North Carolina

1. Marjoleine Kars, *Breaking Loose Together: The Regulator Rebellion in Pre-Revolutionary North Carolina* (Chapel Hill: University of North Carolina Press, 2002), 9–27.

2. Memory F. Mitchell, *North Carolina Signers: Brief Sketches of the Men Who Signed the Declaration of Independence and the Constitution* (Raleigh: Historical Publications Section, North Carolina Division of Archives and History, 1980), 3.

3. David Ramsay, M.D., and Lester H. Cohen, *The History of the American Revolution* (Indianapolis: Liberty Fund, 1990), 1: 237.

4. Catherine S. Crary, *The Price of Loyalty* (New York: McGraw-Hill, 1973), 50.

5. Henry Lee, *Memoirs of the War in the Southern Department of the United States* (New York: University Publishing, 1869); reprinted as *The American Revolution in the South* (New York: Arno Press, 1969): 170–90.

6. Blackwell P. Robinson, *William R. Davie* (Chapel Hill: University of North Carolina Press, 1957), 151.

7. Helen Jenkins, "The Versatile Dr. Hugh Williamson" (master's thesis, University of North Carolina, 1950), 38–39.

8. Ramsay and Cohen, *The History of the American Revolution*, 38–39.

Chapter 6: The Revolutionary War Moves South

1. Justin Winsor, ed., *The American Revolution: A Narrative, Critical and Bibliographical History* (New York: Land's End Press, 1972), 548.

2. Ibid., 473.

3. John Buchanan, *The Road to Guilford Courthouse: The American Revolution in the Carolinas* (New York: John Wiley & Sons, 1997), 151–53.

4. H. L. Landers, *The Battle of Camden, South Carolina, August 16, 1780* (Washington, DC: U.S. Government Printing Office, 1929; reprint, 1997), 1–63.

5. Craig L. Symonds with cartography by William J. Clipson, *A Battlefield Atlas of the American Revolution* (Mount Pleasant, SC: Nautical & Aviation Publishing Company of America, 1986), 87.

6. David Ramsay, M.D., and Lester H. Cohen, *The History of the American Revolution* (Indianapolis, IN: Liberty Fund, 1990), 76.

7. Gen. Richard Caswell to Gov. Abner Nash, Camp, Ancrum's Plantation, July 31, 1780, *The Colonial and State Records of North Carolina*, ed. William Saunders and Walter Clark, 26 vols. (Raleigh: State of North Carolina, 1895–1907), 15: 11, Documenting the American South, University Library, University of North Carolina at Chapel Hill, 2007, http://docsouth.unc.edu/csr/index.html/document/csr15–0009 (accessed March 18, 2009).

8. Ramsay and Cohen, *The History of the American Revolution*, 489–93.

9. Gen. Richard Caswell to Gov. Abner Nash, Salisbury, August

19, 1780, Thomas Addison Emmet Collection (1757–1847), PC.38, State Archives of North Carolina, Raleigh.

10. Dr. Hugh Williamson to Hon. Thomas Benbury, speaker of the House of Commons of the Assembly of North Carolina, Edenton, December 1, 1780, *Colonial and State Records*, 15: 701, http://docsouth.unc.edu/csr/index.html/document/csr15–0121 (accessed March 18, 2009).

11. Hugh Williamson to unknown recipient, Camden, August 1780, *Colonial and State Records*, 15: 166, http://docsouth.unc.edu/csr/index.html/document/csr15–0121 (accessed March 18, 2009), cited in John Washington Neal, "Life and Public Services of Hugh Williamson," *Historical Papers of the Trinity College Historical Society* 13 (1919): 69.

12. Hugh Williamson to Lord Charles Cornwallis, Camden, August 1786, *Colonial and State Records*, 22: 530, http://docsouth.unc.edu/csr/index.html/document/csr15–0121 (accessed March 18, 2009).

13. Hugh Williamson to [Richard?] England, Camden, August 30, 1780, cited in Neal, "Life and Public Services of Hugh Williamson," 70.

14. Neal, "Life and Public Services," 70.

15. Williamson to Benbury, *Colonial and State Records*, 15: 701, http://docsouth.unc.edu/csr/index.html/document/csr15–0121 (accessed March 18, 2009), cited in Neal, "Life and Public Services," 69.

16. Ibid.

17. Neal, "Life and Public Services of Hugh Williamson," 70.

18. Hugh Williamson to Richard Bland Lee, New York, May 19, 1810, cited in Henry Lee, *Memoirs of the War in the Southern Depart-*

ment of the United States (New York: University Publishing, 1869); reprinted as *The American Revolution in the South* (New York: Arno Press, 1969): 586–87.

19. Samuel A. Ashe, *Biographical History of North Carolina* (Greensboro, NC: Van Noppen, 1906), 461–62.

20. Hugh Williamson to Thomas Burke, Halifax, July 5, 1781, *Colonial and State Records*, 15: 507–508, http://docsouth.unc.edu/csr/index.html/document/csr15–0031 (accessed March 19, 2009).

21. Neal, "Life and Public Services of Hugh Williamson," 70.

22. Hugh Talmage Lefler and Albert Ray Newsome, *The History of a Southern State*, 3rd ed. (Chapel Hill: University of North Carolina Press, 1973), 254–55.

23. Ibid., 256.

Chapter 7: State and National Legislator

1. Memory F. Mitchell, *North Carolina Signers: Brief Sketches of the Men Who Signed the Declaration of Independence and the Constitution* (Raleigh: Historical Publications Section North Carolina Division of Archives and History, 1980), 26.

2. Hugh Williamson to Gov. Alexander Martin, Philadelphia, November 1792, Thomas Addison Emmet Collection (1757–1847), PC.38, State Archives of North Carolina, Raleigh.

3. John Jay, *John Jay: Unpublished Papers*, ed. Richard B. Morris (New York: Harper & Row, 1980), vol. 2, *The Winning of the Peace, 1780–1784*, 523.

4. Hugh Williamson to Benjamin Franklin, Philadelphia, August 7, 1782, Library of the American Philosophical Society, Philadelphia.

5. William Bell Clark, *Ben Franklin's Privateers: A Naval Epic of the American Revolution* (Baton Rouge, LA: Louisiana State University Press, 1956), 10–11.

6. Ibid., 72, 171.

7. Minutes of the North Carolina House of Commons, *The Colonial and State Records of North Carolina*, ed. William Saunders and Walter Clark, 26 vols. (Raleigh: State of North Carolina, 1895–1907), 17: 280, 285; 24:747–48.

8. Thomas Jefferson to Hugh Williamson, November 13, 1791, *Colonial and State Records*, 17: 410, http://docsouth.unc.edu/csr/index.html/document/csr15–0031 (accessed March 18, 2009).

9. Minutes of the North Carolina House of Commons, 17: 411.

10. Boyd, "Silas Deane: Death by a Kindly Teacher of Treason," part 1, *William and Mary Quarterly*, 3rd series, 16 (1959): 165–87.

11. Hugh Talmage Lefler and Albert Ray Newsome, *The History of a Southern State*, 3rd ed. (Chapel Hill: University of North Carolina Press, 1973), 274–75.

12. Louis W. Potts, "The Poor Man's Franklin and the National Domain," *North Carolina Historical Review* 64, no. 4 (1987): 371–93.

13. Ibid., 383–84.

14. Burton Craige, *The Federal Convention of 1787: North Carolina in the Great Crisis* (Richmond, VA: Archibald Craige, 1987), 143.

15. Ibid., 131.

Chapter 8: Williamson in the Continental Congress

1. Louis W. Potts, "The Poor Man's Franklin and the National Domain," *North Carolina Historical Review* 64, no. 4 (1987): 382.

2. Ibid., 382–83.

3. Ibid., 384.

4. Ibid., 385.

5. Ibid., 385–86.

6. Ibid., 372.

7. Ibid., 386.

8. *Journals of the Continental Congress*, ed. Worthington C. Ford et al. (Washington, DC, 1904–37), 26: 117–21 (see also Harold Holzer, *Lincoln at Cooper Union: The Speech That Made Abraham Lincoln President* [New York: Simon & Schuster, 2004], 126).

9. Burton Craige, *The Federal Convention of 1787: North Carolina in the Great Crisis* (Richmond, VA: Archibald Craige, 1987), 143–44.

10. Hugh Williamson to Thomas Jefferson, Trenton, December 11, 1784, Ford et al., *Journals of the Continental Congress*, 26: 624.

11. John Jay, *John Jay: Unpublished Papers*, ed. Richard B. Morris (New York: Harper & Row, 1980), vol. 2, *The Winning of the Peace, 1780–1784*, 719.

12. Charles A. Miller, *Jefferson and Nature: An Interpretation* (Baltimore: Johns Hopkins University Press, 1993), 230.

13. Thomas Jefferson to Hugh Williamson, April 1, 1792, *Papers of Continental Congress, January House of Representatives* (*JHR* 1: 525).

14. Hugh Williamson to Thomas Jefferson, New York, May 10, 1803, Thomas Jefferson Papers, Library of Congress, nos. 12606, 12614.

15. Carol Berkin, *A Brilliant Solution: Inventing the American Revolution* (New York: Harcourt, 2002), 22.

16. Hugh Talmage Lefler and Albert Ray Newsome, *The History of a Southern State*, 3rd ed. (Chapel Hill: University of North Carolina Press, 1973), 290.

17. Brian N. Morton and Donald C. Spinelli, *Beaumarchais and the American Revolution* (New York: Lexington Books, 2003), 294.

18. Ibid.

19. Ibid., ix–x.

Chapter 9: The Constitutional Convention

1. Burton Craige, *The Federal Convention of 1787: North Carolina in the Great Crisis* (Richmond, VA: Archibald Craige, 1987), 144–45.

2. Lindley S. Butler and Alan D. Watson, eds., *The North Carolina Experience: An Interpretive and Documentary History* (Chapel Hill: University of North Carolina Press, 1984), 152.

3. Catherine Drinker Bowen, *Miracle at Philadelphia: The Story of the Constitutional Convention, May to September, 1787* (Boston: Little, Brown, 1966), 238–39.

4. William Hogeland, *The Whiskey Rebellion: George Washington, Alexander Hamilton, and the Frontier Rebels Who Challenged America's Newfound Sovereignty* (New York: Scribner, 2006), 237–45.

5. Bowen, *Miracle at Philadelphia*, 11.

6. Hugh Talmage Lefler and Albert Ray Newsome, *The History of a Southern State*, 3rd ed. (Chapel Hill: University of North Carolina Press, 1973), 79.

7. Max Farrand, ed., *The Records of the Federal Convention of 1787* (New Haven, CT: Yale University Press, 1911), 58.

8. Carol Berkin, *A Brilliant Solution: Inventing the American Revolution* (New York: Harcourt, 2002), 66–67.

9. Ibid., 69.

10. Ibid., 116.

11. Ibid., 117.

12. Dorothy Twohig, ed., *The Journal of the Proceedings of the President, 1793–1797* (Charlottesville, VA: University Press of Virginia, 1981), 30, 96–97.

13. Farrand, *The Records of the Federal Convention of 1787*, 150–80.

14. Ibid., 427.

15. Stephen F. Knott, *Secret and Sanctioned: Covert Operations and the American Presidency* (New York: Oxford University Press, 1996), 45.

16. Farrand, *The Records of the Federal Convention of 1787*, 88.

17. Ibid., 301, 358, 386.

18. Bowen, *Miracle at Philadelphia*, 209.

19. "Letter of Sylvius," in series Letters to Freemen Inhabitants of the State of North Carolina, *American Museum*, August 1787; quoted in Helen Jenkins, "The Versatile Dr. Hugh Williamson" (master's thesis, University of North Carolina, 1950), 167.

20. Farrand, *The Records of the Federal Convention of 1787*, 59.

21. Ibid., 373.

22. Craige, *The Federal Convention of 1787*, 146.

23. Ibid., 148.

24. Bernard Bailyn, *To Begin the World Anew: The Genius and Ambiguities of the American Founders* (New York: Alfred A. Knopf, 2003), 53.

25. Craige, *The Federal Convention of 1787*, 148.

26. Bailyn, *To Begin the World Anew*, 33.

27. Craige, *The Federal Convention of 1787*, 147.

28. Robert G. Ferris, ed., *Signers of the Constitution*, Washington, DC: United States Department of the Interior National Park Service, 1976.51

29. H. W. Brands, *The First American: The Life and Times of Benjamin Franklin* (New York: Anchor Books, 2000), 678.

30. Lefler and Newsome, *The History of a Southern State*, 265–66.

31. Craige, *The Federal Convention of 1787: North Carolina in the Great Crisis*, 154.

32. Berkin, *A Brilliant Solution*, 135.

33. Ibid., 149.

34. Ibid., 155.

Chapter 10: The Struggle for Ratification of the Constitution

1. H. W. Brands, *The First American: The Life and Times of Benjamin Franklin* (New York: Anchor Books, 2000), 690.

2. Ibid., 689.

3. Ibid., 693.

4. Ibid., 691.

5. Hugh Talmage Lefler and Albert Ray Newsome, *The History of a Southern State*, 3rd ed. (Chapel Hill: University of North Carolina Press, 1973), 280–81.

6. Ibid., 280.

7. George Washington, *The Papers of George Washington*, ed. W. W. Abbot and Dorothy Twohig, 6 vols. (Charlottesville, VA: University Press of Virginia, 1987), vol. 5, *Colonial Papers August 1787*, 297, quoted in Joseph J. Ellis, *Founding Brothers*.

8. Lefler and Newsome, *The History of a Southern State*, 282.

9. Ibid., 283.

10. Lindley S. Butler and Alan D. Watson, eds., *The North Carolina Experience: An Interpretive and Documentary History* (Chapel Hill NC: University of North Carolina Press, 1984), 167.

11. Hugh Williamson to James Iredell, New York, July 26, 1788, Archives of Continental Congress, no. 917.

12. Ibid.

13. Butler and Watson, *The North Carolina Experience*, 284–85.

14. R. D. W. Connor, *A Documentary History of the University of North Carolina: 1796–1799* (Chapel Hill: University of North Carolina Press, 1953), 1:22.

15. Burton Craige, *The Federal Convention of 1787: North Carolina in the Great Crisis* (Richmond, VA: Archibald Craige, 1987), 155.

16. Butler and Watson, *The North Carolina Experience*, 153–57.

17. Lefler and Newsome, *The History of a Southern State,* 285.

18. New Hampshire State Papers, archives, Concord, NH, 21: 852.

19. Willis P. Whichard, *Justice James Iredell* (Durham, NC: Carolina Academic Press, 2000), 91.

20. Ibid., 288.

21. Lefler and Newsome, *The History of a Southern State,* 254–55.

22. Leonard D. White, *The Federalists: A Study in Administrative History* (New York: Macmillan, 1948), 256, 517.

Chapter 11: Educator

1. Richard Brookhiser, *Founding Father: Rediscovering George Washington* (New York: Free Press Paperbacks, 1996), 195.

2. Matthew H. Kaufman, *Medical Teaching in Edinburgh During the Eighteenth and Nineteenth Centuries* (Edinburgh: Royal College of Surgeons of Edinburgh, 2003), 47.

3. *Boston Post Boy*, October 19, 1767, supplement 1. From *Early American Newspapers, and Archive of Americana Collection*, published by Readex (Readex.com), a division of NewsBank, Inc.

4. Alyn Brodsky, *Benjamin Rush: Patriot and Physician* (New York: St. Martin's Press, 2004), 16–17.

5. "A Tradition of Excellence," http://www.ude/.edu/aboutus/history.html/ (accessed August 19, 2009).

6. The flyers, dated February 4, 1774, are the property of the Historical Society of Pennsylvania, Philadelphia.

7. Historical Society of Pennsylvania, Philadelphia, 64.

8. John Gray Blount, *The John Gray Blount Papers, 1764–1833*, 4 vols., ed. Alice Barnwell Keith, William H. Masterson, and David Morgan (Raleigh: North Carolina Department of Archives and History, 1952–1982) 1: 246.

9. *The State Records of North Carolina*, ed. Walter Clark (Raleigh: State of North Carolina, 1886), 24: 751–52, Documenting the American South, University Library, University of North Carolina at Chapel Hill, 2007, http://docsouth.unc.edu/csr/index.html/document/csr15–0031 (accessed March 18, 2009).

10. Blount, *The John Gray Blount Papers,* 4: 369.

11. Ibid., 1: 402.

12. University Archives and Records, Wilson Library, UNC, Chapel Hill, NC.

13. R. D. W. Connor, *A Documentary History of the University of North Carolina: 1796–1799* (Chapel Hill: University of North Carolina Press, 1953), 2: 449–50.

14. Ibid, 1: 74.

15. Ibid., 1: 99.

16. Ibid., 1: 153.

17. Ibid., 1: 94–95.

18. Kemp P. Battle, *History of the University of North Carolina* (Raleigh NC: Author, 1907), 1: 49–50.

19. Ibid., 54

20. Connor, *A Documentary History of the University of North Carolina: 1796–1799*, 1: 389.

21. Louis W. Potts, "The Poor Man's Franklin and the National Domain," *North Carolina Historical Review* 64, no. 4 (1987): 389.

22. Connor, *A Documentary History of the University of North Carolina: 1796–1799,* 1: 145.

Chapter 12: Entrepreneur

1. *State Gazette of North Carolina*, October 1, 1789.

2. Charles A. Beard, *An Economic Interpretation of the Constitution of the United States* (1935; reprint, New York: Free Press, 1986), 73–152.

3. John Gray Blount, *The John Gray Blount Papers, 1764–1833*, 4 vols., ed. Alice Barnwell Keith, William H. Masterson, and David Morgan (Raleigh: North Carolina Department of Archives and History, 1952–1982), 1: xv.

4. Buckner F. Melton, *The First Impeachment: The Constitution's Framers and the Case of Senator William Blount* (Macon, GA: Mercer University Press, 1998), 4.

5. Thomas P. Abernethy, *The South in the New Nation 1789-1819*, vol. 4 of *A History of the South*, ed. Wendell Holmes Stephenson and E. Merton Coulter (Baton Rouge: Louisiana State University Press, 1961), 5.

6. Thomas Perkins Abernethy, *The Burr Conspiracy* (New York: Oxford University Press, 1954), 274–75; Nancy Isenberg, *Fallen Founder: The Life of Aaron Burr* (New York: Viking Penguin, 2007), 337.

7. Nicholas Romayne to William Blount, 1797, *Annals of the Congress of the United States, 1789–1824* (Washington, DC, 1834–56), 2348, 2352.

8. "The Chisholm-Romayne Scheme," http://www.impeachment.blogspot.com/2004/07/chisholm-romayne-scheme_15.html (accessed August 19, 2009).

9. Blount, *John Gray Blount Papers,* 3: 278.

10. Ibid., 3: 131–32.

11. Ibid., 3: 152–53.

12. Ibid., 3: 163.

13. Melton, *The First Impeachment*, 99–103.

14. United States, Bureau of Rolls and Library, *Documentary History of the Constitution*, 5 vols. (Washington, DC, 1894–1905), 4: 678.

15. Louis W. Potts, "The Poor Man's Franklin and the National Domain,“ *North Carolina Historical Review* 64, no. 4 (1987): 387.

16. Blount, *John Gray Blount Papers*, 2: 473.

17. Ibid., 2: 281–82.

18. Abernethy, *The Burr Conspiracy*, 10; Joseph Wheelan, *Jefferson's Vendetta: The Pursuit of Aaron Burr and the Judiciary* (New York: Carroll & Graf, 2005), 110.

19. Potts, "The Poor Man's Franklin and the National Domain,“ 389–90.

20. Ibid., 389–90.

21. Ibid., 390.

22. William D. Patterson, *Beginnings of the American Rectangular Land Survey System 1784–1800* (Columbus: Ohio Historical Society, 1970), 38–39, 62–66.

23. Potts, "The Poor Man's Franklin and the National Domain," 312.

24. Blackwell P. Robinson, *William R. Davie* (Chapel Hill: University of North Carolina Press, 1957), 393.

25. *New York Daily Advertiser*, May 29, 1817. From *Early American Newspapers, an Archive of Americana Collection*, published by Readex (Readex.com), a division of NewsBook, Inc.

26. *Commercial Advertiser*, March 5, 1812. From *Early American Newspapers, an Archive of Americana Collection*, published by Readex (Readex.com), a division of NewsBook, Inc.

27. *The Columbian*, June 12, 1817. From *Early American Newspapers, an Archive of Americana Collection*, published by Readex (Readex.com), a division of NewsBook, Inc.

28. *The National Advocate*, January 17, 1816, p. 2. From *Early*

American Newspapers, an Archive of Americana Collection, published by Readex (Readex.com), a division of NewsBook, Inc.

29. *New York Gazette*, January 5, 1789, p. 2. From *Early American Newspapers, an Archive of Americana Collection*, published by Readex (Readex.com), a division of NewsBook, Inc.

30. "Discussion of Complexities of Estate Litigation Not Settled Until 1910," *New York Times*, July 31, 1910.

31. Ibid.

32. *City Gazette and Daily Advertiser*, June 11, 1799, p. 3. From *Early American Newspapers, an Archive of Americana Collection*, published by Readex (Readex.com), a division of NewsBook, Inc.

Chapter 13: Williamson the Man

1. Robert K. Wright, Jr., and Morris J. MacGregor, Jr., *Soldier-Statesmen of the Constitution* (Washington, DC: Center of Military History, United States Army, 1987), 126.

2. Burton Craige, *The Federal Convention of 1787: North Carolina in the Great Crisis*. (Richmond, VA: Archibald Craige, 1987), 15.

3. John Washington Neal, "Life and Public Services of Hugh Williamson," *Historical Papers of the Trinity College Historical Society* 13 (1919): 110–11.

4. Winthrop D. Jordan, *White over Black: American Attitudes toward the Negro, 1550–1812* (Chapel Hill: Published for the Institute of Early American History and Culture, Williamsburg, VA, by the University of North Carolina Press, 1968), 540.

5. Louis W. Potts, "The Poor Man's Franklin and the National Domain," *North Carolina Historical Review* 64, no. 4 (1987): 371.

6. Max Farrand, ed., *The Records of the Federal Convention of 1787*, 4 vols. (New Haven: Yale University Press, 1911), 2: 615.

7. Delbert Harold Gilpatrick, "Contemporary Opinion of Hugh Williamson," *North Carolina Historical Review* 17 (January 1940): 33.

8. James Thacher, *American Medical Biography or Memoirs of Eminent Physicians Who Have Flourished in America* (New York: Milford House, 1967), 195.

9. Ibid.

10. Potts, "The Poor Man's Franklin and the National Domain," Benjamin Franklin, *The Papers of Benjamin Franklin*, 39 vols., ed. Leonard W. Labaree, Whitfield J. Bell, Jr., William Bradford Willcox, et al. (New Haven, CT: Yale University Press, 1959–), 1: 374.

11. *Journals of the Continental Congress, 1774–1789*, ed. Worthington C. Ford et al. (Washington, DC, 1904–37), 7: 186, 371–373.

12. Hugh Williamson to Thomas Jefferson, New York, September 1801, Thomas Jefferson Papers, Library of Congress.

13. James Madison, *Papers*, ed. William Thomas Hutchinson, William M. E. Rachal, and Robert Allen Rutland (Chicago: University of Chicago Press, 1962).

14. John Gray Blount, *John Gray Blount Papers, 1764–1833*, 4 vols., ed. Alice Barnwell Keith, William H. Masterson, and David Morgan (Raleigh: North Carolina Department of Archives and History, 1952–1982), 3: 137.

15. Archibald McLean, *French Observer*, quoted in Gilpatrick, "Contemporary Opinion of Hugh Williamson," 33.

16. Gov. Samuel Johnston to Hugh Williamson, February 19, 1789, cited in Neal, *Life and Public Services*, 98.

17. Blount, *The John Gray Blount Papers,* 1: 135.

18. Rufus Wilmot Griswold, *The Republican Court; or, American Society in the Days of Washington* (1867), 102, quoted in Gilpatrick, "Contemporary Opinion of Hugh Williamson,"31.

19. John Dawson to James Madison, January 1789, Edmund C. Burnett, ed., *Letters of Members of the Continental Congress*, 8 vols. (Washington, DC: Government Printing Office, 1921–36), 7: 567.

20. Blount, *John Gray Blount Papers*, 1: 511–12.

21. Charles R. Hildeburn, "An index to the obituary notices published in the 'Pennsylvania Gazette' from 1728–1791," The Pennsylvania Magazine of History and Biography (1886) 10: 349.

22. Hugh Williamson to James McEvers, Philadelphia, July 23, 1791, Pennsylvania Historical Society.

23. *The Columbian*, March 20, 1811, p. 3. From *Early American Newspapers, an Archive of Americana Collection*, published by Readex (Readex.com), a division of NewsBook, Inc.

24. *The Centinel of Freedom*, November 21, 1815, p. 3. From *Early American Newspapers, an Archive of Americana Collection*, published by Readex (Readex.com), a division of NewsBook, Inc.

25. Gilpatrick, "Contemporary Opinion," 28.

26. *Salem Mercury*, August 5, 1788, p. 1. From *Early American Newspapers, an Archive of Americana Collection*, published by Readex (Readex.com), a division of NewsBook, Inc.

Bibliography

Aamon, Harry. *James Monroe: The Quest for National Identity*. 1971; reprint, Charlottesville, VA.: University Press of Virginia, 1990.

Abbot, W. W., ed. *The Papers of George Washington*. Charlottesville, VA.: University Press of Virginia, 1981.

Abernethy, Thomas Perkins. *The Burr Conspiracy*. New York: Oxford University Press, 1954.

Abernethy, Thomas P. *The South in the New Nation, 1789–1819*. Vol. 4 of *A History of the South*, ed. Wendell Holmes Stephenson and E. Merton Coulter. Baton Rouge, LA: Louisiana State University Press, 1961.

Adams, Charles Francis. *The Life and Works of John Adams*. Washington, DC: Ross and Perry, 2002.

Adams, Henry, and Earl N. Harbert, eds. *History of the United States of America During the Administrations of James Madison*. New York: Literary Classics of the United States, 1986.

Adams, Samuel. *The Writings of Samuel Adams, 1773–1777*. Ed. Harry Alonzo Cushing. New York: G. P. Putnam's Sons, 1907.

Bibliography

Allen, Thomas B. *George Washington, Spymaster: How the Americans Outspied the British and Won the Revolutionary War*. Washington, DC: National Geographic, 2004.

Ashe, Samuel A. *Biographical History of North Carolina*. Greensboro, NC: Van Noppen, 1906.

Bailyn, Bernard, ed. *The Debate on the Constitution: Federalist and Antifederalist Speeches, Articles, and Letters During the Struggle over Ratification*. Vol. 1: September 1787 to February 1788. New York: Library of America, 1993.

———. *The Ideological Origins of the American Revolution*. Enlarged ed. Cambridge, MA: Belknap Press, 1992.

———. *The Ordeal of Thomas Hutchinson*. Cambridge, MA: Belknap Press, 1974.

———. *To Begin the World Anew: The Genius and Ambiguities of the American Founders*. New York: Alfred A. Knopf, 2003.

Bakeless, John. *Turncoats, Traitors and Heroes: Espionage in the American Revolution*. New York: Da Capo Press, 1998.

Banning, Lance, ed. *Liberty and Order: The First American Party Struggle*. Indianapolis, IN: Liberty Fund, 2004.

Barnum, H. L. *The Spy Unmasked; Or, Memoirs of Enoch Crosby, Alias Harvey Birch, the Hero of James Fenimore Cooper's* The Spy. 1828; reprint, Harrison, NY: Harbor Hill Books, 1975.

Barton, David. *Benjamin Rush: Signer of the Declaration of Independence*. Aledo, TX: WallBuilder, 1999.

Battle, Kemp P. *History of the University of North Carolina*. 2 vols. Raleigh, NC: Author, 1907–12.

Beard, Charles A. *An Economic Interpretation of the Constitution of the United States*. 1935; reprint, New York: Free Press, 1986.

Bibliography

Berkin, Carol. *A Brilliant Solution: Inventing the American Revolution.* New York: Harcourt, 2002.

Bernstein, Peter L. *Wedding of the Waters: The Erie Canal and the Making of a Great Nation.* New York: W. W. Norton, 2005.

Bishop, Jim. *The Birth of the United States.* New York: William Morrow, 1976.

Blount, John Gray. *The John Gray Blount Papers.* Ed. Alice Barnwell Keith and William H. Masterson. 3 vols. Raleigh: North Carolina Department of Archives and History, 1952.

Boorstin, Daniel J. *The Americans: The Colonial Experience.* New York: Vintage Books, 1958.

———. *The Lost World of Thomas Jefferson.* Chicago: University of Chicago Press, 1981.

Bowen, Catherine Drinker. *Miracle at Philadelphia: The Story of the Constitutional Convention, May to September, 1787.* Boston: Little, Brown, 1966.

Bowling, Kenneth R., and Helen E. Weit, eds. *The Diary of William Maclay: And Other Notes on Senate Debates.* Documentary History of the First Federal Congress of the United States, ed. Charlene Bangs Bickford, vol. 9. Baltimore: Johns Hopkins University Press, 1988.

Boyd, Julian P. "Silas Deane: Death by a Kindly Teacher of Treason, Part I." *William and Mary Quarterly* 3rd series, 16 (1959): 165–87.

Brands, H. W. *The First American: The Life and Times of Benjamin Franklin.* New York: Anchor Books, 2000.

Bridenbaugh, Carl, and Jessica Bridenbaugh. *Rebels and Gentlemen: Philadelphia in the Age of Franklin.* 1942; reprint, New York: Oxford University Press, 1968.

Bibliography

Broadwater, Jeff. *George Mason: Forgotten Founder*. Chapel Hill: University of North Carolina Press, 2006.

Brodsky, Alyn. *Benjamin Rush: Patriot and Physician*. New York: St. Martin's Press, 2004.

Brookhiser, Richard. *Founding Father: Rediscovering George Washington*. New York: Free Press, 1996.

———. *Gentleman Revolutionary: Gouverneur Morris, the Rake Who Wrote the Constitution*. New York: Free Press, 2003.

Buchan, James. *Crowded with Genius: The Scottish Enlightenment—Edinburgh's Moment of the Mind*. 2003; reprint, New York: Perennial, 2004.

Buchanan, John. *The Road to Guilford Courthouse: The American Revolution in the Carolinas*. New York: John Wiley & Sons, 1997.

Burns, Edward McNall. *James Madison: Philosopher of the Constitution*. Rutgers University Studies in History, vol 1. New York: Octagon Books, 1968.

Butler, Lindley S., and Alan D. Watson, eds. *The North Carolina Experience: An Interpretive and Documentary History*. Chapel Hill: University of North Carolina Press, 1984.

Cerami, Charles. *Young Patriots: The Remarkable Story of Two Men, Their Impossible Plan and the Revolution That Created the Constitution*. Naperville, IL: Sourcebooks, 2005.

Chaplin, Joyce E. *The First Scientific American: Benjamin Franklin and the Pursuit of Genius*. New York: Basic Books, 2006.

Chernow, Ron. *Alexander Hamilton*. New York: Penguin, 2004.

Clarfield, Gerard H. *Timothy Pickering and the American Republic*. Pittsburgh, PA: University of Pittsburgh Press, 1980.

Clark, Walter, ed. *State Records of North Carolina*. 16 vols. Raleigh: State of North Carolina, 1895–1907.

Bibliography

Clark, William Bell. *Ben Franklin's Privateers: A Naval Epic of the American Revolution*. Baton Rouge, La.: Louisiana State University Press, 1956.

Clary, David A. *Adopted Son: Washington, Lafayette, and the Friendship That Saved the Revolution*. New York: Bantam Dell, 2007.

Collier, Christopher, and James Lincoln Collier. *Decision in Philadelphia: The Constitutional Convention of 1787*. 1986; reprint, New York: Ballantine Books, 2007.

Commager, Henry Steele, and Richard B. Morris, eds. *The Spirit of Seventy-Six: The Story of the American Revolution as Told by Participants*. 1958; reprint, New York: Da Capo Press, 1995.

Connor, R. D. W. *A Documentary History of the University of North Carolina, 1776–1799*. 2 vols. Chapel Hill: The University of North Carolina Press, 1953.

Corner, George W., ed. *The Autobiography of Benjamin Rush: His "Travels through Life" Together with His Commonplace Book for 1789–1813*. Princeton, N.J.: Princeton University Press, 1948.

Cornog, Evan. *The Birth of Empire: Dewitt Clinton and the American Experience, 1769–1828*. New York: Oxford University Press, 1998.

Craige, Burton. *The Federal Convention of 1787: North Carolina in the Great Crisis*. Richmond, VA: Archibald Craige, 1987.

Crow, Jeffrey J. *A Chronicle of North Carolina During the American Revolution, 1763–1789*. Raleigh: North Carolina Division of Archives and History, 1975.

———. *The Black Experience in Revolutionary North Carolina*. Raleigh, NC: Division of Archives and History, 1977.

Cunningham, Noble E. Jr. *The Jeffersonian Republicans in Power: Party

Operations, 1801–1809. Chapel Hill: University of North Carolina Press, 1963.

De Roulhac Hamilton, J. G. "Historic Medicine." *Southern Medicine and Surgery* (1931): 58–59.

Dobson, Jessie. John Hunter. London: E & S Livingstone, 1969.

Documents Illustrative of the Formation of the Union of the American States. Washington, DC: Government Printing Office, 1927.

Draper, Theodore. *A Struggle for Power: The American Revolution*. New York: Times Books, 1996.

Duncan, Louis C. *Medical Men in the American Revolution, 1775–1788*. Reprint ed., Carlisle Barracks, PA: Medical Field Service School, 1931; reprint, New York: Augustus M. Kelley, 1970.

Ekirch, A. Roger. *"Poor Carolina": Politics and Society in Colonial North Carolina*. Chapel Hill: University of North Carolina Press, 1981.

Elkins, Stanley, and Eric McKitrick. *The Age of Federalism: The Early American Republic, 1788–1800*. New York: Oxford University Press, 1993.

Ellis, Joseph J. *Founding Brothers: The Revolutionary Generation*. New York: Alfred A. Knopf, 2000; reprint, New York: Vintage Books, 2002.

———. *His Excellency: George Washington*. New York: Alfred A. Knopf, 2004.

Ewing, Lucy E. Lee. *Dr. John Ewing and Some of His Noted Connections*. Philadelphia: Allen, Lane & Scott, 1924.

Farrand, Max, ed. *The Records of the Federal Convention of 1787*. New Haven, CT: Yale University Press, 1911.

Ferling, John. *A Leap in the Dark: The Struggle to Create the American Republic*. New York: Oxford University Press, 2003.

———. *Adams Versus Jefferson: The Tumultuous Election of 1800*. New York: Oxford University Press, 2004.

Ferris, Robert G., ed. *Signers of the Constitution*. Washington, DC: United States Department of the Interior National Park Service, 1976.

Flavell, J. M. "Lord North's Conciliatory Proposal and the Patriots in London." *English Historical Review* April (1992): 302–22.

Fleming, Thomas. *Duel: Alexander Hamilton, Aaron Burr and the Future of America*. New York: Basic Books, 1999.

The Formation of the Union: A Documentary History Based Upon an Exhibit in the National Archives Building. Washington, DC: National Archives, 1970.

Fothergill, John. *Chain of Friendship: Selected Letters of Dr. John Fothergill of London, 1735–1780*. Cambridge, MA: Belknap Press, 1971.

Franklin, Benjamin. *Benjamin Franklin's Autobiographical Writings*. Ed. Carl van Doren. New York: Viking Press, 1945.

———, *The Papers of Benjamin Franklin*. Ed. Leonard W. Labaree, Whitfield J. Bell Jr., William Bradford Willcox, et al. 39 vols. New Haven, CT: Yale University Press, 1959– .

———, *The Compleated Autobiography by Benjamin Franklin*. Ed. Mark Skousen. Washington DC: Regnery, 2006.

Frohen, Bruce, ed. *The American Republic: Primary Sources*. Indianapolis, Ind.: Liberty Fund, 2002.

Ganyard, Robert L. *The Emergence of North Carolina's Revolutionary State Government*. Raleigh: North Carolina Division of Archives and History, 1978.

Gilpatrick, Delbert H. "Contemporary Opinion of Hugh Williamson." *North Carolina Historical Review* 17 (1941): 26–36.

Gladstone, William E. "Kin Beyond the Sea." *North American Review* 127 (1878): 185.

Golway, Terry. *Washington's General: Nathanael Greene and the Triumph of the American Revolution*. New York: Henry Holt, 2005.

Hendrickson, Robert. *Hamilton I (1757–1789)*. New York: Mason/Charter, 1976.

Higginbotham, Don. *The War of American Independence: Military Attitudes, Policies, and Practice, 1763–1789*. Boston: Northeastern University Press, 1983.

Hindle, Brooke. *The Pursuit of Science in Revolutionary America, 1735–1789*. 1956; reprint, New York: W. W. Norton, 1974.

Hogan, Margaret A., and C. James Taylor, eds. *My Dearest Friend: Letters of Abigail and John Adams*. Cambridge, MA: Harvard University Press, 2007.

Hogeland, William. *The Whiskey Rebellion: George Washington, Alexander Hamilton, and the Frontier Rebels Who Challenged America's Newfound Sovereignty*. New York: Scribner, 2006.

Hosack, David. *Biographical Memoir of Hugh Williams, M.D., LL.D.* New York: New York Historical Society, 1820.

Isenberg, Nancy. *Fallen Founder: The Life of Aaron Burr*. New York: Viking Penguin, 2007.

Jay, John. *John Jay: Unpublished Papers, 1745–1784*. Ed. Richard B. Morris. 2 vols. New York: Harper & Row, 1975–80.

Jefferson, Thomas. *The Papers of Thomas Jefferson*. Library of Congress, Washington, DC.

Jenkins, Helen. "The Versatile Dr. Hugh Williamson." Master's thesis, University of North Carolina, 1950.

Jillson, Calvin C. *Constitution Making: Conflict and Consensus in the Federal Convention of 1787*. New York: Agathon Press, 1988.

Kars, Marjoleine. *Breaking Loose Together: The Regulator Rebellion in Pre-Revolutionary North Carolina*. Chapel Hill: University of North Carolina Press, 2002.

Kaufman, Matthew H. *Medical Teaching in Edinburgh During the Eighteenth and Nineteenth Centuries*. Edinburgh: Royal College of Surgeons of Edinburgh, 2003.

Ketcham, Ralph. *James Madison: A Biography*. Charlottesville: University Press of Virginia, 1990.

Ketchum, Richard M. *The Winter Soldiers: The Battles for Trenton and Princeton*. New York: Henry Holt, 1973.

Knott, Stephen F. *Secret and Sanctioned: Covert Operations and the American Presidency*. New York: Oxford University Press, 1996.

Labaree, Benjamin Woods. *The Boston Tea Party*. New York: Oxford University Press, 1966.

Landers, H. L. *The Battle of Camden, South Carolina, August 16, 1780*. 1929; reprint, Washington, DC: U.S. Government Printing Office, 1997.

Lee, Henry, ed. *Memoirs of the War in the Southern Department of the United States*. New York: University Publishing, 1869; reprint, *The American Revolution in the South*, New York: Arno Press, 1969.

Lefler, Hugh Talmage, and Albert Ray Newsome. *The History of a Southern State*. 3rd ed. Chapel Hill: University of North Carolina Press, 1973.

Madison, James. *Notes of Debates in the Federal Convention of 1787 Reported by James Madison*. Athens: Ohio University Press, 1966.

Main, Jackson Turner. *The Upper House in Revolutionary America, 1763–1788*. Madison: University of Wisconsin Press, 1967.

Marshall, James V. *The United States Manual of Biography and History*. Philadelphia: James B. Smith, 1856.

Martin, James Kirby. *Benedict Arnold: Revolutionary Hero—An American Warrior Reconsidered*. New York: New York University Press, 1997.

Massengill, Stephen E., ed. *North Carolina Votes on the Constitution: A Roster of Delegates to the State Ratification Conventions of 1788 and 1789*. Raleigh: North Carolina Division of Archives and History, 1988.

McAnear, Beverly. "The Raising of Funds by the Colonial Colleges." *Mississippi Valley Historical Review* 38, no. 4 (1952): 591–611.

McCaughey, Elizabeth P. *From Loyalist to Founding Father: The Political Odyssey of William Samuel Johnson*. New York: Columbia University Press, 1980.

McCoy, Drew R. *The Last of the Fathers: James Madison and the Republican Legacy*. New York: Cambridge University Press, 1989.

McCullough, David. *John Adams*. New York: Simon & Schuster, 2001.

McFarland, Philip. *The Brave Bostonians: Hutchinson, Quincy, Franklin, and the Coming of the American Revolution*. Boulder, CO: Westview Press, 1998.

Melton, Buckner F. *The First Impeachment: The Constitution's Framers and the Case of Senator William Blount*. Macon, GA: Mercer University Press, 1998.

Middlekauff, Robert. *The Glorious Cause: The American Revolution*. New York: Oxford University Press, 1982.

Miller, Charles A. *Jefferson and Nature: An Interpretation*. Baltimore: Johns Hopkins University Press, 1993.

Mitchell, Memory F. *North Carolina Signers: Brief Sketches of the Men Who Signed the Declaration of Independence and the Constitution*. Raleigh: North Carolina Division of Archives and History, 1980.

Moore, Wendy. *The Knife Man*. London: Transworld Publishers, 2005.

Morgan, David T., ed. *The John Gray Blount Papers, 1803–1833*. Vol. 4. Raleigh: North Carolina Division of Archives and History, 1982.

———. *The Devious Dr. Franklin, Colonial Agent: Benjamin Franklin's Years in London*. Macon, GA: Mercer University Press, 1996.

Morgan, David T., and William J. Schmidt, eds. *North Carolinians in the Continental Congress*. Winston-Salem, NC: John F. Blair, 1976.

Morton, Brian N., and Donald C. Spinelli. *Beaumarchais and the American Revolution*. New York: Lexington Books, 2003.

Neal, John Washington. "Life and Public Services of Hugh Williamson." *Historical Papers of the Trinity College Historical Society* 13 (1919): 62–111.

Nevin, David. *Treason*. New York: Forge, 2001.

Numbers, Ronald L., and Todd L. Savitt, eds. *Science and Medicine in the Old South*. Baton Rouge: Louisiana State University Press, 1989.

O'Brian, Patrick. *Joseph Banks: A Life*. Chicago: University of Chicago Press, 1987.

Oppenheimer, Jane M. *New Aspects of John and William Hunter*. New York: Henry Schuman, 1946.

Patterson, William D. *Beginnings of the American Rectangular Land*

Survey System, 1784–1800. Columbus, OH: Ohio Historical Society, 1970.

Peters, William. *A More Perfect Union: The Making of the United States Constitution*. New York: Crown, 1987.

Potts, Louis W. "The Poor Man's Franklin and the National Domain." *North Carolina Historical Review* 64, no. 4 (1987): 371–93.

Puls, Mark. *Henry Knox: Visionary General of the American Revolution*. New York: Palgrave Macmillan, 2008.

———. *Samuel Adams: Father of the American Revolution*. New York: Palgrave Macmillan, 2006.

Rakove, Jack N. *James Madison and the Creation of the American Republic*. Ed. Oscar Handlin. 2nd ed. Library of American Biography. New York: Longman, 2002.

Ramsay, David, M.D., and Lester H. Cohen. *The History of the American Revolution*. Ed. Lester H. Cohen. 2 vols. Indianapolis, IN: Liberty Fund, 1990.

Rankin, Hugh F. *North Carolina in the American Revolution*. Raleigh: North Carolina Division of Archives and History, 1959.

Rhodehamel, John, ed. *The American Revolution: Writings from the War of Independence*. New York: Library of America, 2001.

———, ed. *Washington Writings*. New York: Library of America, 1997.

Robbins, Christine Chapman. *David Hosack: Citizen of New York*. Philadelphia: American Philosophical Society, 1964.

Robinson, Blackwell P. *The Revolutionary War Sketches of William R. Davie*. Raleigh: North Carolina Division of Archives and History, 1976.

———. *William R. Davie*. Chapel Hill: University of North Carolina Press, 1957.

Rodell, Fred. *Fifty-Five Men*. New York: Telegraph Press, 1936.

Rose, Alexander. *Washington's Spies: The Story of America's First Spy Ring*. New York: Bantam Dell, 2006.

Rossiter, Clinton. *1787 the Grand Convention*. New York: Macmillan, 1966.

Royster, Charles. *The Fabulous History of the Dismal Swamp Company*. New York: Alfred A. Knopf, 1999.

Saunders, William, ed. *The Colonial Records of North Carolina*. 10 vols. Raleigh: State of North Carolina, 1886–1890.

Schiff, Stacy. *A Great Improvisation: Franklin, France, and the Birth of America*. New York: Henry Holt, 2005.

Schiffer, Michael Brian. *Draw the Lightning Down: Benjamin Franklin and Electrical Technology in the Age of Enlightenment*. Berkeley, CA: University of California Press, 2003.

Sheehan, Colleen A., and Gary L. McDowell, eds. *Friends of the Constitution: Writings of the "Other" Federalists, 1787–1788*. Indianapolis, IN: Liberty Fund, 1998.

Sheldon, Garrett Ward. *The Political Philosophy of James Madison*. Baltimore: Johns Hopkins University Press, 2001.

Simon, James F. *What Kind of Nation: Thomas Jefferson, John Marshall, and the Epic Struggle to Create a United States*. New York: Simon & Schuster, 2002.

Sizer, Theodore. *The Works of Colonel John Trumbull: Artist of the American Revolution*. New Haven, CT: Yale University Press, 1950.

Smith, Page. *The Constitution: A Documentary and Narrative History*. New York: Morrow Quill, 1980.

Smith, Richard Norton. *Patriarch*. New York: Houghton Mifflin, 1993.

Stahr, Walter. John Jay: *Founding Father*. New York: Hambledon and London, 2005.

Stephenson, Michael. *Patriot Battles: How the War of Independence Was Fought*. New York: Harper Perennial, 2007.

Symonds, Craig L., with Cartography by William J. Clipson. *A Battlefield Atlas of the American Revolution*. Mount Pleasant, S.C.: Nautical & Aviation Publishing Company of America, 1986.

Thacher, James. *American Medical Biography; Or, Memoirs of Eminent Physicians Who Have Flourished in America*. 1828; reprint, New York: Milford House, 1967.

Thomas, Evan. *John Paul Jones: Sailor, Hero, Father of the American Navy*. New York: Simon & Schuster, 2003.

Twohig, Dorothy, ed. *The Journal of the Proceedings of the President 1793–1797*. Charlottesville, VA: University Press of Virginia, 1981.

Van Doren, Carl. *Benjamin Franklin*. New York: Viking Press, 1938.

Van Tyne, Claude Halstead. *Loyalists in the American Revolution*. Gansevoort, NY: Corner House Historical Publications, 1999.

Ward, Christopher, and John Richard Alden, ed. *The War of the Revolution*. 2 vols. New York: Macmillan, 1952.

Wheelan, Joseph. *Jefferson's Vendetta: The Pursuit of Aaron Burr and the Judiciary*. New York: Carroll & Graf, 2005.

Whichard, Willis P. *Justice James Iredell*. Durham, NC: Carolina Academic Press, 2000.

White, Leonard D. *The Federalists: A Study in Administrative History*. New York: Macmillan, 1948.

Williams, Stephen W. *American Medical Biography; Or, Memoirs of Eminent Physicians Who Have Flourished in America: Embracing Principally Those Who Have Died since the Publication of Dr. Thacher's Initial Work in 1828 on the Same Subject*. 1845; reprint, New York: Milford House, 1967.

Williamson, Hugh. *Experiments and Observations*. Vol. 8. London: Philosophical Transactions of the Royal Society of London, 1775.

———. *The History of North Carolina*. 2 vols. Philadelphia: Thomas Dobson, 1812.

Wills, Garry. *Henry Adams and the Making of America*. New York: Houghton Mifflin, 2005.

Winsor, Justin, ed. *The American Revolution: A Narrative, Critical and Bibliographical History*. New York: Land's End Press, 1972.

Wood, Gordon S. *The Creation of the American Republic, 1776–1787*. Chapel Hill: Published for the Institute of Early American History and Culture at Williamsburg, VA, by the University of North Carolina Press, 1969.

———. *The Radicalism of the American Revolution*. 1991; reprint, New York: Vintage Books, 1993.

———. *Revolutionary Characters: What Made the Founders Different*. New York: Penguin, 2006.

Wright, Robert K., Jr., and Morris J. MacGregor Jr. *Soldier-Statesmen of the Constitution*. Washington, DC: Center of Military History, United States Army, 1987.

Index

Index

Index

Index

Index

Index

Index

Index

Index

Index

Index